« Philosophical Witnessing »

THE TAUBER INSTITUTE FOR THE STUDY OF EUROPEAN JEWRY SERIES

The Tauber Institute Series is dedicated to publishing compelling and innovative approaches to the study of modern European Jewish history, thought, culture, and society. The series features scholarly works related to the Enlightenment, modern Judaism and the struggle for emancipation, the rise of nationalism and the spread of antisemitism, the Holocaust and its aftermath, as well as the contemporary Jewish experience. The series is published under the auspices of the Tauber Institute for the Study of European Jewry—established by a gift to Brandeis University from Dr. Laszlo N. Tauber—and is supported, in part, by the Tauber Foundation and the Valya and Robert Shapiro Endowment.

For the complete list of books that are available in this series, please see www.upne.com and www.upne.com/series/TAUB.html

Berel Lang
Philosophical Witnessing: The Holocaust as Presence

David N. Myers
Between Jew and Arab: The Lost Voice of Simon Rawidowicz

Sara Bender
The Jews of Białystock during World War II and the Holocaust

Nili Scharf Gold
Yehuda Amichai: The Making of Israel's National Poet

Hans Jonas
Memoirs

Itamar Rabinovich and Jehuda Reinharz, editors
Israel in the Middle East: Documents and Readings on Society, Politics, and Foreign Relations, Pre-1948 to the Present

Christian Wiese
The Life and Thought of Hans Jonas: Jewish Dimensions

ALSO BY BEREL LANG

Art and Inquiry

The Human Bestiary

Faces, and Other Ironies of Writing and Reading

Philosophy and the Art of Writing

Act and Idea in the Nazi Genocide

The Anatomy of Philosophical Style: Literary Philosophy and the Philosophy of Literature

Writing and the Moral Self

Mind's Bodies: Thought in the Act

Heidegger's Silence

The Future of the Holocaust: Between History and Memory

Holocaust Representation: Art within the Limits of History and Ethics

Post-Holocaust: Interpretation, Misinterpretation, and the Claims of History

EDITED VOLUMES

Marxism and Art: Writings in Aesthetics and Criticism

The Concept of Style

Philosophical Style: An Anthology about the Writing and Reading of Philosophy

Philosophy and the Holocaust

The Philosopher in the Community: Essays in Memory of Bertram Morris

The Death of Art

Writing and the Holocaust

Race and Racism in Theory and Practice

The Holocaust: A Reader

BRANDEIS UNIVERSITY PRESS

WALTHAM, MASSACHUSETTS

PUBLISHED BY

UNIVERSITY PRESS OF NEW ENGLAND

HANOVER AND LONDON

Philosophical Witnessing

The Holocaust as Presence

BEREL LANG

BRANDEIS UNIVERSITY PRESS
Published by University Press of New England
One Court Street, Lebanon, NH 03766
www.upne.com

Printed in U.S.A.
5 4 3 2 1

Library of Congress
Cataloging-in-Publication Data
Lang, Berel.
Philosophical witnessing: the Holocaust as presence / [Berel Lang].
p. cm. — (The Tauber Institute
for the Study of European Jewry series)
Includes bibliographical references and index.
ISBN 978-1-58465-741-5 (cloth: alk. paper)
1. Holocaust, Jewish (1939–1945)—Moral and ethical aspects.
2. Holocaust, Jewish (1939–1945)—Influence. 3. Good and evil.
4. Philosophy, Jewish. I. Title.
D804.3.L3573 2009
940.53'1801—dc22 2009006597

University Press of New England is a member of the Green Press Initiative. The paper used in this book meets their minimum requirement for recycled paper.

TO LELA, NINA, & GABRIEL,

TO HANNAH & LEAH

—and the world before you

« Contents »

« Preface »

The themes of "philosophical witnessing" and "presence" that balance the two sides of my book's title have shaped its writing, often explicitly, but always at least tacitly. "Presence" refers to the continuing place of the Holocaust in the contemporary world more than sixty years after its nominal end. This sustained aftermath is not unique in the history of atrocity or destruction, and it would be an indignity to argue comparative degrees of wrong or suffering in that dense history. But neither of these considerations is a deterrent to writing about the presence of the Holocaust in the post-Holocaust world, many-sided and startling as its appearances there have been. Much of that expression, predictably, has come from individuals and groups tracing and analyzing the complex combinations of acts and ideas that constituted "the Holocaust" in which they had been enmeshed. And then, too, there are the shock waves from that past that continue to ripple forward, shaping both institutional structures—international, national, cultural—and individuals. Although many in both these groups may be far removed from the event itself, an impulse to confront that past has often come to the surface in them.

It is aspects of this presence that I consider here, both looking back to moments or aspects of the Holocaust that warrant attention they have not received and looking forward to a future that the consequences of the Holocaust may, even *should*, affect in shape and direction and then finally in practice. These appearances have assumed various forms, as expressions of memory (individual and collective) for those who lived through the Holocaust, and through the faculty of moral imagination for the by-now majority of others born only after that event. Both memory and imagination seem in the end private or inward, but both also reveal themselves in the public face of practice: in political and legal determinations of policy, in literary and other artistic representations to which the Holocaust gives voice, in public ritual and commemorative institutions, in the reach of historical and philosophical reflection.

To be sure, the intense aftermath of the Nazis' war against the Jews has not reflected a consensus. Internal disagreements about the character of that "presence" have ranged from flat denials of its legitimacy (echoing denials of the Holocaust itself) to the metahistorical claim of the Holocaust's uniqueness—opening the space between them to a large number of more nuanced but equally deep issues. So, for examples, the related questions of historical causality and moral responsibility leading up to and in the Holocaust; or the consequences of the Holocaust for the principal groups caught up in it; and finally, to the daunting question of how this past event *should* be incorporated in the present. Even to acknowledge that last question points to the continuing presence of the Holocaust as itself a moral decision, a biting reminder of the convergence, often denied or ignored, of history and ethics. On this count, one has only to recall the names or terms encapsulated from the Holocaust that stand now as shorthand markers—"Auschwitz," "Final Solution," "Kapo"—to recognize the spread of its effects in the discourse of everyday life.

Indefinite boundaries mark out all presence, and I make no attempt to impose stricter ones here. Anyone thinking about the Holocaust in a sustained way will be aware of the new details of its course that have continually come to light—a pattern unlikely to end soon. One such instance recalled here (chapter 8) is the odd phenomenon of Theodore Kaufman's slight pamphlet, *Germany Must Perish*, which had consequences during World War II far beyond what its author or anyone else anticipated; it remains relatively unknown, but in this, too, it is emblematic of the way in which a causal—and casual—improbability may find itself part of a central and disturbing historical current. Karl Jaspers' brave, almost instantaneous postwar analysis of German guilt in his 1945 book *Die Schuldfrage* warrants reflection from a later perspective, designed to consider what his philosophical and juridical analysis both saw and ignored in the immediate Nazi past that he observed from the outpost of his own "internal migration" (chapter 4). Are there, amidst the profusion of writings about the Holocaust, *omissions* even among them that are no less "telling" and present than what has been said explicitly? This, at least, is a claim made and returned to here—at times referring for evidence to literary and other artistic representations of the Holocaust (chapters 6 and 7), at times building on what purports to be straightforward historical discourse, and then, too, on philosophy's own address (chapters 1 and 2). Silence itself also has its genres, elaborated through the arts of repression or deliberate concealment. That the presence of the Holocaust is so often and largely on display as to suggest that nothing has been "left out" runs up against evidence of just such absences.

The book's second theme is less obvious than the first—indeed, more a question than an assertion. What, after all, would be distinctive about *philosophical* witnessing? (And how many types of witnessing *are* there, anyway?) From my first writing about the Holocaust in *Act and Idea in the Nazi Genocide* (1990), I have both pursued and been pursued by the question of what philosophy could add to the understanding of that subject that other disciplines and research had missed or slighted. I have since carried on this search by considering many of the same questions addressed elsewhere to see what differences might be uncovered from other answers to them, but also by looking for questions that otherwise had not been asked. I am uncertain still of the answer to the question of what philosophy's contribution might be, as I remain more widely skeptical on the distinctiveness of philosophical thought or analysis about *any* subject. It seems at least possible, however, that philosophy may be more inclined toward certain perspectives, angles of vision, or types of analysis than turn up elsewhere: a directive to the understanding, if not in itself a means. Admittedly, the question of whether even these limited possibilities hold can be answered only externally, by judging the work itself rather than by studying its intentions: also for philosophy, the principle, "Trust the tale, not the teller," applies. (In this sense, too, the title, "philosopher"—like that of "poet"—would be honorific, achieved by accomplishment, not self-ascribed.)

In any event, the connections between the account given here and certain traditional philosophical positions will be apparent. The problem of evil, for one example, has loomed as large in philosophy as it has in theology, and for the span of history in which that problem rises to the surface, the Holocaust represents an obvious occasion. Thus, in chapter 3, I consider responses to the Holocaust within the bounds of both philosophy and theology, weighing the strains in their convergence that the Holocaust's enormity imposes. That the concept of genocide itself emerged in the context of the Holocaust is generally acknowledged, although it is less often understood how the *concept* of genocide has affected other important conceptual features in the long tradition of individual and natural (latterly re-titled "human") rights. My claim of a progression leading from the Holocaust to "genocide" to our contemporary emphasis on group rights thus becomes the subject of chapter 10 (and of part III more broadly).

The topic of "philosophical witnessing," a motif throughout the volume, figures explicitly in chapter 1, in which the concept of the witness *in* philosophy is analyzed, on the grounds that the witness's role in that (and indeed, in any) context is more than only a vicarious or imaginative projection; that its significance is both moral and epistemic, involving work that philosophy not only can but ought to undertake. The relative absence of this practice in contemporary philosophical writing has, in my view, reflected an underlying a- or even antihistorical presentation of philosophy's self among the most influential twentieth-century "schools" and continuing into the present. A professional deformation, I would charge—and propose to contest.

The reader will judge whether or how an understanding of aspects of the Holocaust is advanced in *these* pages. But that risk is constant for philosophical discourse—more so than in other forms of discourse, since here the question of whether what is written contributes to understanding its occasion differently or more fully is linked always to the broader question of what philosophy *ever* adds to what is already othewise known or understood.

« » « »

In extending acknowledgments and thanks to friends and colleagues, I recognize the dangers of naming (so too, of omitting) names. But this risk seems preferable to either a collective nod or to silence, and I hope that mentioning them may at least stir further discussions. And if those to whom I express a debt do not recall it or want to dispute it on other grounds, I either would try to remind them or, failing that, would simply register the objections. But before any of this can happen, varieties of thanks to Lawrence Baron, Judith Baskin, Hedva Ben-Israel, Richard Bernstein, Claudia Card, Robert Fogarty, Esia Friedman, Simone Gigliotti, Warren Ginsberg, Laurence Goldstein, Rebecca Goldstein, Jacob Golomb, Shelly Hornstein, Sam Kassow, Joel Kraemer, Paul Levitt, Michael Morgan, Leslie Morris, Dalia Ofer, Marc Lee Raphael, Joerg Riegel, Alvin Rosenfeld, John Roth, Steve Stern, Gerhard Weinberg, Carol Zemel, Yael Zerubavel, Anna Ziebinska, and Steven Zipperstein. The late Raul Hilberg was a generous source for me as he was for all Holocaust students (including our conversation in a memorable walk in Washington, D.C., on 9/11—much of the city was then walking—that took us from the Holocaust Museum with the smoke from the Pentagon rising in the background, around the White House, and on to Dupont Circle).

For the past three years, I have had the good fortune to be a "visitor" in the Department of Philosophy and the College of Letters of Wesleyan University, and I am grateful to colleagues and students there for a combination of challenge and sustenance; special thanks on both those accounts to Howard Needler and Ethan Kleinberg. Barbara Estrin, a remarkable reader in and beyond texts, provided both light and warmth when they mattered most; words mark but do not measure her help. I began to write about the Holocaust twenty-five years ago when my daughters, Ariella Lang and Jessica Lang, were in grade school. Since then, that work has also been for me a means of speaking to them about that event, and in a notable turn, I have recently been able to read and learn from them in some of their own writings on the same subject. This, in its turn, has brought me to think of *their* children—and it is to them, in their new, very new generation, that the book inscribed here is dedicated.

Middletown, Connecticut
Riverdale, New York
July 2008

« Acknowledgments »

Early versions of chapters 3, 4, 6, 7, and 11 — all of them substantially revised since — appeared (respectively) in Michael Morgan and Peter Gordon, eds., *The Cambridge Companion to Modern Jewish Philosophy* (2007); *Review of Metaphysics* (2007); Marc Lee Raphael, ed., *The Representation of the Holocaust in Literature and Film* (2007); *Antioch Review* (2006), and *Jewish Social Studies* (2005). I am indebted to Phyllis Deutsch, editor of the University Press of New England, and an anonymous reader for the Press for their very helpful readings and suggestions about the text. Erinn Savage has been generous in her attention and efforts in preparation of the manuscript.

I

The Holocaust at Philosophy's Address

« 1 »

Philosophical Witnessing

"... And only I have survived to tell you"

To consider the concept of philosophical witnessing in relation to the Holocaust and to genocide more generally, I set out from two classical texts. The first of these is the fragmented quotation from the Book of Job in this chapter's title: "And only I have survived to tell you." Job himself appears in that narrative as the victim of a series of afflictions he suffers after God has in effect made a bet with Satan. God is so confident of "his servant Job" that he boasts to Satan that no matter how much Job might be made to suffer, he would remain faithful; Satan disputes this prediction, appealing to a theory of human nature currently familiar as "rational self-interest": "*Of course*, Job has been faithful," Satan challenges God; "why shouldn't he be? Look at the good life you've given him: family, prosperity, health. Change *those*, however, and see *then* how he acts." God rises to the bait and allows Satan to test Job. That takes the form of a series of disasters, beginning with four separate attacks on Job's possessions and family, each destroying more than the preceding one: property, herds, family members. From each attack, a lone surviving messenger arrives to report to Job his new losses. All four announcements (could it have been the same messenger each time? the narrator does not tell us) conclude with the same statement by the witness: "And only I have survived to tell you."

This refrain identifies an archetypal motif of witnessing—of cultural or collective witnessing, and more specifically, of individual testimonies transmitted from the Holocaust—with the repeated statement of Job's messenger conveying both a literal and a metaphoric reference. In its literal reference, it resembles accounts written from the Holocaust by people who believed that without their words, no record at all would remain of the events engulfing them; nobody would know how what happened happened, perhaps not even *that* it happened; in effect, they thought of their writing as if "only *it* alone would survive." Some of these witnesses survived themselves, some did not. We recall the dramatic statement of Simcha Rotem from the Warsaw Ghetto, who, after having hidden in the ghetto's sewers during its razing, came to the surface afterward, and reported that, "I said to myself, 'I am the last Jew.'" Also in the Warsaw Ghetto, Immanuel Ringelblum, organizer of the Oneg Shabbas archives (unequaled as a record of *collective* witnessing), anticipated the same possibility when he buried in milk cans and other containers the collection of data his team of collectors had assembled, gathering side by side such varied "witness" information as the numbers of the ghetto's daily death rate together with the programs of evening nightclub acts put on there.[1]

Even witnesses aware of the existence of other survivors, however, might be inclined to say with Job's herdsmen that "only I have survived," and here we encounter that statement's metaphorical cast. For it is a feature of witnessing that although variant accounts of the same event usually will have *some* common elements, differences frequently occur among them—some of them evident contradictions, but also others that call attention to aspects of the event that simply have passed unnoticed in other accounts. The contradictions and other extreme differences in such accounts have raised suspicions about the reliability of eye-witness testimony as such, but discrepancies in witnesses' accounts otherwise may *add* weight to the testimony they give by citing details that other witnesses had not noticed or had not thought worth the telling.[2] For two remarkable examples, we find Primo Levi and Thadeusz Borowski reporting aspects of their "survival in Auschwitz" that others who suffered there had not taken note of or at least did not write about (or not as fully): the role of chance in his survival that Levi elaborates and the anger toward the camp victims that Borowski experiences, with striking differences between them also in their reactions overall to what they had confronted.[3] Undoubtedly, the motivations and abilities of Levi and Borowski as writers made a difference in their reports as witnesses, but it would be a mistake to analyze witness-narratives as if they had nothing to do with the act (or art) of seeing. A writer's rhetorical skill would amount to little unless joined to an unusual sense of sight that singled out what was significant to write *about*. These two capacities in effect act on each other; certainly their connection seems crucial in the act of witnessing. The messenger(s) who brought news to Job had relatively simple events to report on, however distressing; industrial and state-killing on the scale of genocide imposes greater demands on its witnesses—first, in order to survive, but also in order to report.

The second text invoked here is the Passover Haggadah, specifically the brief paragraph in it that mandates *within* the text, for those reading the account of the Exodus at the Seder, that they should recite the narrative as if they themselves had been present at the events re-told, as though the experience described had been their own. This imperative is intensified by the Haggadah's status as a performance-text: It is not a script being read *to* an audience by an authority or representative, nor one to be read in silent unison, as certain prayers are in the Jewish liturgy. Rather, its historical account—for it *is* represented as history if not only that—is to be read aloud and collectively, the participants speaking it as a means of making it their own; thus also, as recollecting, as themselves *remembering* the events recounted. The history ostensibly fixed in the distant past, we understand, is the history of the present-day reciter, with the difference between reading collectively and aloud and reading singly and silently emphasizing the former process as a medium of group autobiography. (When else does an informal group read a lengthy text aloud and collectively?)

But this manner of witnessing is also literal and not only imaginative —and here, too, is a dramatic connection to the Holocaust. For it is a matter of fact that the Exodus from Egypt and its consummation at Sinai, whether one understands that account as theology or politics or myth, concluded in the shaping of a people or nation. The group that arrived at Sinai had a common language and a leader; they acquired there also a system of law and the promise of a land. These elements, welded together in the peril of their escape—the danger together with the overcoming—reiterate conditions formulated in numerous studies of nationalism as characteristic of the formation of a people or nation.[4] And, surely, without the events retold there (or analogous ones), the group-identity that emerged would not have been possible. Still more decisively—but less often considered—the present-day reciters of the Haggadah not only would not be doing that, but arguably would not *be*, certainly not in their current identities. In this sense, for reciters of the Haggadah to identify with the people spoken of in the text—in effect, to re-witness that event—has literal and not only figurative force: The re-tellers are what they are only because those whom they "tell" about were what they were.

Here a connection also emerges to writing about the Holocaust, with a special relation to Holocaust-witnessing, and with a similarly broad reach. The Nazi goal in the Holocaust, in what their coded language named the "Final Solution of the Jewish Question," was the destruction not only of the Jews of Europe, but of the Jews as a people (in chapter 9, I trace more systematically the history of the concept, the term, and the fact of "genocide"). Hitler's designs were directed primarily against the Jews of mainland Europe and Western Asia, but they extended southward (with concentration camps in North Africa) and westward—as in the concentration camps planted on the small Channel Isles, the one part of Great Britain that the Nazis occupied—with plans for persecuting England's Jews in the principal island once that was conquered and with threats, beyond that, for the Jews of the Americas. (The latter plans were epitomized in the working title of the "New York Bomber," a warplane, the Junker 390, designed to bring the United States within bombing range and at least two prototypes of which were flown.)[5]

More simply: Hitler's intentions were directed against Jews every place they lived, the more deliberately so because of his view of them as a unified group, plotting the limitless spread of their designs. It was the latter, allegedly cosmopolitan impulse, emanating from its particularist source, that the Nazis construed as threatening German national and racial purity. That the Nazis failed to realize their intention to destroy this source should not obscure the intention itself, and here also we see the parallel implication for Holocaust-witnessing in the Haggadah's stipulation that its readers should read it as if they, too, had been present at the Exodus. For as certainly as any extrapolation from history can be, it follows that if Hitler's design had succeeded, people living now as Jews would not be—either Jews or alive. Both the group and its individual members would have been destroyed, with the consequence that those born since Hitler's defeat would remain unborn, adding their numbers to the millions murdered. Understandably, we think first of the actual victims of genocide—those physically destroyed—but what was lost with them also must include those who would have come to life in their vanished futures.

Thus, witnessing becomes a *current* imperative for Jews alive now who were not in the Holocaust or even born at the time. It is, after all, sheer chance—geographical distance, the vagaries of emigration and immigration, Hitler's own tactical blunders—that they were not caught up in the sweep of the destruction; the intention underlying that effort certainly would not have exempted them. It is as if they too may—*ought* to—count themselves as survivors: not as having suffered the physical wounds, but as having escaped an ominous near-miss. Such witnessing is more immediate and personal—and historical—than the projective identification associated with the vivid, larger-than-life characters of literary fictions, for example, intense as these associations often are. The identification involved in this witnessing is not only imaginative, but factual: the life, or more precisely the death, that might have been.

« » « »

These general comments on witnessing in relation to the Holocaust and genocide do not yet address the promise in this chapter's title of "*philosophical* witnessing"—"philosophical" appearing there not in its colloquial usage (as in "keeping a stiff upper lip")—but referring to "professional" philosophers (and philosophy in *its* profession) as they have been or might be witnesses. For surely one might expect the "lovers of wisdom," as their title nominates them, in their constant search for ethical and political foundations, to confront the moral enormity of the Holocaust and of genocide more generally. If not unique in their twentieth-century appearances, these came center-stage during that time and with great intensity: sufficient warrant, it would seem, to hold the attention of anyone thinking seriously about the human condition.

But this has not been the case, and my discussion here turns to the likely reasons for that omission and what might be done to repair it. One preliminary issue, however, arises before those more substantive ones are considered. "Philosophical *witnessing*?" Is that what philosophers expect or are expected to do? Well, yes, this is the question—although even before responding to it, a related, still more rudimentary question occurs about exactly who is being examined here. There is an evident difference between professors of philosophy and philosophers, and this, from both directions: the very idea of "professional" philosophy would have been unrecognizable (arguably unintelligible) to Plato or Aristotle, for example, who were indisputably philosophers, but no less indisputably *not* professors. But a group of people now by training and certification "do" philosophy—in teaching and writing, and often as a livelihood—dedicated ostensibly to philosophy's traditional ideal of a search for understanding (if with various understandings of what *that* understanding is). It is about this group that the question of the role of the philosopher as witness appears here: partly as a general question, but more immediately in considering the philosopher as witness, actual or potential, to the particular historical event of the Holocaust, with its large moral and political and (as I elaborate in chapter 2) epistemic implications. How, in the face of the Holocaust and the generic phenomenon of genocide, have philosophers served as witnesses *there*? This is a question that quickly evokes a corollary: What witness could or should philosophers have provided that they did not? And then, also, what might they yet aim at?

Different groups of philosophers warrant consideration here, including some who had direct contact with the Holocaust and others—much the largest (and younger) group—who did not. A relatively small group that is nonetheless notable in this connection includes those philosophers who were natives of Germany and Austria or of countries occupied by the Nazis, but who succeeded in emigrating prior to the worst ravages of the

"Final Solution" and who thus, although experiencing the hardship of dislocation and in some instances family losses, did not themselves undergo the brutalities later suffered by others. Some of the names that might be mentioned here are well-known, some not; the group as a whole is formidable, although quite noticeably it is rarely cited *as* a group (why this should be echoes the issue being raised). The United States was the principal destination of this emigrant wave of philosophers that includes Herbert Marcuse, Theodor Adorno, Hans Jonas, Leo Strauss, Herbert Feigl, Marvin Farber, Aron Gurwitsch, Carl Hempel, Paul Oskar Kristeller, and perhaps most widely known (although she herself objected to the designation of "philosopher"), Hannah Arendt. A number of others, including Martin Buber and Ernst Simon, left Germany for then-Palestine (later joined there, after a detour through Canada, by Emil Fackenheim); a number of émigrés arrived, sometimes by a circuitous route, in Great Britain, including Karl Popper and Friedrich Waismann. For many of these figures, their own sense of Jewish identity had been marginal; some recognized that identity as though for the first time when they were forced to flee. But one might anticipate that as a consequence of this personal dislocation and the enormity that then transformed their native grounds, the Holocaust would have become a preoccupation of these philosophers in their subsequent thought and writing. This proved true, however, for only a small number of them; for most, it either did not appear explicitly in their later work at all or affected it in such subtle ways below the surface as to be difficult to trace. Of the figures mentioned, Arendt is arguably the best known for work related to then-current history—for *The Origins of Totalitarianism*; and then, specifically in relation to the Holocaust, through *Eichmann in Jerusalem: A Report on the Banality of Evil* (more about this below). Adorno, together with Horkheimer, wrote *The Dialectic of Enlightenment*, a sustained attempt to trace the origins of the Holocaust to the Enlightenment; in other writings (for example, *Minima Moralia* and *The Authoritarian Personality*), the shadow of Nazism is strongly evident. Fackenheim, after a delay, turned from his principal interest in Hegel and nineteenth-century philosophy to a sustained, albeit quasi-theological focus on the Holocaust.

From these several figures outward, however, the emphasis diminishes sharply. Leo Strauss was deeply engaged personally with the Holocaust, but this expressed itself professionally more in occasional essays and his correspondence than in his systematic works (as in his books on Maimonides, Spinoza, and Machiavelli). Buber wrote extensively about issues in Jewish history and thought, but comparatively little specifically about the Holocaust; Popper wrote a sweeping critique of totalitarianism (initiated, as he saw it, in Plato), but as a general concept remote from the events that took him from Vienna to years in New Zealand before reaching England. Emmanuel Levinas does not quite fit in this group, since he was held captive as a French soldier in a German prisoner-of-war camp, thus escaping the brutalities of the other "camps." But the family he had left behind in Lithuania suffered sharp losses. Although the turn to ethics as prior to ontology and thus as fundamental intensifies after that, the Holocaust as such never becomes a sustained historical subject of his analysis.[6] For the other members of this group mentioned, their philosophical (i.e., professional) work proceeded as if the decade between 1935 and 1945 had not differed significantly from the one preceeding it. (A statement epitomizing this detachment appears in A. J. Ayer's 1946 introduction to that year's new edition of his *Language, Truth and Logic*: "In the ten years since *Language, Truth and Logic* was first published, I have come to see that the questions with which it deals are not in all respects so simple as it makes them appear; but I still believe that the point of view which it expresses is substantially correct"—a notably subdued reaction to a decade that had been anything but subdued.[7] Ayer, when he first published his book in 1936, introducing the Logical Positivism of the Vienna Circle to the English-speaking world and concluding there, among other claims, that ethical judgments were noncognitive—more than that, nonsensical—found nothing in the events of that subsequent decade that would lead him to re-think that conclusion.)

Insofar as this minimal response characterizes the work of philosophers in immediate proximity to the Holocaust, it is less surprising that silence about it or genocide more broadly should characterize the work of philosophers at a greater, more impersonal distance. And indeed, in philosophy as a *field*, the proportionate attention to the Holocaust or the phenomenon of genocide has been slight, even in the book-filled cognate fields of ethics and political or social theory. The exceptions to this generalization, including those mentioned, underscore their status *as* exceptions. (More practical, albeit anecdotal evidence of this figured recently at a major conference on the Holocaust, where among two hundred participants and thirty conference sessions, one session was devoted to philosophy, with the three philosophers attending the conference the speakers at that one session.)

A partial explanation of this phenomenon would, I believe, point to the general "culture" of contemporary philosophy and the a- or even antihistorical tendencies evident in it. Explanations for these tendencies range from philosophy's efforts to fashion itself in the image of science (in which history has at most an antiquarian role) to a reaction against the historicist thinking often accused of conspiring in the rise of totalitarianism itself. However we judge such explanations, the characteristic they are meant to explain has been evident—with history as a subject or source of examples a minor consideration, if one at all, in philosophical reflection. This appears vividly in Anglo-American analytic philosophy in relation to the kinds of examples (and counterexamples) typically adduced in its argumentation. At the same time (and soon after) that the moral extremities of the mid-twentieth century were occurring (and continuing afterward), examples cited in that writing would still focus on the moral problem of what might justify breaking a promise to go on a picnic or the epistemic problem of how (or if) one can know the pain of a toothache. (Would Wittgenstein's philosophical writings provide even a hint of the circumstances that led him along the way [in 1939] to arrange a large payment from the family fortune to the Nazi hierarchy that enabled his two sisters still living in Vienna to be re-classified as racially "mixed" (Mischlinge) rather than as (full) Jews, and so, probably, to save their lives?)[8] And if the "continental" philosophical tradition in phenomenology and existentialism or their recent successors has both attacked and been attacked by analytic critics on grounds of both methodological and substantive "softness," a similar disposition to antihistoricism figures largely there as well. (Neither Husserl's sloganeering for a return "to the things themselves" nor his own troubled place in Freiburg's University in the 1930s sufficed to make the events of that history a subject of philosophical interest for him.)[9]

Furthermore and independently of these circumstantial antihistoricist tendencies, philosophy draws on a characteristic ground that also works against historical reference. A common theme of many (arguably all) philosophical discourse, including much of it that disagrees about many other matters, has been a requirement of generality for philosophical conclusions: that the latter—theories of human nature or stipulated conditions for knowledge, definitions of justice, conceptions of history as well—should apply universally, not to a single, time- or culture-bound set of examples. (This move to generalization holds at some level, I should argue, even for nominalist-inclined views like pragmatism or existentialism.) And this disposition leads readily to the view that specific historical examples or occurrences *should* be viewed only as ancillary, as springboards for jumping elsewhere, and thus as comparatively unimportant, certainly as subordinate to the general conclusions drawn from them.[10]

The problem that this methodological commitment raises for the present discussion is evident: How could we hold philosophical witnessing as a standard, with its required investment in an historical moment, conceptually and methodologically—if the moment, however weighty, is then to be pushed aside in favor of a broader conclusion for which particular identity is largely irrelevant? Or, more concretely: Is it plausible to ask if Aristotle or Kant would have altered their thinking on ethics or political theory if *they* had witnessed an event like the Holocaust or the phenomenon of genocide? In point of fact, those two thinkers *were* conscious of the historical settings in which they lived and wrote. Aristotle in his work on political theory analyzed 26 constitutions of Greek city-states, and Kant held the dramatic example of the French Revolution (and a portrait of Rousseau) clearly before him when he wrote about the prospects for perpetual peace and the possibility (or liabilities) of a world government. What more could have been expected or required?

But certain aspects of philosophy's history itself hint at the possibility of what I call philosophical witnessing, and a number of these converge in the close proximity to the themes of these pages in the admittedly contentious example of Hannah Arendt's *Eichmann in Jerusalem: A Report on the Banality of Evil.* The controversy stirred by that book when it first appeared was sharp and deep, and continues to some extent into the present. I offer no brief here for Arendt's account of Eichmann's character as proof of the "banality of evil," or of the conduct of the ghetto councils as evidence for Jewish complicity in their own destruction—the two main "flash-points" in that controversy. But what Arendt attempted in that book and *did* (again, apart from her specific conclusions) was to exemplify a form of philosophical witnessing in which a thinker, face-to-face with a significant historical "moment," infused that moment in her reflection on broader philosophical themes, at once elaborating them but always in close contact with the source from which the discussion set out, and thus constantly joining the two, as though history itself were given a voice. Eichmann is clearly not a pretext for Arendt's analysis even if she could arguably have based a similar, perhaps almost identical account (of the "banality of evil") on certain other Nazi figures. The enduring impression that Arendt's book has made is thus not an endorsement of its individual conclusions, many of which have been discredited historically or disputed philosophically. It reflects rather her *project*, with its focus on a juncture between historical particularity and philosophical generalization: What I have been proposing as philosophical witnessing. The process involved here resembles in important ways witnessing's more standard appearances, with the role of witness including even those who were immediately present in an event actualized as witnesses only as they revive the past in the present and bring the one to bear on the other. Witnessing is always of the past, but only as it moves the past into the present. Arendt had had direct contact with Nazi Germany (she had also been interned briefly in the camp at Gurs in France), but her role as author of the Eichmann book did not invoke or depend on that part of her past. She chose to "think-Eichmann" as a means of establishing the immediacy and detail of the Nazi-project within (but also as affecting) a framework of philosophical concepts (beginning, perhaps also ending with the concept of evil). The conception of philosophical witnessing is, it seems to me, a way of characterizing that role.

I do not imply with this that thinking with one's mind is identical to seeing with one's eyes or to feeling one's own (let alone another's) pain. But there are more than mere parallels among these: As certain eyes are keener than others in picking out and translating into feeling traces, symptoms, details; so there are minds that think—see, in that sense—both concretely *and* abstractly, even (on a classical account of what knowing is, as the mind and its object become *one)*. And even if philosophers characteristically aim for generality, the pre-eminent canonical figures in the history of philosophy invariably extend themselves also in the opposite direction, to the intelligibility of concrete moments and instances. The conclusions or principles they arrive at, furthermore, invariably are measured—tested—by particular instances; and even if many such instances would be required in order to assess claims about human nature or the ideal state, that requirement need not assume the homogenizing effect aimed at in scientific explanation, where all examples used as evidence are viewed as essentially equivalent. Philosophical reflection thus can be a form of witnessing, but only insofar as it draws specific, historical moments into principles that build on them not as mere occasions but as components. With this, also the philosopher brings the past into the present, much in the way that personal eye-witnesses of the events of everyday life bring and sustain *their* pasts into the present.

Admittedly, this expanded concept of witnessing does not indicate which moments of history or experience the philosopher ought to turn to, or how they would be selected. About this, it seems, one can say only the obvious: that a combination of moral imagination, reflective depth, and good eye-sight must be put to work here, distinguishing what is important from what is not, predicting where larger or lesser consequences follow. Tradition undoubtedly exerts influence here as elsewhere in the history of ideas and culture, and even the extraordinary improbability of an event like the Holocaust (also partly responsible for the philosophical silence that followed it) should itself be registered philosophically in any reflections on it.

Is this not openly to use the term "witness" as a metaphor? Yes, but . . . . For although it is implausible to suggest that thinking about the Holocaust or even "thinking-the-Holocaust" are identical with the experience or the fact of those who lived through it, it is not exactly or only the immediate physical experience that constitutes the testimony of those who lived through it and then appear as witnesses. There seems to me an intrinsic metaphoric component in the concept of the witness *whenever* that term applies. What makes witness testimony distinctive and compelling, after all, is not the historical detail it yields; as has been noted above, we recognize from disputes about such testimony even in commonplace settings that its factual accuracy is often questionable. (And if the detail of witness testimony were known not through witnesses, but only by impersonal but substantial documentation, would its force as historical fact be in any way diminished?) It is, then, less the specific details in such accounts that give them their special force, but the fact of their speaker's presence in the event witnessed, and the persistence of *that* fact in the continuing (in this sense, perpetual) present. The metaphoric aspect of witnessing thus adds itself to the historical reference, even for those who were physically present: the fact *that* they were there, that the events recounted were seen through the eyes, bodies, and minds of those who speak of them in witness. It is the medium, in effect, as distinguishable from its particular assertions. In this sense, then, thinking-the-Holocaust can also become a form of witnessing; insofar as that prospect is accepted as possible, it then also becomes an obligation.

« » « »

This chapter began with certain comments about witnessing in general; so too, in conclusion, I return after considering a particular application to a more general consideration that, by implication, reflects on the Holocaust as such and its relation to the broader phenomenon of genocide. Genocide by definition involves the intentional destruction of a group. Even as a group, however, those murdered in genocide die individually; in this, genocide is identical to mass murder and also, for that matter, to individual murder, however basic other conceptual and moral differences are among these. Furthermore, even if genocide is perpetrated against victims who are themselves assembled in groups, as has typically been the case, it is unlikely that a single group of the *whole* (that is, the genos) will be affected within sight or consciousness of the members of that group. More concisely: When reference is made to "witnessing genocide," it must be the rare exception that anyone would or could witness "genocide" as such, if only because of the scale on which that act is committed. This does not make the suffering or witnessing *within* genocide less horrific—but it does mean that references to witnessing genocide, or specifically, to witnessing the Holocaust, require caution. This is more than a truism or a quibble, more also than the moralistic observation that where the ethical stakes are so high, accuracy in language and fact-finding becomes especially urgent. The danger pointed to here is the application of the concept of "Holocaust-witnessing" anachronistically—as those who speak of it from outside and after the fact analyze what occurred within it from their quite different vantage point that includes fuller knowledge of both the outcome of the Holocaust and its process. But to project this awareness back into the consciousness of those inside the events—where what was occurring was invariably contingent, fragmentary, incomplete—skews the representation. It also makes increasingly likely discrepancies in any (present) judgment of the (past) events, especially of both the intentions and capacities in their settings of agents, victims, and bystanders alike.

This caution on writing and thinking about witnessing in general originates, again, in the witnesses themselves. It is generally recognized, for example, that by the end of 1942 about half the total of six million Jewish victims of the Nazi genocide had been killed. But the decision about the Nazis' "Final Solution" transmitted as policy at Wannsee in January 1942 was known even by the end of that year only to relatively few officials in the Nazi hierarchy; it was grasped only by inference from fragments of evidence among the Jewish populace themselves, including the immediate victims and still more certainly by the potential victims, a considerable number of whom were then still relatively secure (for example, the Jews of Hungary or Italy). This "fog" of genocide was in good measure a deliberate feature of Nazi efforts to conceal the plan for genocide under a cloak of secrecy and deception. (The very phrase, "The Final Solution of the Jewish Question," was forbidden for use in official documents; substitute terms were to be cited, like "resettlement" or "special treatment"—the Nazis thus creating a code within a code.) But that policy converged on an understandable impulse in the Jewish communities to believe that the worst *might* not occur: the very possibility of genocide seemed unreal. Many, arguably most, prospective and even actual victims did not comprehend the extent or nature of what we now refer to familiarly as the Holocaust or genocide. (Remember, again, that the term, "genocide," appeared publicly only near the end of World War II; and the term "Holocaust" gained currency only more than a decade later.)

Thus, in addition to the standard questions about the reliability of individual witness-reports, still larger questions apply and still more pressingly to events on the scale of genocide, including a question about what witnesses reasonably can be said to attest to in it. To speak after the fact about that act as if it had provided a view of the whole risks projecting backwards a consciousness that could not have been present. This caution in no way diminishes the role of Holocaust-witnessing, although it also bears recalling that in the face of moral enormity, historical accuracy becomes an ever more pressing imperative. Indeed, the claim seems pertinent that what witnesses attest to in the Holocaust was so horrific that to exaggerate it in any way must have the effect only of diminishing it. And then, too, as we consider the varieties and structure of witnessing, we do well to recall Primo Levi's chilling reminder that the truest witnesses of the Holocaust were not those whose testimony has survived and to which we have access, but those who died voiceless, whose words we do *not* have.

« 2 »

Truth at Risk and the Holocaust's Response

The title of "humanist" emerged as a recognizable if loosely defined norm in the "humanistic" Renaissance.[1] Vague as its boundaries were, the emphasis of that norm on human nature and history and thus *away* from God's nature and rule—both tendencies furthered by an ambitious retrieval of the classical past—distinguished its advocates from contemporaries still fixed in place by the theological anchor of scholastic learning. As with all paradigm shifts, to be sure, the drama of this revolution gradually lost its edge, but its focus on the human as a *match* for nature (literally and figuratively) persisted, overcoming sporadic dissent and eventually being absorbed and advanced by the Enlightenment in the seventeenth and eighteenth centuries. Near the end of the latter period, however, a countermovement stirred from small beginnings that eventually would challenge the intellectual and moral optimism of this stride into modernity, one with sufficient staying power to sustain itself into our own present. This reaction was impelled by a number of "philosophers of suspicion" who, more or less independently and often at odds with each other on other matters, launched an attack in various registers against the philosophical foundations of the humanist tradition (indeed, against the idea of foundations as such), pushing forward in virtually all areas of thought, within but also outside the humanities.[2] In biology, economics, theology, geology, linguistics, psychology, and of course philosophy, an incipient skepticism gained momentum against the essentialist grounds on which the Renaissance and the Enlightenment following it had depended, protesting (among other things) that the very concept of a human *nature* was misbegotten—and that even if one sidestepped this issue, the claims that had been asserted of what human nature was were tendentious and empty, conclusive evidence (if more were needed) of the very concept's problematic status.

The "humane sciences" that over time built on this intervention focused increasingly on the *way* in which the world and its human inhabitants could be represented or known rather than any basis they might have in the metaphysical natures or essences emphasized previously. This shift of attention—in effect, of commitment—would subsequently (and still now, into the present) spread broadly, extending from interpretations of literary texts to those of theories in quantum physics, from the anthropological study of cultures to justifications for human rights in political theory. The effect of the shift heralded a radical conceptual reformation: replacing substances or essences by emphasizing method and perspective; foregoing the search for the *real* in favor of the *means* by which knowledge might (or might not) emerge; subordinating historical or social or linguistic "facts" to systems-analysis of the signs or symbols used to represent them. So far as philosophy was concerned, this revision was still more fundamental, since the revision positioned itself against the metaphysical tradition that had been a traditional center, shifting that center to epistemology, with the assurance that the latter would not only survive but thrive with the displacement.

To be sure, achievements in the "hard" sciences and technology realized during the same span of time seemed from their practical results alone to contravert these currents of skepticism and antifoundationalism, but as "science" they also could be (and were) viewed as extraterritorial in contrast to what was *humanly* significant. In the event, they hardly deterred the revisionary arguments for suspending or bracketing traditional (or as the philosophers of suspicion would have it, ideological) claims in philosophical realism of truth or fact.

Admittedly, this same reflexive impulse produced findings that were familiar from earlier motifs of the humanities and philosophy. The stipulation, for example, that philosophical (indeed, all) discourse also must consider its own structure as part of its subject does not entail giving up the independence of either speaker or object: knower and known may still retain a certain autonomy. But the rising tide of suspicion came to view even such minimal concessions as unnecessarily generous. At the farthest extreme of this view, then, consciousness or reason would appear not only as "slaves of the passions," in Hume's daring pronouncement, but because of the passions' newly extended reach as expressing an indefinite variety of forces, no potential source of displacement would be excluded. There could be no reason to do so.

Into this unstable setting, the mid-twentieth-century Holocaust injected through its brute facticity a conceptual dilemma. On the one hand, that event's occurrence was held on some accounts to *follow* from the narrative just described, directly or by its own version of the "transvaluation of all values"; that is, its own version of the reduction of humanity (and human nature) to the "superfluousness" of which Hannah Arendt would speak.[3] From this perspective, the Holocaust as an event confirmed the narrative as given, informing us of our own condition, even now, in 2008. It not only happened in or to our culture—it was and arguably *is* our culture. On this highly compressed account, then, the Renaissance commitment to human creativity and originality, complemented by the Enlightenment's faith in reason, also found accommodation for an intense dogmatism and a depersonalized bureaucracy—the two of these eventually converging in genocide.[4]

But this provocative and much-debated hypothesis addressed only one side of a two-sided narrative, acknowledging one aspect of the new suspicion (in its motivation) but not the second side that emerges only as the impulse of suspicion is pushed further to its own conclusion, where it poses what seems in effect to be a contradiction to its first side. It is at this juncture, too, I would argue, that the event and then the concept of the Holocaust make unavoidable a countermove to the motif of suspicion as it is embedded in recent theory, disclosing in that motif, for all its critical incisiveness, the seeds of its own deconstruction. It did not *require* an event of the Holocaust's enormity to bring this implication into the open, nor did the Holocaust compel that disclosure by itself (a disclosure still in process, and still, it has to be said, contested). But the moral and social impact of the Holocaust has been—is—a powerful force in asserting not only a place for itself historically, but a place as well for its continuing presence, one whose weight carries it *beyond* suspicion. Thus, the view to be developed here of the Holocaust as a challenge to a newly prominent conception of truth at work in contemporary philosophy and the humanities, specifically in the role accorded there to a conceptual skepticism that has, on the one hand, taken history for granted, but on the other hand, has ignored skepticism's own conceptual foundations that preclude any such assumption.

In certain respects, this second side of what is here challenged in the philosophical substructure of research in the humanities remains consistent with its Renaissance origins. Certainly, emphasis on the person, the human self, as at once the agent and subject of culture, both shaping and shaped by it, is a variant of the earlier movement's motifs. But the more recent elaborations of that theme have moved further than its predecessor and exacted a higher price; it is in this connection that the status of truth comes to the fore as an issue in the humanities that pushes us back to its philosophical grounds. The same juncture marks the occasion of my reference to the Holocaust and the post-Holocaust, with the event, the fact, of the Holocaust, standing as a challenge to the latter-day misconception (in my view) of truth that has on many fronts become a dominating presence. The stance on display in that presence—truth as intrinsically defeasible, contextual, always (explicitly or not) to be set in scare quotes ("as it were")—has itself emerged on two different tracks. In few of that doctrine's appearances in historiography or epistemology or cultural theory has the Holocaust figured largely—and that absence seems to me precisely the issue here, with the conception of truth that often has been assumed easily and uncritically avoiding the tests that might indeed push it to or (as it has happened) *over* its limits.

I do not mean to suggest that this philosophical ground or the humanities more generally have set themselves formally or by implication on the side of what has come to be known as "Holocaust-denial." But it is important to note that the latter view invokes not only a particular set of historical data but still more basically (as I will attempt to show) a related concept of truth. It should not be surprising, then, to find ramifications of the issue of truth extending also to that extreme view—extreme in method as well as in consequence. But still more concretely: It is an essential part of my claim that the more general conception of truth at work in that structure—and the one challenged here—could have no grounds in principle or application for *disputing* assertions of Holocaust-denial. None, that is, in any deeper sense than as one of a number of possible deviations from current epistemological conventions (with the concept of "deviation" here entirely descriptive, not evaluative). Admittedly, the absence of a hedge or fence against Holocaust-denial is not equivalent to affirming that view, but it raises serious problems related directly to the latter position.

The latter point is intended not only as a generic caution; it focuses on an influential conception and application of the criteria of truth in the humanities that, in their efforts at historical contextualization, make all claims of truth, irrespective of differences in the evidence supporting them, questionable, disputable, and in that sense equal and alike. And so then, too, the injection here into the thicket of epistemology of the Holocaust as an historical event, both in its particular role as a subject of discourse *and* as exemplary for philosophy of both an expression and standard of truth applicable more generally. In other words, I am suggesting that as much as we require conceptual instruments with which to view—to analyze, understand, assess—historical events and the moral issues to be found in them, those events themselves (here, specifically the Holocaust) are also significant for shaping the instruments of analysis and assessment themselves. This would in any event explain (as a corollary) how the contemporary presence of the Holocaust would impress itself not only through the many works that explicitly cite it as a subject, but also as a tacit presence in texts and discourse with little or nothing to say explicitly about the Holocaust as such.

The first of the "two tracks" I have mentioned as ingredient in the conception of truth disputed here is a wariness or distancing from individual historical events—especially in philosophy, but also in literary theory and even, odd as this may seem, in historical discourse. In all of these, the paradigm of "hard" science has obtruded, with those soft disciplines attempting to emulate the methods (also, they hope, the success) of the sciences for which universal or general principles stand as ideals. The confidence of science in moving beyond individual "events" to more inclusive and abstract generalizations drew much of its force from variations of the "covering law" model that attempts to provide explanations of particular occurrences by placing them under general formulas that themselves, of course, had to be derived.[5] The latter then represented a more fundamental claim on reality than the individual historical instances "covered." In supporting this formulation, any single occurrence would count as an instance or example, relatively insignificant in itself.

Unlikely as it might seem to find evidence of this same disposition in historical discourse, its influence nonetheless has been apparent there as well, in part, as residual scientism working to impose general patterns of explanation on disparate individual events; in part through an often exclusionary emphasis on "alltäglich" history that in focussing on the significant commonplace of daily life (unnecessarily) blurred the distinction on its *other* side between major and lesser historical events.[6] It hardly needs to be said that history as a discipline has been foremost among the humanities in marking the complexities—and *facts*—of the Holocaust; to accomplish this, however, it has had to counter pressures from both outside and inside the discipline, which, although weakened by the tide of Holocaust scholarship itself, still persist.[7]

To be sure, it was the Holocaust itself, as the detail of its planning and evolution, and then more slowly, the more abstract questions of historical causality and moral responsibility began to be systematically addressed, that was decisive in this development. Even when viewed abstractly or formally in conceptual terms, the Holocaust cast a shadow backward and forward from the mid-point of the twentieth century, magnified by its source in a nation that had been a center of the Western humanistic tradition, and carried on in near or full view (and often with the collaboration) of other nations sharing that tradition. It is too much to claim (and is, at any rate, unverifiable) that since the occurrence of the Holocaust, *all* thinking about culture and the place of the human within it has been affected by that event's moral weight and consequence. But it would be no less remiss to deny the impact of the Holocaust, its presence in the study and scholarship of the humanities — overtly, with the Holocaust as an announced subject or participant, but also and still more importantly, in challenging the moral and epistemic limits that have flourished mainly by ignoring that event together with the more common friction of history. For there has been a tension here — as it is impossible to ignore the presence of a nearby mountain even when clouds or fog obscure it. Even as *general* philosophical and epistemological arguments have been urged for the intrinsic fallibility of all truth claims, the shadow of this particular event has stood in the background, and it is from this source that the challenge I note here stems.

Admittedly, the same presence also has fostered a distortion at the opposite extreme, in the numerous literary, historical, and philosophical representations of the Holocaust as extraterritorial, *outside* history (or reason or psychology), beyond understanding. Such accounts characterize the Holocaust as unclassifiable, "unique," modifiers that in the end are both confused and confusing in positioning the Holocaust beyond the reach of history itself. On this view, what was so determinately and emphatically an historical occurrence — evident in the motivating, planning, and implementing of the "Final Solution" — appears not as *more* difficult to understand than other historical events, but *impossible* to understand, a claim of an entirely different order.[8]

The second of the two tracks leading to the formulation for which the Holocaust stands as a challenge is conceptually deeper than the first, spanning a broader expanse of modern intellectual history. Even to abbreviate that development requires a reach back to the Enlightenment "project" of the seventeenth and eighteenth centuries and the turn it gave to the concept of truth. The 150-year span between Descartes and Kant saw truth that was fully representational for the former (a gleaming "mirror of nature") blurred by a growing self-consciousness and related skepticism ensuing later in Kant's version of the Copernican Revolution in which the knower became co-author in shaping whatever came to be known: thus, a founding source of what has since emerged as the "constructivist" theory of knowledge.

Radical as Kant's Revolution was, with human reason and understanding ingredients in the "known," it did not imply that the knowledge gained—its *content*—is fully individuated or "subjective." For Kant and the Enlightenment more generally, reason and judgment were at the least intersubjective, reaching beyond their human agents, insofar as they could put aside accidental historical conditions. (A vivid example of this principle is the conjunction of universality and subjectivity claimed by Kant for aesthetic judgment.[9]) In this sense, Kant's Revolution traversed only a half-turn, not a full one, with knowers and the known linked in a common project, but with both retaining a significant measure of independence. It would be just this "half-turn" that the post-Enlightenment philosophers of suspicion would propel into a full turn by further increasing the responsibilities of the knower—to the point that what had remained for Kant *facts* of experience (and knowledge) also began to waver and vanish. Like the smile of Lewis Carroll's Cheshire Cat, they became apparently real, and that, only transiently.

It might be objected to this linear and much condensed summary of modern intellectual history that it finds no place for the totalizing impulse of the nineteenth-century combination of Idealism and Romanticism that opposed the rationalist optimism of the Enlightenment mind with an even more ambitious optimism of the will. But both these visions soon provoked their own reactions that in common further expanded the role of the self or "knower" that Kant's Revolution had set in motion. They did this by enlarging the subject's role in the construction of knowledge and practical (moral) judgment, going so far, in fact, as to claim to dispense even with the ladder that the subject had climbed in order to do the work of construction. At its conclusion, it arrived at a full "inwardness" (in Charles Taylor's term) for which history and its material (and a fortiori, any metaphysical) means were in the end irrelevant.[10] The ladder that had been climbed was not only kicked away but somehow made to disappear; history itself would thus be overcome.

Truth in this context becomes a function of language, not of events or actions or things; thus, self-referential or contextual *and* measured by its own criteria (like a bull's-eye drawn around the arrow after it has struck). So William James cited the "cash-value" of truth claims, with the rate of exchange set by the pragmatists' own bank; the phenomenologists, bracketing the domain of individual experience, insisted that there was no indication within those brackets of what (if anything) existed outside it; existentialists, rejecting the moral and conceptual force of general "principle" as such, placed the burden of all justification on individual assertion (*as* assertion); "ordinary language" analysis would rely on the context of discourse closest to the analysts themselves for the definition of truth (or other key terms), effectively precluding any question of how linguistic or cultural communities had come to assume the forms they had.

The common source—and it has to be said, truth—from which these views set out is evident. The flaw in traditional rationalistic claims for "immaculate" perception or knowledge—perception or knowledge as frictionless (and fictionless)—has been widely acknowledged, and the modernist project of constructivism sets out from that objection, although then carrying it farther. Furthermore, the conceptual dogmatism that is the object of that criticism has held on despite it: the racist and nationalist ideologies that fueled the Holocaust themselves exemplify the staying power of what its adherents viewed clearly as a "*non*-constructed" theory of truth, a position that has persisted in the post-Holocaust world in *its* varieties of atrocity. That this inflated version of a realist epistemology goes beyond and in certain respects against the latter's minimal requirements, however, raises the question of whether there is any correspondingly minimalist version of the constructivist position. It is difficult to see how—for example, in Nietzsche or Foucault, for whom truth is a direct function of persuasion or power—there could be limits to that view that did not also give up its essential condition (power up to the point where reason takes over?), and few of its recent advocates have ventured anything like that.[11]

It is at this point, then, that the presence—beginning with the *fact*—of the Holocaust becomes an issue within the broad penumbra of the status of truth. For, again, if the constructivist view of history and truth has not become dominant currently in the humanities, it has been an urgent presence, using not only arguments but the shame conveyed by subtlety, claiming always to look below the surface that others seem content to linger on, in order to make its case.[12] The pressure from this culture of shaming has been especially prominent in literary theory, but extends to historiography, cultural studies, psychology, and philosophy. At times contested on all these fronts, it remains a force, epitomized by the flurry of scandal that at first surrounded the publication in a literary journal of a deliberately garbled proof in "physics" presented as supporting a constructivist epistemology, but which seemed subsequently to effect little general change even, for that matter, in the particular journal's direction.[13] Indeed, the controversy's focus on pseudo-truth and evidence in science may have had the effect of diverting attention from those same issues in nonscientific fields and especially in the humanities.

At this point in the conceptual struggle, the Holocaust as an event, I would argue, becomes an unavoidable issue, raising as dramatically and forcefully as it has ever been, the question of the status of truth. The very phrase "the Holocaust"—that substantive identification, in all its given-ness—has acquired an epistemic weight; the portmanteau reach of the general term has been reinforced continuously as the details of its historical sequence have come to light: the development of the "Final Solution" in Nazi thinking; the organizing of the concentration camps and then the death camps—and the intricacies (sometimes the blunders) of experimentation in devising the latter (how *does* one invent a production line for the killing of millions?) The phrase, "the six million," has become a metonymy for Holocaust history as such, with that obviously approximate number a shorthand summary of the scattered, willfully selected victims who were joined in common only by an identity that the Nazis and their collaborators had defined.

The phenomenon of "Holocaust-denial" is well-known, far exceeding the reach or number or standing of its advocates. This disparity itself underscores the question that underlies the challenge to the concept of truth at issue here: Why, with the historical, cultural, and conceptual status of Holocaust-denial as feeble as it has been, should it have caused the stir it has?[14] This question is the more pointed because of the divisions and vagaries in the denial itself: whether it is the number of Jews who were or were not killed in the (alleged) Holocaust, what was responsible for the deaths of those who were killed (or died); what the Nazi (or Hitler's) intentions *were* vis-à-vis the Jews. (A point often left unremarked in the discussion of Holocaust-denial is the implied concession by deniers that *if* the Holocaust had occurred, it would have been evil and wrong; what they deny is "only" that it *did* occur: a shady difference between the "deniers" and those who acknowledge its occurrence and continue to defend it.)

The question of "truth" or "fact" in relation to Holocaust-denial thus arises at a number of levels: most generally, in the ascription of intention, but more immediately in empirical questions (such as whether there *were* gas chambers or crematoria in which camps, or if there were, whether they could have accomplished the killing alleged, and so on). That such questions are raised tendentiously does not mean that they are meaningless or do not require answers; in fact they bear directly on the status of truth and its standing for the humanities—literature, history, philosophy—in the "post-Holocaust" world. For even after allowing for interpretive differences of the "fine" anatomy of the Holocaust (like the causal role of anti-semitism in Nazi policy) as distinct from the Holocaust's "gross" anatomy about which there is little to *argue*; and after acknowledging that historical discourse never brings back to life for scrutiny the events it purports to reconstruct (or even attempts to). After all this, there remains a ground of fact about the Holocaust as strongly supported as any claim of fact ever has been. Indeed, for the post-Holocaust world, that ground serves itself, I should argue, as a *criterion* for truth, with this function serving as a crucial point at which the Holocaust and the humanities converge (or, as it seems, collide).

Consider the following statement: "On January 20, 1942, fifteen Nazi officials, at a meeting in Wannsee, discussed plans for implementing the 'Final Solution of the Jewish Question.'" This statement does not speculate on the background of the meeting or the decisions that led up to it, nor does it assume the implementation of plans discussed at the meeting. The statement itself, however, is attested by the Protocol of the meeting—its authenticity attested by other evidence, much of it consisting of independent items of evidence.[15] The weight of supporting material here does not mean that to deny the truth of the statement as cited is *impossible*, but it does mean that denial of that assertion (one piece, after all, of a much more extensive whole) is also a piece of a larger whole that, pushed further, would seem in the end to amount to denial of the concept of evidence or, no less fundamentally, of historical truth. There is a difference between interpretive alternatives of a sequence of events or acts, on the one hand, and the factual ground, on the other, that stands at the basis of such a sequence: the difference between a narrative and a chronicle. And if ever the distance between the terms of this difference demands attention, reflection, and caution, it would be in the circumstances of the sort referred to in statements integral as pieces in the articulation of the Holocaust—and then, as that follows, the broader assertion of the occurrence of the Holocaust itself.

Admittedly, the statement about the Wannsee Conference formally resembles innumerable others in historical accounts of events much less highly charged than the Holocaust. The claim here, however, is not for uniqueness, but for the exemplary force of the statement, as it stands (together with others, related or not to the Holocaust) in a ground-zero for historical and, more generally, empirical assertions, and then for their verification. That such assertions also reflect varied motivations (psychological, moral, ideological) is a separate, ad hominem consideration from the question of the truth or falsity of the claims registered, which also, in this sense, cross the boundaries of otherwise separate contexts.

Again, it is not necessary to base this realist epistemology on the single claim that the Holocaust did occur. But precisely because that event is so highly charged, the assertion of its occurrence compels reflection on the discomfort in the humanities about the boundaries of interpretation, the referentiality of texts (historical as well as literary), and the criteria by which narratives (grand or not) can be assessed. The pressure here from the side of suspicion, evolving as I have condensed it, has reached the point where, as Rorty asserted, so far as truth is concerned, "everything is up for grabs"; it is at this juncture that, notwithstanding the innovations also fostered by this view, the argument for closure appears.[16] This, in the brute facts of the events of the Holocaust and in the either/or that those facts pose: *either* the Nazis initiated a systematic genocide against the Jews *or* they did not—with no third way open. The choice between the two alternatives itself appears as a matter of fact, an historical condition.

The argument here involves more than only historical texts. Literary representations of the Holocaust have less evidentiary or epistemic force than straightforward empirical claims; but that these literary representations invariably incorporate—in effect, presuppose—historical evidence, and commonly assumed historical evidence at that, adds its weight to the historical ground. Not because "fiction" is not inventive, but because the most inventive fictions build on empirical and historical grounds; for example, in commonplace details of human appearance, or, at the other, individualized extreme, the specific historical settings in which individual characters and events are portrayed. In the otherwise radically different appearances of the Holocaust that figure in the writings of Jerszy Kosinski, Philip Roth, Bernard Schlink, Jakov Lind, Aharon Appelfeld, Paul Celan, Vassily Grossman, Art Spiegelman, all of them nonetheless posit, tacitly but unmistakably, a historical ground (thus also of truth) that assumes the view, in general and specifically, that has been proposed here. One has only to attempt to imagine what even these imaginative and creative authors would have written *without* this common historical foundation in their otherwise varied representations. The interpretive space beyond that base, the space of the creative imagination (or even of ideology), is not at all at odds with this common starting point. The greatest artists do not spin out of whole cloth, and nowhere is this clearer than in the imaginative diversity of the strongest examples of Holocaust "literature." In other words, whatever view one has of the adequacy of literary (fictional, poetic) representation to depict an event with the Holocaust's dimensions, the event remains as both a feature of the representation and *beyond* it; that is, beyond interpretation. And this occurs even if one agrees on a certain limited indeterminacy of interpretation, as Umberto Eco convincingly argues; that is, only by ruling *out* some possibilities.

Nor is the status or role of truth in the humanities confined to the reach of literary analysis only in relation to literature conventionally defined, since that reach has been extended also to historiography. Here, too, notwithstanding claims made about historical writing for the particular (or generic) forms of historical narratives, or attempts to map out historiography in terms of literary tropes or "figures in the carpet" (as in Hayden White's influential *Metahistory*), or conceiving of historical discourse on the order of even small, not grand narratives, unless such efforts, in addition to what they contribute to understanding the rhetoric of history, *also* deny the differences, any differences, between fictional and historical discourse, they too will be caught by that last step and forced to stop there.[17] The alternative is stark: that (for example) the statement cited above about the Wannsee Conference (and the assembly of statements like it that constitute the historical Holocaust in memory and reflection) might *equally credibly*—evidentially, causally, consequentially—be false as true. And thus, too, their summary equivalent: the explosive claim that "The Holocaust did *not* occur."[18]

That truth as such and not only one or another particular claim is at risk here also indicates that what may seem exclusively an epistemic or cognitive issue is equally an ethical one. It is not only that recognition of the Holocaust has acted on a broad variety of political and social legislation and institution-building in the post-Holocaust period (for a small sample: the Nuremberg Trials [1945], the U.N. Convention on the Prevention and Punishment of the Crime of Genocide [1948], or, more currently, the

International Criminal Court [2002] which is empowered to try and punish genocide and related crimes). Nor is it only that the term and concept of "genocide" as articulated by Rafael Lemkin in the context of the Holocaust have been so fully absorbed into social discourse as to serve often as a synonym for atrocity as such, or that a broader vocabulary drawn from the Holocaust has entered the language as metaphors. "Auschwitz," "Nazi," "Kapo," "Final Solution," "Musselman," and "Hitler" all recur, standing on their own, with their individual histories assumed as subtexts for use in the now-conventional references made to them.

The common implications of these examples converge on the characterization given here of the Holocaust as serving now as a criterion of truth as such, most pointedly in the areas of the humanities where that criterion has been placed at risk. But a more basic issue is also at stake here, which is the common assumption of a sharp line between fact and value, between theoretical and moral reasoning; this division, too, circulated as a shibboleth in contemporary discourse in the humanities and social sciences, is breached in the conceptual limit (now ethical as well as epistemic) asserted in the Holocaust.[19] Plato found an intrinsic relation between the True and the Good in his "theory of forms"—but the connection can be argued apart from that theory, and not only by considering the moral *consequences* of the difference between truth and its opposite. The claim that the Holocaust occurred not only refers to an assembly of individual historical assertions (like that about the Wannsee Conference), since the individual assertions incorporate a valuation in themselves; what they refer to warrants consideration with its ethical quality a substantial part of that warrant. The outrage provoked by claims that the Holocaust did not occur is not merely a protest against historical or empirical misrepresentation or falsification (a common enough feature of everyday discourse); nor is it motivated only by concern for particular individuals—the survivors or their descendants. The fact at risk here has unusual significance and weight *because* of its moral standing.[20] That the claim for a realist conception of truth becomes more intense in the affirmation or denial of the Holocaust's occurrence of the Holocaust than for many other historical claims means only—equally importantly—that in the end, it remains an aspect of all findings of truth (or falsity). Why, otherwise, would truth *matter*?

« » « »

It may be objected to the account given of the relation between the status of truth and the Holocaust that it is less descriptive than prescriptive; that it identifies turning points or shifts of which their agents have themselves been unconscious or even that they explicitly rejected, that I am in effect contriving an argument rather than describing one that has figured historically. Furthermore, the premise that the Holocaust has been a large background presence in the humanities even when not explicitly noted would be difficult to verify even in principle: the humanities are too scattered, various, multitasking, to submit readily to such a characterization; any claim of a presence "in principle"—like Marx and Engels' proclamation of the "specter haunting Europe"—raises immediate doubts. And then, too, even if such claims were credited, the conclusion drawn from them here may be read as an apologia for reaction, a plea for return to the Enlightenment project, with all the baggage of essentialism, dominance, and master narratives associated with that project, at times for better, but certainly, at other times, for worse.

Well, perhaps, although at most only in part. To be sure, the account here affirms and not only describes the contention that where truth is at risk, as it has been placed in the contemporary humanities, the Holocaust exemplifies a ground by which the status of truth, *wherever* its presence is in question, can be tested. But here "prescription" merges with "description": Either the claim for such a ground is warranted or it isn't, and if it is, it must be so acknowledged (here the prescription) whatever else is then built on it or taken from it. No particular epistemic assertion is at issue here, nor is the possibility of disagreement, as in conflicts of evidence, ruled out. But that there is a ground-zero in any such procedure, and that the occurrence of the Holocaust has come to stand for that in much contemporary discourse—for good reason—seems also itself a matter of fact. Again, not because the Holocaust is "unique," and not because no other historical event *could* lead to the same conclusion, but because in the context of our own present, the combination of the dimensions of the Holocaust, its proximity, and the threatening repetition of certain of its features commands attention and recognition. The limits indicated in that basis are more general and applicable than the basis itself, but this seems all the more reason for acknowledging them when we see them.

It is in this sense that I have been proposing a ground for the humanities wherever the claims made in its fields of discourse are subject to assessment as true or false — a ground that provides assurance of the choice to be made, an either/or, with no third or intermediate way. That there are *some* such cruxes would not often be denied, but they typically are set aside as exotic or special cases, remote from everyday life as well as from the abstract findings or conclusions that typically characterize the humanities, in literary or historical or philosophical accounts and judgments. But epistemic skepticism and moral openness must themselves concede limits if they are to be intelligible or applicable (beginning with self-referentiality, their willingness to question their own questions). One can see the force of this stricture as clearly as it can be seen in the superficially simple move that would put the Holocaust in scare quotes, as "the Holocaust": that is, as the "so-called" Holocaust, the Holocaust "as it were," or — more deeply — "as it is claimed to have been."

The classic imperative "Know thyself" resonated in directing human vision and understanding to the person whose vision and understanding it was. The humanities have grown through and past this ideal, recognizing its contingency and thus also disputing the vacuum or airlessness of the "view from nowhere" by means of which Enlightenment thinking had then come to elevate man himself in his capacity for knowledge. A line of argument that evolved in the aftermath of that period did make the effort to introduce inhabitants of flesh and blood, particular ones; but it did this without providing those inhabitants with the means of sustenance or survival, as if they could thrive and have their say about the world if only they were first able either to supply themselves with oxygen or to find a means of living without it. A further alternative is the one proposed here, in the stark irony of the claim that recognition of the Holocaust, that symbol of death and brutality, may convey and sustain the life of truth. The basic question for philosophy and other fields of the humanities is not how to re-do or re-imagine history, but how to countenance and imagine the present through the history that has been and that remains now, in its basic modality, fixed in place. The fact that individual historical events had been contingent in their occurrence does not mean that the future in which they then, having occurred, became incorporated also is contingent. Quite the contrary: The one-time contingency endures later as fact. The Holocaust in *its* two-fold role — that it need not have occurred, but that it did — exemplifies this, making the Holocaust more than only a lesson in history, as it continues to assert its own presence.

As far as human eyes can judge, the degree of evil
might have been less without any impediment to good.

SAMUEL JOHNSON

« 3 »

Evil and Understanding

A Holocaust Dilemma

The need to account for the appearance of evil in a world assumed to be ruled by goodness and justice provoked Jewish religious and philosophical reflection long before the Holocaust. The "problem" of evil, pointed most sharply in the phenomenon of human suffering and loss, figured in the very origins of Jewish philosophy (as in Saadya's commentary on Job [c. 935 C.E.]), and Genesis itself provided an earlier view of the knowledge of good and evil in its synthesis of cosmology and genealogy: the entry into human nature of moral conscience that ensured that man would then make his own way across the grain of historical contingency *and* face divine judgment for his actions in that process.[1] It was this *second* nature that would impel the Biblical narrative and subsequent Jewish ethical reflection.

Nothing in this history, however, suggests a distinctively Jewish representation of the "problem of evil" or of the connection it involves between ontology and ethics—the substantive connection between the world as it is and the world as it ought to be. The common, and commonsensical, assumption of a relation between the "is" and the "ought" has figured prominently in theoretical and practical ethics for as long as records exist of either, and the twentieth-century disclaimer of that relation in the "Naturalistic Fallacy" (and its empiricist predecessors) should be viewed in the context of this larger, contrary tradition rather than the other way round.[2] What, after all, would be a stronger incentive for moral analysis (also, admittedly, for moralizing) than to consider how badly some human lives have fared under a supposedly beneficent and all-powerful ruler?

The skeptical reminder that righteous people suffer and wicked ones prosper does not hold universally, but it does not have to. Even a few local examples—always available—underscore this imbalance, and it seems impossible to find a culture or age from which awareness of it is absent. An obvious reason for this widespread recognition is that illness and death are cultural as well as biological universals: However inventive a society's rationalized accounts of loss and suffering, those disruptions lodge in the social fabric and recur in its "thick" descriptions. Furthermore, the issue they pose dramatically in a divinely ordered world figures in other settings as well, for one example, in the problem of voluntary evil-doing: how, or whether, a person can choose to do evil in full knowledge of what he is doing (human rationality as an analogue here to divine omniscience). The sophisticated debate reported in Job about the gap between divine justice and human suffering suggests a history in Jewish thought antedating that book's composition (c. 500 B.C.E.); the "consolation" of his comforters as they urge Job to examine his own responsibility for his suffering rather than to dispute its justice—an early version of theodicy—is unlikely to have been invented for that occasion.

Motivation for philosophical and religious reflection on evil, then, is ample, and if that background presses no more urgently in Jewish thought than in other religious or philosophical traditions, it is no less evident there. On the one hand, the world was found "good" at each stage of the Biblical creation, and except for scattered moments of mystical enthusiasm, subsequent Jewish commentary never disputed that judgment. On the other hand, a profusion of evidence attests to individual and group suffering in people who appear to deserve that condition no more (often much less) than contemporaries who fare better, often, *much* better. At least from the time of Rabbinic Judaism, in any event, the issue thus stated would recur in Jewish theological and philosophical discussion: how to reconcile misfortune, suffering or persecution, and exile with the goodness of creation and the authority of an all-powerful and beneficent creator. And if modern *pre*-Holocaust Jewish thinkers, from Spinoza to Hermann Cohen, seem less troubled than their predecessors by the phenomenon of evil as a historical and then religious or metaphysical factor, this reflected new anxieties about epistemological themes more than the diminished significance of ethical issues themselves.

The constancy in the conceptualization of evil is further underscored when compared to changes in other cultural themes. For in contrast to the variations in other traditional beliefs, few surface in the idiom of "normal" representations of evil. This persistence appears also in the avoidance even among historical accounts of culture of anything like a "history of evil"—this, *against* the evidence that conceptions and practices of evil, like other ideas and practices, have altered over time (and might even, like those others, comprise a *progressive* history). Western ethical thinking, both in and outside Judaism, has emphasized the contrary view, treating evil rather as all-of-a-kind, effectively settled in its character and motivation from its first occurrence. Here the capacity for evil-doing reflects an assumed constancy in human nature, appearing full-grown even in its first Biblical appearance: the disobedience in the Garden and its attempted cover-up seem, after all, quite effortless—if one did not know better, as if they reflected long practice. However one understands the "Yetzer Ha-rah" ["evil impulse"] ascribed to man in the Biblical account of Noah, furthermore, it too remains unaltered in later sources as an aspect of human nature. In contrast to the varieties of its expression, then, the *character* of evil-doing—the evil in it—appears unchanging. If goodness or justice remain goals to be realized in the future (if ever), the option of evil seems always present and immediately available.

Admittedly, except for the quasi-mythical Draconian law of a single and harsh punishment for all crimes, ethical violations and their corresponding punishments are typically distinguished by degrees of severity (again, both within and outside Judaism). The idea that "punishment ought to fit the crime" thus appears historically as a bedrock principle in systems of justice, notwithstanding other differences as to *which* acts count as crimes or how to measure their relative severity.[3] The largest instances of suffering or affliction in group-histories, furthermore, tend to appear as quantitatively, not qualitatively different from others: more or fewer victims, a longer or shorter period of persecution. What typically is *not* considered is the evil in the evil-doing itself. (Stalin's responsibility for a larger number of murderous deaths than Hitler, for example, is sometimes cited as if there were no differences in what led to those ends.)[4]

Divergent judgments of the same event often obscure questions about the judging itself. A war that is catastrophic for the loser and thus (for him) challenges the claim of Providence, is to the victor additional evidence *for* that role. From the one side, then, evil and injustice; from the other, well and good—although both conclusions derive from the same evidence. Survivors of a massacre or catastrophe may thank God and cite that outcome as miraculous, but this reaction ignores its theological and ethical implications for the victims who did not survive and who, we may assume, would not be thankful at all. To see evildoing as part of an historical process already moves beyond the immediacy of personal agency or suffering, but even then the latter typically overshadow the structure and form of the acts involved. That people differ about which acts are unforgivable—one mark of evil at its extreme—is another indicator of the historicity of evildoing, but this implication, too, often gives way to the conclusion that ultimately, evildoing and its corollary, evil-suffering, are essentially all-of-a-kind. Differences in individual moral character generally have been recognized; evil itself has been viewed as constant and common.[5]

« » « »

History, however, has a way of undoing the most conscientious expectations, and the Holocaust has had just that unsettling effect on moral history and theory. Evidence of this appears in the assembly of claims representing the Holocaust as unique or as a "novum," a breach or turning point in moral history generally and in Jewish history specifically.[6] Such characterizations start out from the systematic cruelty inflicted in the Holocaust, with that enormity also expressed in a related set of terms that call the Holocaust "indescribable," "beyond words," "ineffable."[7] Often such terms are figurative, hyperbolic (this issue is discussed at greater length in chapter 5), but even allowing for this rhetorical element, their literal core remains: the *fact* of the Holocaust, involving systematic cruelty on a scale that portends a rupture or paradigm shift in moral understanding generally and opens the issue for Jewish thought and consciousness in particular. The metahistorical implications thus noted evidently presuppose the historical ground: a dependence of moral or religious conclusions on historical premises, a dependence that although not unique to accounts of the Holocaust, requires closer than usual scrutiny because of the scale of the issues.

This requirement is not without its own difficulties, however, as even common references to the phenomenon of evil make clear. On the one hand, if evil were not apparent, there would be no moral "problem" to discuss. On the other hand, to speak of evil as real—without scare-quotes—turns out, on inspection, to be tendentious, since a significant philosophical tradition has argued that evil is *only* apparent. On this account, any assumption that evil is more than that shows only a lack of understanding, since whatever else evil is, it is *not* real. In this way, the "problem" of evil proves itself to be a problem.

Even this deflationary conclusion, however, cannot obscure the occurrence of human suffering and loss, and it is these, after all, that on the scale of the Holocaust impel the claim of a breach or transformation in moral history, necessitating the revision and possibly the abandonment of traditional moral categories. Again, the prima facie grounds are clear for both the historical and the metahistorical sides of this thesis: the distinctive cruelty in the agents and the suffering in the victims impel the finding of a metahistorical breach in moral and religious history. Viewed against that background, the question, "Where was God in Auschwitz?" has become formulaic, recurring in Jewish and other religious reflections on the Holocaust (slightly altered, in secular accounts as well). With Auschwitz itself a metonymy for Nazism, furthermore, "*After* Auschwitz" also now designates a metonymic line of (chronological) demarcation—a transformative moment in moral and social and religious history.[8]

This line of reasoning underscores the need to assess the historical basis for the metahistorical conclusion that regards the Holocaust as having broken the traditional instruments of moral measurement. Here I can sketch only this comparative historical critique, recognizing also that comparisons among such instances of suffering are necessarily invidious and themselves cruel. But the conception of the Holocaust as a moral turning point is (also necessarily) comparative, requiring that the event itself be scrutinized in the same terms, whether in relation to Jewish or to world history. Perhaps surprisingly, the former—the Holocaust viewed in the context of Jewish history—has been attempted less often than assessment of the Holocaust on a global scale. Common to both views, however, has been the finding of rupture in the post-Holocaust moral universe—a transformation in moral conscience and consciousness. Thus, the need for testing the historical ground, since unless that ground is substantiated, the *contrary* view would hold, of continuity between pre- and post-Holocaust consciousness in Jewish and/or world history, with the Holocaust making no essential difference to the philosophical or theological analysis of evil. That, too, remains a possibility, and indeed the burden of proof seems to rest on the other side; that is, of demonstrating discontinuity: the breach or revolution.

The turning points in Jewish history that suggest likely comparison to the Holocaust are both few and evident: the destruction of the two Temples (586 B.C.E and 70 C.E.); the destruction and disruption accompanying the Crusades beginning in 1096 C.E.; the natural disaster of the Black Death (1348–1350 C.E.) and the related massacres of Jews who were blamed for it; the expulsion of the Jews from Spain and Portugal (1492 and 1497); the Chmielnicki "riots" (1648–1649)—are all obvious, if not the only candidates. The numbers or percentages of Jews killed in these catastrophes are not the only measure of their significance, but they provide a starting place for any comparison. So, for example, the sweep of the First Crusade through Central Europe that began in 1096 caused the estimated deaths of five thousand Jews and corresponding communal disruption. But the communities evidently overcame the shock of those events with "no substantial discontinuity in Franco-German [Jewish] society as a whole. . . . The towns were quickly resettled, commerce and trade were reconstructed."[9] The Jewish suicides in Mainz at this time (choosing death rather than capture) made an enduring impression within and beyond the local communities, and some contemporary accounts of the persecution understood it as a "trial of the righteous" rather than (as others did) a form of collective punishment. But both these explanations had precedents in Jewish history, and cruel as the pressures were, there seems no basis for regarding the events themselves as a caesura or turning point in the collective moral consciousness (even taking into account the difficulty of any such assessment).[10] Similarly, the expulsions from Spain and Portugal involved the dislocation of a Jewish populace numbering in various estimates between one hundred and three hundred thousand, with the deaths caused by the expulsion or otherwise by the Inquisition at the time (at most) in the thousands. The communal upheaval and the crisis in the flourishing "Golden Age" of Sephardic Jewry were evident; but again, the survival through emigration of much the largest part of that group allowed for continuity among those expelled and even enrichment for the Jewish communities that absorbed them.

For its proportion of victims, the Black Death of 1348 to 1350 arguably looms larger than any other recorded natural catastrophe, having killed between a quarter and a half of the populace of Europe and approximately the same proportion of Jews (250,000 of 500,000). To the latter figure must be added Jewish victims of related massacres, as Jews were variously held responsible for the Plague itself (for example, through the libel of well-poisoning). The number of victims in this related persecution was certainly in the thousands, possibly in the tens of thousands, and the period of recovery required by the Jewish communities was proportionately large. But in part because the plague affected all groups in its path, its impact, in terms of moral or religious upheaval, seems to have been relatively subdued; the Polish and Lithuanian Jewish communities, not very far distant, were nonetheless relatively unaffected by the plague or the associated persecution. Estimates of the Chmielnicki Massacres of 1648 to 1649 refer to victims in the tens of thousands, with a round figure of one hundred thousand sometimes cited (and up to three hundred communities destroyed). The period was spoken of at the time by R. Shabbetai Sheftel Horowitz as the "Third Destruction" (after the First and Second Temples), but if the massacres seemed from within to warrant that label, it was also apparent, to some extent even at the time, that the Jewish communities in Western and other parts of Eastern Europe were relatively unaffected.

Even the admittedly vague numbers in these instances are unavailable for the conflicts that ensued in the destruction of the First and Second Temples and the exiles that followed them. What evidence there is suggests a minimal number of deaths, but it is also clear that in their communal and religious (and conceptual) consequences, the destruction of the temples was at least equal to and probably greater than any of the later events mentioned. The religious prophecies prior to the first destruction and the ensuing exile that apparently validated them, effecting a revolution in religious thought and practice—the confluence threatening a breach in God's covenant with Israel—loom larger in their impact than any of the later events. This would include the Holocaust itself, which in a number of ways allowed for regeneration and communal continuity (more about this below).

Such doubts about the breach caused by the Holocaust in *Jewish* history leave untouched, however, the analogous claim in world-historical terms. Here the argument has a sharper edge, as the Holocaust represents a paradigm (whether or not the first) instance of genocide: the intentional, state-sponsored, and systematic attempt to erase "that" people "from the face of the earth" (in Himmler's wording). To be sure, "uniqueness" claims for the Holocaust often build on subordinate rather than essential features of the Holocaust. That the Nazi genocide against the Jews was initiated by a nation closely tied to both the Christian tradition and the Enlightenment; that it was carried on in view of other countries with the same traditions; that it implemented a process of industrialized killing "invented" for the occasion; that aside from its principal purpose of annihilation, it constantly applied what Primo Levi chillingly calls "useless violence"—these remarkable features do not alter the basic structure of the genocidal act itself.[11]

The same claim applies to the extreme consequences of the Holocaust *within* the Jewish community. The murder of two-thirds of the European Jews ended the role of Eastern Europe as a primary source of Jewish communal existence; it was also a death sentence for Yiddish as a language and cultural means. Most basically, of course, it cut off the lives and futures of six million people. That the Nazis did not succeed in fully implementing their "Final Solution" is, furthermore, also "accidental"; they advanced sufficiently far on that goal, in any event, to mark their action as genocide (a conceptual feature of genocide—in contrast to homicide—is that it need not be "complete"). And it remains the phenomenon of genocide itself that ultimately distinguishes what the Nazis intended and did, and which also may render it no less significant in moral history than specifically in Jewish history. It does not diminish the enormity of the Holocaust to acknowledge that it left important centers of Jewish life physically untouched (except by the influx of Jewish refugees and all the changes this entailed) in North and South America, to some extent in Great Britain, in Palestine, in the Islamic countries of Asia and in North Africa; and that it thus subsequently allowed both for communal continuity there and for those communities' valuable—arguably, decisive—contributions to the State of Israel's independence and development. Certain commentators who emphasize the continuity of Jewish history as a whole, view that continuity as also a primary "lesson" of the Holocaust: another threat to Jewish existence as added to earlier ones that were *also* thwarted. Only on this basis could as measured a post-Holocaust writer as Eliezer Berkowitz conclude that "We [Jews] have had innumerable Auschwitzes . . . Each generation had its Auschwitz problem."[12] Continuity indeed.

« » « »

On the one hand, then, post-Holocaust Jewish ethical reflection faces the large-scale and systematic destruction caused by the Holocaust; on the other hand, the evidence remains of comparable or larger breaches in the moral and religious fabric of Jewish history and consciousness. In this sense, the claim for the Holocaust as indicating or demanding a moral transformation applies more clearly to world-history; that the Jews were the principal victims of the Holocaust only intensifies the irony here. But this does not mean that post-Holocaust Jewish thinkers have not *claimed* that the Holocaust demands a transformative moral and religious response in Judaism itself. On the other hand, although many such claims have been made, they turn out on examination to represent a minority view, and one that arguably overstates its conclusions even in its own terms. Even if one grants this, it would not follow that formulations that place the Holocaust on a continuum with prior events of Jewish history are by *that* fact adequate, but even the possibility that the enormity of the Holocaust might leave the status of evil in Jewish thought unaltered is significant.[13] Admittedly, the question would then arise of how far the metahistorical claim of continuity extends. But a limited claim of continuity would bear directly on post-Holocaust Jewish thought, among other things, providing a baseline for assessing accounts that emphasize *dis*continuity.

Thus, the conceptualization of the Holocaust "within the bounds of Jewish history" appears in various formulations, with several versions of the most common formulation revolving around a single thesis: That since whatever occurs in history reflects divine intention (at least, concurrence), all such events are also justified or good, *and* that this holds whether the rationale for such events is humanly intelligible or not. This "theodicy" (in Leibniz's coinage of 1710)—"God-justice"—has itself appeared in philosophical and theological variants, but also with a constant basis: That God, himself outside history, nonetheless governs it through his qualities of goodness and omnipotence.[14] *Apparent* evil is, in these terms, only that; in fact, whatever occurs is not evil, but justified, good—a view originating perhaps in direct response to specific historical events, but also there as part of a larger, metahistorical framework. Anything not so justified would, quite simply, not have occurred.

The most urgent application of this principle is to actions or events that ensue in suffering or loss and thus invite interpretation as punishment. Traditional claims in Judaism for such divine supervision have been widespread and substantial. So, for example, Maimonides writes in the *Guide* about "our" [the central Jewish] view: "It is in no way possible that He [God] should be unjust . . . All the calamities that befall men and all the good things that come to men, be it a single individual or a group, are all of them determined according to the deserts of the men concerned through equitable judgment which is no injustice whatsoever."[15] An earlier, more specific formulation (cited by Maimonides in the same context) is R. Ammi's: "There is no death without sin and no suffering without transgression."[16] A prayer recited in the Jewish prayer for the "new month" and in the Holiday service points to the same principle in collective form: "*Mip'ne Chata'enu, Ga-linu Me'artzenu*" ("Because of our sins, we have been exiled from our land").[17]

The implications of this "punishment-reward" model are evident. For the Holocaust, it implies that victims suffer only and always for reason, because of their own wrongdoing or because of someone else's for which they were responsible or because, on balance, the whole of which a particular event was part warranted its occurrence. As directed at the Holocaust, furthermore, this conclusion applies equally to the children and the aged among the victims, to the pious and the unbelievers, the criminal and the righteous, as for every other exemplar of religious or moral practice in the afflicted Jewish communities of Europe: all of them, now, justly punished.

The evident harshness of this judgment as applied to the Holocaust has provoked numerous objections, some of which extend the argument beyond that event. For example, Berkowitz's sharp dissent: "That all suffering is due to [sin] is simply not true. The idea that the Jewish martyrology through the ages can be explained as divine judgment is obscene."[18] Yet, "obscene" as the interpretation may appear, it has recurred, and if its formulations seem marginal or problematic philosophically, their cultural and religious significance is undeniable. So, for example, Rabbi Yoel Taitlebaum, the then-Satmar Rebi, finds Zionism the wrong that precipitated and so warranted the Holocaust: due punishment for its effort to preempt the Messiah's role in initiating the return to Zion. An analogous rendering is Rabbi Elhanan Wasserman's rhetorical tour de force: "In those [pre-Holocaust] days, the Jews chose for themselves two forms of idolatry . . . socialism and nationalism . . . A miraculous event occurred: in Heaven the two idolatries were combined into one—National Socialism. A terrible staff of ire was created which extends harm to all the ends of the earth."[19] A more recent expression of the punishment-and-reward view was Rabbi Ovadiah Yosef's, in 2001, who found in the Jewish victims of the Holocaust "reincarnations of earlier souls, who sinned and caused others to sin."[20] (The logic here is both swift and circumspect: The appeal to reincarnation anticipates the objection that apparent innocents—children and pious elders—were among the Holocaust victims; there could be due cause from their prior existence for *their* suffering.)[21]

Again, the severity of this position is clear: The cruelty and suffering inflicted in the Holocaust seem disproportionate to any possible wrongdoing by its victims. A further problematic implication is this view's representation of the perpetrators of such suffering (indeed, Hitler himself) as instruments of divine justice, in effect doing God's work. That consequence is unavoidable: if the punishment is just, whoever administers it must also, ultimately, be acting justly.[22] Yet, despite these implications, the view's persistence is in its own terms not arbitrary or groundless, as becomes evident in more nuanced explanations that hope to avoid the notion of suffering as divine justice by shifting responsibility for it from God to man, but which are in the end forced to revert to the same source: God's sanction for the events of world history.

The principal argument in this second variant of the punishment-reward model emphasizes man's free moral agency. Acting on his own, man rather than God becomes responsible for any evil that occurs in human history, even on the scale of the Holocaust. It is not that the victims always bring their fate on themselves, but that *some* human agents act in such a way as to produce the harm to them. Again, the logic here is straightforward: Man has the freedom to do good or evil—a (arguably, *the*) distinctive human attribute. Given God's benevolence and omnipotence, evil when it does occur—inflicting suffering and loss on the innocent—expresses human not divine character and choice. God *could* not have a role here if man's freedom is to be preserved—and the result of human agency and decision is what one would expect: human responsibility. So Berkowitz writes, "[Human] freedom must be respected by God himself. God cannot as a rule intervene whenever man's use of freedom displeases him. It is true, if he did so, the perpetration of evil would be rendered impossible, but so would the possibility for good."[23]

The reason for this effort to shift responsibility from God to man is evident. But the move also invites the charge of question-begging on the issue of whether man's freedom is worth the price of a world that includes the Holocaust—and of how to settle *that* question. The response of theodicy here would be certain: "Yes, of course: human freedom, whatever its consequences." And more generally: "Better the world as it is, including the Holocaust, than otherwise, or any other world." This version of the "Continuum" argument avoids finding fault in the specific victims, but the omission counts for little in distinguishing this from the earlier version because of its insistence in turn that *on the whole* whatever happens is justified. The question of who specifically provoked a certain punishment thus becomes irrelevant, in deference to the interest of justice "on the whole." All this, again, follows the principle that whatever happens in history is finally justified.

A third variant of the punishment-reward account of evil situates the Holocaust on a continuum of Jewish history within the framework of that history's redemptive features, often citing the 1948 establishment of Israel as a central item of evidence. This assertion of the good that may come out of evil is sometimes set within a religious framework, but it also occurs in versions of secular redemption (for the establishment of Israel, on the principles of nationalism and self-determination). Both these lines of interpretation, however, find the Holocaust an important, even necessary stage on the way to Israel's statehood, itself viewed as a consummatory moment in Jewish history. Thus, the Holocaust is redeemed, whether partly or in full, by the creation of Israel that *would not* have occurred (this, as either a tacit or explicit assumption) had there been no Holocaust. The latter claim is itself a straightforward historical assertion, albeit with the problems of any counterfactual conditional. In strictly historical terms, the claim has often been disputed. But such objections do not, of course, address the "meta"-historical elements in the redemptive theory of Jewish history that finds hardship and suffering ultimately, and necessarily, transfigured. The significance claimed for the connection between the Holocaust and the establishment of the State of Israel is an especially dramatic application of this theory.

The fourth and last variant of the punishment-reward model invokes the concept of "Hester Panim"—[God's] "hiding of the [his] face"—as a means of preserving God's justice and power and yet leaving room for (localized) injustice. The metaphor of "hiding" describes a divine withdrawal from history that allows events to occur that God otherwise would have prevented—the withdrawal occurring not because God wills the events but because he wills man's freedom more. So Norman Lamm writes: "[In a period of Hester Panim] . . . we are given over to the uncertainties of nature and history where we can be raised . . . to the crest of the world's waves—or herded pitilessly into the fierce troughs of life."[24] And Berkowitz, with further emphasis on the role of human freedom, adds: ". . . If man alone is the creator of value . . . then he must have freedom of choice and freedom of decision . . . That man may be, God must absent himself . . . He hides his presence."[25] This view has the (temporary) advantage of dividing history into divine and human parts: the former where God is active, the latter that moves by human decision. To be sure, God *could* control the human part if he chose to, but he chooses not to, in order to ensure man's freedom. "Hester Panim" thus intensifies the shift of evil-doing (and suffering) to man as initiator; also here (as in the second version above of the punishment-reward argument), the privileging of human freedom above other, possibly conflicting values is unquestioned. But once again, since "Hester Panim" must acknowledge that God *chooses* to hide when he does (he could not, after all, be forced to do that), this "choice," too, emerges as a version of theodicy: Whatever happens—including God's withdrawal—reflects a decision to do so, an *intention*. Thus, too, the claim, even for the prospect of the Holocaust, that what occurs must be "for the best."[26]

The "punishment-reward" interpretation of the Holocaust in these four versions is one of three formulations of the "Continuum" view that finds the Holocaust unexceptional in terms of traditional Jewish thought and texts—*and* in terms of justification. The second formulation, also with a lengthy past, interprets apparently unwarranted suffering not as punishment, but as something quite different; thus, a "Reductive" account. One version of this conceives of suffering as a test, with its "proof-text" in the Biblical "Akedah"—the "binding" of Isaac—where God commands Abraham to sacrifice his son *as* a test. Other "tests" also appear in the Bible (for example, in Job), and indeed, conceptually, treating suffering or harm as a test has a dialectical advantage, since even a just ruler might reasonably test a blameless subject, in contrast to punishing him wrongly. But this conceptual looseness also comes at a price, since unless there are limits to what counts as a test, what could be said about victims of the Holocaust who died in the "test" would remain unclear (unless the deaths of some are to be understood as a test of the survivors, with the dead themselves left entirely bereft.).

A second variant of this "Reductive" interpretation views suffering as having positive value in itself. At times echoing Rabbi Akiba's statement that "suffering is precious," suffering is accorded a justified place in the world—as it anticipates future reward, or as the price to be paid in the present for the goodness of the whole, or as proof of faith in the present, or (most basically), for the experience of suffering itself.[27] Versions of this view range from a flat denial of the experience (so, Reb Zusya of Anipol: "I don't understand why you ask me this question [about *my* suffering]. Ask it of someone who has known such evil. As for me, this does not apply, for nothing ill has ever happened to me"[28]) to the near-utilitarian justification that Rabbi Joseph Soloveitchik offers even in reference to the Holocaust: "Suffering occurs in the world in order to contribute something to man, in order that atonement be made for him, in order to redeem him from corruption, vulgarity, and depravity."[29]

The third formulation of the Continuum position, overarching the others, accounts for evil by *refusing* to account for it; that is, by falling back on the limits of human comprehension: For certain "difficult" events, human understanding finds *no* adequate ground—not because there is none, but because of its own incapacity. Such limits, if invoked for an event like the Holocaust, would apply more generally as well, and the arguments to this effect have a lengthy tradition both within and outside Judaism. Thus we hear that God's ways are not man's ways, that the difference between finite and infinite understanding makes access impossible from the one to the other—in short, that there *is* no way of comprehending the rationale for human history, whatever its turns, since that would require, per impossibile, a human grasp of God's reasons.[30]

Superficially, this account might seem to replace theodicy with agnosticism—the view, for example, that "A certain event *appears* to have resulted in terrible injustice, but this is because our limited understanding cannot fathom the true reasons for it." The implied directive here, however, is not agnostic at all, since its claim of incomprehensibility concludes finally by justifying the occasion considered (and its apparent injustice), *not* of raising or substantiating doubts about them: "There *are* reasons—if only we could grasp them." If this were not the case, as Hugh Rice points out, consistency would require the tag of incomprehensibility also for occasions of rejoicing or what we take to be justice realized, indeed, for all God's actions, whatever their consequences.[31] The unstated assumption of the Argument from Incomprehensibility, then, is that there are reasons—more specifically, *good* ones—for suffering and loss that seem senseless and unjustifiable in terms of man's limited understanding. Far from putting God's supervision of history in question, this argument advocates its acceptance as just, attesting to human limits, not God's. Thus again, theodicy survives.

« » « »

Despite their recognition of cruelty and suffering in the Holocaust, none of the accounts of evil noted so far finds in that event a basis for reconceptualizating moral principle or religious commitment within the context of Judaism. Whatever the Continuum view finds demanded of moral conscience "after Auschwitz," the traditional principles and texts of Jewish thought remain adequate, in both explanation and justification. That the principal sources for this view come from religious "Orthodoxy" may not be surprising, but neither should it discount the response itself. Indeed, the Continuum position appears also in secular writers and in others who, although religiously committed, address the Holocaust in the context of ethical judgment as such. So, for example, Emmanuel Levinas acknowledges the Holocaust as a "paradigm" of suffering, but also finds it parallel to "the Gulag and all other places of suffering in our political century"—in other words, part of a broader, and in that sense, nonspecific, historical tendency.[32] It is significant, furthermore, that most of the influential Jewish thinkers who write after the Holocaust, wherever they place themselves in respect to the Jewish tradition and even when they allude (as virtually all do) to the Holocaust, do not find that event as pivotal in their own rendering of Jewish history or thought. (I consider here such otherwise different figures as Martin Buber, A. J. Heschel, Mordechai Kaplan, Yeshayahu Leibowitz, Emmanuel Levinas, Nathan Rotenstreich, and Gershom Scholem.) Certain commentators, apart from any judgment on the character of evil in the Holocaust, call attention to the psychological or social grounds that, within the context of Jewish thought, influence responses to that aspect of the Holocaust. Thus, David Hartman writes, "For some, suffering is bearable if it results from the limitations of finite human beings, but it becomes terrifying and demonic if it is seen as part of the scheme of their all-powerful creator. Others would find life unbearably chaotic if they did *not* believe that suffering, tragedy, and death were part of God's plan for the world."[33] Undoubtedly, these ad hominem considerations affect responses to the Holocaust, and it would be valuable to have them systematically analyzed, but even if the difficulty of effectively carrying out such analysis were overcome, we would still have to consider the reasoning in the responses as reasoning, a process that would, in my view, bring us back to assessing the views of evil as they are outlined here.

The "Continuum" position reflects a conception of evil on which distinctions among its instances (in their explanation or justification) are finally irrelevant. And indeed, it seems to follow logically that the slightest occurrence of evil is as much a test of theodicy as any larger one, since for a just and all-powerful God, *no* evil or injustice should have a place. The Continuum position, drawing mainly on variations of theodicy, readily accommodates this implication, as in Berkowitz's summing-up: "As far as our faith in an absolutely just and merciful God is concerned, the suffering of a single innocent child poses no less a problem to faith than the undeserved suffering of millions."[34] That conclusion by itself is noncommittal on whether evil *does* occur, but this point is then addressed in the several versions of the Continuum argument (including Berkowitz's) that displace or simply deny all such occurrence.

The claim of a rupture or caesura caused by the Holocaust in Jewish history must then argue against the Continuum position on grounds not of logic, but of substance, asserting in both historical and moral terms that events are *not* all of a kind; that their differences may be qualitative as well as quantitative; and, in more specific reference, that the scope and scale of murder in the Holocaust marks a quantum jump from "ordinary" wrongdoing. On this account, the Holocaust is sufficiently distinctive to require new categories of moral understanding in the context of Jewish history and arguably for world history as well. On this view, too, variant accounts emerge concerning the nature and consequences of the breach alleged in moral consciousness. Thus, the dramatic thesis that even the extremity of the Holocaust makes no essential difference to moral understanding in the context of Jewish thought shifts to the drama of its opposite, which then faces the problem of showing how the Holocaust makes such an essential difference, but without either severing post-Holocaust Jewish thought from characteristic elements of its religious and philosophical past, however difficult or contentious the process of identifying them is.

The most extreme example of this response was as clear in anticipation as it has proved difficult to sustain. If the traditional view of evil in Jewish thought was obliged to confront God's role as omnipotent and benevolent, the most obvious break with the tradition would be to argue *against* that role, and this indeed is the direction taken by Richard Rubenstein, first in *After Auschwitz* and then in later writings.[35] *After Auschwitz* itself appeared in a setting not specifically related to the Holocaust, through the "death of God" theme that, echoing Nietzsche's Zarathustra, was at the time circulating among non-Jewish theologians like Thomas Altizer, Harvey Cox, and William Hamilton.[36] Indeed, Rubenstein's own earlier "Reconstructionist" leanings laid the ground for this move in its Deweyan (by way of Mordechai Kaplan) denial of God's transcendence. But Rubenstein, arguing "*after Auschwitz*," believed there was now a still stronger case against Judaism's traditional conception of God, one that extended to what he regarded as the cultural and social liabilities to which such belief contributed.

This meant also that there was (and in the event, would remain) a question about what Rubenstein could *affirm* in Jewish principle or thought, and his subsequent writings seem at once to have sought and to have avoided such affirmation. Their dominant theme has combined a view of truth and knowledge as functions of power (after Nietzsche and, latterly, Foucault) with a social or cultural definition of Judaism centered on the entry into history and power of the State of Israel. This emphasis on political rather than moral or religious factors offers a prescription for Jewish survival *given* the narrowed and shaken world articulated in the aftermath of the Holocaust; it says little about any specifically Jewish religious or social link to the past as an essential element. The lesson of the Holocaust disclosed for Rubenstein through the lens of powerlessness affords little positive basis for Jewish—indeed, for any religious or even ethnic—particularism, and little more for the institution of religion as such. The metaphor of "triage" to which Rubenstein later turns as a basis for political theory seems at once to epitomize the break he sees in Jewish history as caused by the Holocaust and the difficulty of finding a source of continuity for that tradition—other than force itself—to overcome the breach.[37]

A less radical reaction against the traditional view of transcendence appears in Hans Jonas, who finds in the limitation in contrast to the denial of God's power a means of accounting for the breach caused by the Holocaust. For Jonas, the Holocaust serves not as disproof of God's existence or of his justice but as evidence of certain constraints that bind even him. It is not, in this view, that God could have acted in that history and chose not to, but that he could not act, however much he wished to. Jonas thus argues for a conception of God as limited by his own earlier choices—if not to the same extent as man in *his* history, analogously. Admittedly, the logical limitations of omnipotence (as in the challenge of whether God could create a rock so heavy that he could not pick it up) had been long discussed, but for Jonas, the issue is directed at a particular context. It is not the priority of human freedom that motivates the shift of moral responsibility for the Holocaust away from God (although Jonas affirms such freedom), but that, given his own earlier decisions, God *could* not have intervened to deter or even to mitigate it.[38] On the terms of this account, evil becomes an ingredient in existence, with the responsibility for its occurrence neither God's nor man's exclusively, but shared between them and including constraints of history that are beyond the capacity of either of them to overcome. This view does not exonerate God any more than it does man, nor does it depict evil as an impersonal and independent force. Evil appears rather as friction that might in some circumstances be mitigated or redirected but never entirely avoided, since its occurrence does not depend only on acts of will, human or divine; history itself accounts for its occurrence, with God himself inside as well as outside it.

Neither Rubenstein's nor Jonas's response to the Holocaust is rooted specifically in that event. Like other "death of God" pronouncements, Rubenstein's would apply retroactively, implying not that Judaism's transcendent God had suddenly died but that he had never actually lived. And for Jonas as well, the limits on God's power did not *originate* with the Holocaust. For both writers, however, it was the breach they find in the Holocaust that provoked the turn in their thinking about the status of evil.

A second version of the Holocaust viewed as transformative in Jewish thought and practice uses law or Halakah as a bridge to the past that now, post-Holocaust, is elaborated or changed *because* of the Holocaust. The reason for considering this an example of "discontinuity" is its reference to the law that, immutable for subtraction *or* addition in Orthodox terms, retains a privileged position also for others who would now add to it. The most notable advocate of this view is Emil Fackenheim, who proposed a 614th commandment—"not to give Hitler posthumous victories"—as a literal commandment, not a figurative expression.[39] The ground for Fackenheim's proposal was two-fold: first, the extraordinary—for him, unique—evil that found expression in the Holocaust; and second, his understanding of Halakah as such as involving an historical or contextual dimension throughout its past. In other words, all the mitzvoth, in Fackenheim's view, have emerged in response to historical conditions that then also contributed to the shape they took; given this general feature, also the extraordinary character of the Holocaust *ought* to be reflected in the law. This principle would not by itself determine what the 614th commandment would be; for that, Fackenheim draws on the distinctive goal of the Nazi genocide to destroy the Jewish people. The fitting response to this, as he judges it, should then be a corresponding affirmation of Jewish existence: a commitment by its members to its (and their own) continuity. Sometimes charged by his critics with basing his apparently positive commitment on negative grounds—as reactive or ressentiment, part of a critical tradition that regards antisemitism as at once cause and reason for Jewish survival[40]—Fackenheim's basis seems broader than only that, encompassing other commandments and sources and indeed (as suggested) a general theory of Jewish law.

The starting point for Fackenheim's reflections on the Holocaust, again, is the "rupture in history" he finds in that event as an unparalleled example of evil committed for the sake of doing evil, unparalleled, as he sees it, either in Jewish or in world history.[41] As argued here earlier, the historical claim that serves as the basis for any such metahistorical claim would have to stand on its own historical grounds—as compared to other events in Jewish and world history. Fackenheim's contention that the evil in Nazism is unparalleled stands on the border between the historical and metahistorical, and is no easier either to demonstrate or disprove because of that. Most notable about Fackenheim's account is the correspondence he affirms between the distinctive historical "moment" of the Holocaust and the addition he infers from that for Jewish law as serving as mark at once of a breach and a bridge. The general question of who has the authority, and on what grounds, to add "laws" to long-established and acknowledged precedent remains a problem for Fackenheim's account.[42] His suggestion that the absolute evil which he finds evident in the Holocaust can only be shown, not explained, adds to the difficulty of assessing the premise itself.

A third position in the view of the Holocaust as a rupture or caesura—both historical *and* metahistorical—resembles the last position mentioned in connection with the Continuum model in its reference to the Holocaust's "incomprehensibility." By contrast to the Continuum model, however, this one offers no assurance of a positive outcome even in its conclusion. A compelling statement of this view appears in the work of Arthur A. Cohen, who, transposing Rudolf Otto's conception of the "tremendum" onto the Holocaust, finds the latter "beyond the discourse of morality and rational condemnation."[43] This stance might seem to bring Cohen back (full circle) to Rubenstein's skepticism about the possibility of a religious covenant—to say nothing about the improbability of a living God who would allow such an event to occur. But Cohen rejects that rejection, although acknowledging at least certain of its features. Thus, evil, as Cohen finds it in the Holocaust, *is* real, "no less than good." Yet God is also present and active, almost in partnership with man: ". . . God describes the limits but man sets them . . . God engenders possibilities but . . . man enacts them" (93). One problem, of course, for any claim of incomprehensibility is that it must itself be articulated and explained, and Cohen, as he analyzes the concept, seems at times to make the Holocaust less incomprehensible than it otherwise appears to him (as for example, in the comparison he defends between the impact of the Holocaust and that of the Jewish expulsion from Spain; or when he notes that the Jewish finding of uniqueness in the Holocaust is a feature of every group's response to *its* genocide). There is, then, a question of consistency here, together with a question of exactly what Cohen's conclusion excludes and includes. The stark terms of the opposition that Cohen reiterates dramatize the issue that the Holocaust poses for him: on the one hand, the "tremendum"—in effect, atrocity that is outside history; on the other hand, the affirmation nonetheless not only of the Jewish people but of the God who did not prevent it and yet who, in Cohen's view, remains as a "source of hope."

« » « »

The schematism of moral analysis presented of Jewish religious responses to the Holocaust has been divided between those in which issues raised by that event are seen as continuous with issues raised by prior instances of collective Jewish suffering and responses that regard the Holocaust as a genuine "novum" historically, and then, because of that, in its moral and religious implications. Undoubtedly the single most widely discussed analysis of evil in relation to the Holocaust remains Hannah Arendt's *Eichmann in Jerusalem: A Report on the Banality of Evil*, which has been discussed in a different context in chapter 1. Although in that book and elsewhere, Arendt views the Holocaust in its relation to the rise of totalitarianism historically as a novum, in the conclusions she draws about the nature of its evil (through Eichmann himself), she endorses a "Continuum" view that links up with elements of theodicy from which the present discussion set out. Arendt is rarely counted a "Jewish" philosopher, but her conclusions on Eichmann's "evil" would be significant for reflections on the Holocaust even if it did not (as it does) underscore a basic crux in the understanding of evil that impinges both on Jewish thought and on moral conceptualization more generally.[44] On the one hand, Arendt's view of Eichmann echoes in a shadowy way the aspect of the Continuum view that, in agreement with theodicy, disputes the depth and even the reality of evil. On the other hand, Arendt has no doubt, despite her procedural misgivings about the Eichmann trial, that Eichmann was criminally responsible and that he should have been, as he was, executed. If the tension between these claims is puzzling, that says as much about the issues at stake as it does about her specific account.

The meaning of the phrase, "banality of evil," has been often misrepresented, partly because it is sometimes confused with other issues in Arendt's analysis, partly because of Arendt's own unsystematic development of her own concept. What is clear in her usage and her subsequent reflections on it, however, is that the phrase opens a question that goes to the center of the analysis of evil. The first step in this progression is Arendt's rejection of the view of Eichmann as demonic or as an agent of "radical" evil. Compared to such stereotypic evildoers as Iago or Richard III, she insists, Eichmann does not come close; he is, by contrast, "thoughtless," "a clown," dependent on clichés in his speaking and, still more fundamentally, in his thinking. This is, in fact, the source of his evil-doing even in the monstrousness of the "Final Solution"; the source or agent himself was and remained "banal," his actions not so much unintentional as "non-intentional"; he did not, in Arendt's depiction, *think* about what he was doing and its consequences.

This view of Eichmann has been disputed by critics who question the disproportion that Arendt claims between source and effect in an event of the scope of the Holocaust. In this contentious aftermath, Arendt herself began to see that a general theory of evil-doing was at issue in the contrast she had at first only assumed between "radical" evil (as in Kant's rendering and in the conventional view of Nazism) and evil as banal, in her understanding of *that*. Perhaps in part because of misgivings over the examples of radical evil she had cited as drawn from literary, not historical sources, Arendt began to question whether historical evil was itself *ever* "radical" in the sense of being fully intended or committed "thoughtfully" — that is, with true reflection or full knowledge of its character. The outcome of this deliberation was anticlimactic, and perhaps because of that was not much attended to in the literature about the "banality" of evil. But that outcome is clear, and reveals itself as standing in the lengthy rationalist tradition of ethics initiated by Plato (then also in Platonism) and reappearing in such modern rationalists as Spinoza and Leibniz. In this view, evil, whatever its scale, is nothing positive but a privation; those who commit it act not from deliberation and choice — thoughtfully, knowledgeably — but precisely because they have *not* adequately considered or understood what they were doing. Certainly Eichmann, in Arendt's terms, did not know better. And the crucial implication following from this—albeit one that she herself does not articulate—that if he *had* been more thoughtful, had understood more or more adequately, he would not, and arguably could not, have done what he did. Why Arendt did not go on to acknowledge this point herself may have various explanations, but more important than that issue is the implication's status as a corollary of her view of the banality of evil and its reference to Eichmann's conduct.

The latter view, it should be noted, notwithstanding the special historical circumstances to which it responds, has ample precedent in the Platonic doctrine that "To know the good is to do the good" (or, in its contrapositive, "Not to do the good means not to know the good"). Evildoing in this view reflects a failure of understanding—or, in Arendt's term, "banality." And this, it seems, would for her characterize not only the trivial wrongs commonly cited as "thoughtless" but extreme wrongs as well; it marks off what evil *is*. Thus, in a letter to Gershom Scholem (shortly before he cut off communication with her *because* of the Eichmann book), Arendt wrote: "It is indeed my opinion now that evil is never radical, that it is only extreme, and that it possesses neither depth nor any demonic dimension. It can overgrow and lay waste the whole world precisely because it spreads like a fungus. . . . It is 'thought-defying' . . . because thought tries to reach some depth, to go to the roots, and the moment it concerns itself with evil, it is frustrated because there is nothing. That is its banality. Only the Good has depth and can be radical."[45]

Arendt adds certain nuances to this position in her subsequent writings, but the view indicated remains essentially unchanged, as do its grave implications for her account of evil in or after the Holocaust. For if the charge against Eichmann—and, as it might be extrapolated, Nazism more generally; a large step, but implicit in Arendt's rendering—is one of "thoughtlessness," of such terrible wrongdoing as having been committed mindlessly and without deliberation (and committed *because* of this), then the character of Holocaust-evil, together with related questions of moral responsibility for it, become quite different from what they would be for evil as the outcome of meditated or deliberate intention and act. At issue here is not Nazi "pseudo-science" as simple mistaken (in their biological rationale for racism); it is a question of a failure to "think" in the face of atrocity. Arendt's analysis in these terms had begun more than twenty years earlier in her conception of totalitarianism as rendering the individual person "superfluous," as depriving him of all agency.[46] Compelling as that account is in political terms, however—arguably more dramatic even than Socrates's individual encounter with Protagoras in Plato's dialogue by that name—neither in that earlier work nor in her analysis of Eichmann does she provide an explanation of what happens to moral agency or responsibility under what now turns out to be the universal condition of evil as "banal." Eichmann, she concludes, *should* have been hanged as he was, and the implication of this is that banality does not preclude that verdict. But she does not explain the basis for that judgment on her part (or of the prior finding of his guilt) in relation to the concept of banality, although the way is open here to a charge of inconsistency: Why, to put it bluntly, if Eichmann was incapable of thinking before acting should he have been held responsible at all? (Arendt's contention that his punishment was warranted because he did not want to "share the world" with *his* victims shifts the justification to a quite different principle.

The first phase of the circle traced in the present discussion of evil in the post-Holocaust—a beginning that also denied the possibility of radical or "real" evil—offered by contrast a solution to what, at the closing of the circle in Arendt, seems to become, and to remain, a problem. In those first discussions, human agency and responsibility were asserted as constant even in a divinely ordered world, and irrespective of the social conditions under which any particular individual person or agent lives. The "Yetzer Ha'rah" introduced in Genesis had the function of asserting the lure of evil (not necessarily its triumph, but its presence) even in the presence of understanding and thinking that would *always* be options. The problem for this juxtaposition, we saw, concerned the imposed resolution of theodicy—that whatever happened in history, up to and including the Holocaust, was ultimately for the best, with God and man thus appearing as collaborative agents. Arendt would certainly reject this verdict on history—on world history, on Jewish history, *and* on Eichmann's history. But the terms that she herself sets for the problem of Holocaust-evil by insisting at once on its banality and its extraordinary criminality afford her no ready way of reconciling the two sides of that tension. As has been shown here, she is hardly alone in facing this difficulty, and no doubt Jewish thought in the post-Holocaust will continue to wrestle with it.

« 4 »

Karl Jaspers' *Die Schuldfrage*

A Presence Early and Late

Two conflicting views divide contemporary philosophers in reading the history of philosophy. One group reads that history and the philosophers in it as if they were their own academic contemporaries, measuring their predecessors by what they would have to say (or more often, not say) about current philosophical issues. On this view, the fact that philosophers may have lived centuries ago, working in distinct cultures, traditions, and languages, makes no difference to any later assessment; philosophy, in this view, lives in a timeless present. The second group of contemporary philosophers regards the history of philosophy as embodying history *and* philosophy, accepting that relation as significant in assessing and, before that, in understanding the work of thinkers from the past. On this second account, philosophical writing is inseparable from its historical context, including its linguistic and literary medium as well as the social conditions and the "climate of ideas" at the time: To read a text while ignoring such contextual conditions will almost inevitably be to *mis*read it.

Sixty years after its publication, Karl Jaspers' *Die Schuldfrage* [literally, "The Guilt-Question"] rewards reading from both these perspectives.[1] And if the same claim can to some extent be made for philosophical texts more generally, it has a distinctive applicability to *Die Schuldfrage*. The importance of the historical setting for understanding Jaspers' book is evident. The lectures on which it is based were delivered in January and February 1946, little more than a half year after the Nazi surrender to the Allies and with the populace and cities of Germany still in chaos, with hundreds of thousands of Germans—those left homeless by the war's destruction, former soldiers and prisoners of war, others who had been displaced from countries in the East—still streaming through the countryside and cities. It was in this context that German civil institutions (not fully "German," since they were still under the authority of the four occupying powers) began the effort at revival, hoping to reclaim the "normal" character that twelve years of Nazi dictatorship and the war it initiated had violated. It was also in this context that Jaspers himself, who in 1937 had been "retired" from his position as Professor of Philosophy in the University of Heidelberg—mainly because his wife was Jewish[2]—was reinstated in September 1945; soon after that, he began to prepare the lectures that he delivered in January and February and from which *Die Schuldfrage* would emerge, to be published in Heidelberg later in the same year.[3]

But this historical setting, which provided both the pretext and context of Jaspers' book, is but one element of its structure. For although *Die Schuldfrage* appeared soon after the war's end, it is clearly a meditated work, intended in both the questions it raises and Jaspers' responses to them to go beyond the particular historical occasion from which it sets out. The concerns and issues at its focus, moreover, had held Jaspers' attention well before Germany's official surrender in May 1945 and the opportunity that that provided for a public examination within Germany of its "guilt." The internal evidence of Jaspers' early concern with the "Schuldfrage" is as strong as its external evidence; the book's phenomenology of German reactions to the Nazi regime provides so acute an analysis that recent historians, more than a half-century later, have been deliberating on many of the issues anticipated and confronted by Jaspers (although there is slight evidence of any direct influence).[4] So, for example, Jaspers refers to the role of the Wehrmacht and not only the S.S in implementing Nazi "criminal orders" (48)—arguing against what became a standard postwar narrative to the effect that the Wehrmacht, in contrast to the S.S., had no part in Nazi atrocities. So too, Jaspers writes explicitly and critically about apologetic accounts at the time that stress *Germany's* suffering during the war (from military casualties and civilian bomb damage), a recurrent (in his judgment, misleading) motif at the time, and also one that has flourished recently in German public discourse.[5]

Such insight into the historical situation of Germans and Germany during the war and its immediate aftermath attests to Jaspers' acumen (and courage), but it also reflects a philosophical and moral awareness that goes beyond the specific points addressed, notably through the relationship asserted in the text between the author and its likely readers. Some version of that relation is undoubtedly a factor in all texts (philosophical as well as "literary" ones), but for *Die Schuldfrage*, that relation is central. Part of its importance there stems from the transparency of Jaspers' own history in his writing. He had, after all, remained in Germany throughout the war; more than that, he had remained essentially passive in the presence of a regime that he recognized to be committing moral outrage. In writing about German "guilt," then, he acknowledges as a starting point his own history (and failings) among the varieties he then goes on to discuss.[6]

This by itself, however, need not have brought him to the rhetorical perspective in the book that has readers and writer appearing as equals being judged for their actions and inactions. Jaspers is certainly aware of differences in conduct among Germans during the war. (He also knows, and details, the rationalizations they have given themselves and others for both what they did and what they did not do.) But he makes it clear that he wants his German readers of 1946 to set out with him in thinking about these matters with no presumption of difference or invidious comparison either among themselves or in relation to him as author. The book is about guilt in the context of Germany's war as that might be established for *all* Germans—at least for all those Germans willing to confront a book with the title *Die Schuldfrage* that appeared so quickly after the conclusion of a devastating war in which their own country (and almost all families) had suffered greatly, whatever judgment could have been made at the time about the causes of that suffering.

The book's audience would in this sense be self-selective, with Jaspers' assertion of German guilt putting off some readers and with the title alone putting off others. But there was little Jaspers could do about this even if he had wished to, so long as he was raising the subject of German guilt at all. What he could do, and what he accomplished with remarkable even-handedness, was to speak from the inside about the German people as both individuals and Germans, and most importantly, in relation to both these aspects of identity, to treat his readers as equals in their (and his) relation to the Nazi regime. This sense of equality or likeness is sustained in his book even after the conceptual distinctions he introduces; for he then seeks his readers' concurrence for the types and degrees of guilt he lays out.[7] Readers and author alike are thus asked to scrutinize themselves as they would be forced to if they were facing crossexamination in court; that Jaspers himself was both prosecutor and defendant adds to the drama of the interrogation.

Viewed in this light, we understand that *Die Schuldfrage* not only had been meditated before it was written, but that it embodies key features of "the meditation" as one among other traditional philosophical genres, a genre designed not only for an audience to read, but more than that, for them to *do* (as evident, for example, in such otherwise different meditations as those by Marcus Aurelius and Descartes.) *Die Schuldfrage*'s readers are thus posed a two-fold task: to shape certain actions in the future, but to do this only as the past is incorporated in the judgment leading to those actions in recognition of the reader's responsibility. And if much of the evidence of guilt that Jaspers cites directly touches only some of his readers, certain of the issues raised apply to them *all*, German or not, contemporary with Jaspers or later, and for all of them equally. The conclusions of his moral or political judgment, his analysis of responsibility and guilt, are thus not restricted to one historical moment, however unusual his particular "moment" was. Given that time and place, with its proximity to the evidence of extreme violence and suffering, and with the temptations close to hand of high-handed moralizing or equally disingenuous mea culpas, the equable relation constructed by Jaspers in his writing between author and reader remains a remarkable accomplishment.

Admittedly, in attempting to achieve this effect, Jaspers excludes two groups of potential readers, one of them central to the events he analyzes, the other peripheral but nonetheless significant. For the "implied readers" of Jaspers' book are limited to those who during the Nazi period or afterward acknowledged a distance first between Nazi ideology and their own convictions, and then between the latter convictions and their conduct under Nazi rule. This requirement would exclude Germans who *remained* committed to Nazi principles—not because the types of guilt that Jaspers identifies do not apply to them, but because there could be no point in addressing them about "guilt" when they still believed in the legitimacy of what the Nazis did. "Hitler and his accomplices, that small minority of tens of thousands [!], are beyond moral guilt for as long as they do not feel it. They seem incapable of repentance and change . . . Force alone can deal with such men who live by force alone" (57). The second group whom Jaspers does not directly address are those known in the Holocaust's aftermath as "bystanders": individuals or groups not under immediate threat (even if living under Nazi Occupation) who had the option of deciding whether (and if so, how) to oppose them, with the choice possible on its other side of passivity and relative security. Jaspers does not entirely exclude the latter group from his discussion, since he does write about the "others" (than the Nazis or the German populace at large) who bear responsibility for not opposing certain Nazi actions in a way that might have deterred later ones. (His examples here are pointed: the negligible reaction in the 1930s by other European countries to Hitler's violations of extant treaties—including the blind eye to Mussolini's attack on Ethiopia and France's acquiescence in Germany's occupation of the Rhineland; the Vatican pact with Germany soon after Hitler came to power in 1933; the 1936 Berlin Olympic games in which the world's democracies participated—as well as the ways in which the officially "neutral" countries of Europe cooperated with Germany after the outbreak of war in 1939 (85–89).[8]

That Jaspers excludes the first of these two groups from "the question of guilt" might seem a serious flaw: If anyone deserved to be confronted by a discussion of guilt, surely it would be those who supported Nazi ideology and practice in its time and (still more) who held to that commitment even after the war's end and the fuller public disclosure of its atrocities. The reason for this exclusion, however, is integral to the condition that Jaspers sets for any judgment of *moral* guilt; namely, the person judged must himself concur in the finding. I indicate below my own substantive objections to this requirement, but for the moment note it only as a feature of his analysis. It does not, at any rate, disrupt the parity that Jaspers asserts in the relation between him as author and the readers whom he *does* mean to address.

« » « »

Jaspers' detailed account of the "guilt-question" revolves around a fourfold distinction in terms of which he asks German readers who lived through the war years to examine and judge their conduct. These four types of guilt are: (1) criminal guilt; (2) political guilt; (3) moral guilt; and (4) metaphysical guilt. In identifying these categories, Jaspers intends primarily to bring his fellow Germans face-to-face with the situation in which they (and he) now, in 1946, find themselves, possessed of the freedom to judge and to reconsider their own actions (or inactions) during the twelve years of the Nazi regime. Jaspers is aware that this purpose would carry no conviction unless the categories proposed were broadly applicable: there should be no special pleading in relation to the charge of guilt in this case more than in others. And if he most directly addressed himself to the audience of 1946 German nationals, Jaspers' readers in 2009 are more than justified, *required* to assess his account for its relevance sixty years later as well. State-sponsored atrocity and the questions of responsibility or guilt on the part of the states's citizens did not originate with the Third Reich nor did they lose their point with that regime's fall. Even for much less extreme actions than those of Nazi Germany, questions about the nature and differences of individual and group responsibility (in the event, guilt) have been seen as increasingly important, and there, too, Jaspers' analysis is pertinent.

"Criminal guilt," the first type noted and analyzed by Jaspers, is quite straightforward, and he devotes less space to it than to his other categories. "Criminal guilt" implies the breaking of a recognized law at whatever level the law applies: local, national, international. Such guilt (Jaspers' view here is unequivocal) is individual, the outcome of an act committed always by some*one* (the exclusion of corporate or group criminal guilt is explicit). The determination of criminal guilt, Jaspers further notes, falls under the jurisdiction of "the court"; a premise of the argument here is that if laws exist that can be violated, courts must also exist in a position to judge those violations.

Jaspers seems to sidestep the question here of whether disobedience to *bad* laws incurs "criminal guilt," although strictly speaking, it would have to: the violation of a law remains a violation apart from the merits of the law itself (and indeed, the façade of legality within Germany applied to many of the harshest decrees of the Nazi regime; the "Nuremberg Laws" of 1935 were a decisive step but by no means the most severe). On the other hand, Jaspers also, although without elaborating on this, alludes to a role in determining criminal guilt for violations of "*natural* law" (38), implying that the laws of governments can be scrutinized from that quite different vantage point that (he implies) overrides any involved in national or even international law. (He specifically appeals to natural law later as well, when he rejects the criticism of "illegality" against the postwar Nuremberg trials on the grounds that the charges brought there applied "laws" that did not exist as laws when the "crimes" alleged were committed (with this criticism based on the traditional principle of "No punishment without a law"; 49–50). Jaspers here invokes a "natural law" justification, for example, for the charge (one among others brought at Nuremberg) of "crimes against humanity" even if those "crimes" had not been codifed in binding national or international law. The first of the Nuremberg Trials, ongoing when Jaspers delivered the lectures at the university from which *Die Schuldfrage* emerged, was thus in his view a legitimate forum for judging the Nazi defendants on grounds of their criminal violations as individuals. (That first trial began in Nuremberg on November 20, 1945, with the verdict handed down on October 1, 1946; Jaspers did not oppose the death penalty at the outcome of this trial—the verdict reached for twelve of the twenty-four defendants and carried out for ten of them.)

Jaspers' second category of "political guilt" is the most conceptually complex of the four types of guilt he distinguishes; it stems, he asserts, from "the deeds of the state whose power governs me and under whose order I live. Everybody is responsible for the way he is governed" (25). Guilt of this sort is a function of states or governments; thus, he recognizes, judgments of political guilt typically will be determined by the victors in a conflict, at any rate as a function of political power (although even these judgments, he comments, may be "mitigated" by appeal to "natural and international law" (25). Here, too, the guilt ascribed is individual, but it is incurred by acts of state that often if not always may be difficult to trace in any specific way to individual agency.

At the core of this conception of political guilt is Jaspers' address to the German public at large: "You must answer for the acts of the regime you tolerated" (43). Even Hitler's Germany, in this sense, becomes an expression of collective acceptance and thus of complicity. In this sense, and notwithstanding the fact that the Nazi party never achieved a freely won national majority vote when that was still possible (i.e., prior to January 30, 1933), *Nazi* Germany represented a collective will, with Germans as a people then responsible for acts committed by its leaders. That responsibility, in Jaspers' view, extended to citizens who had no direct part in atrocities, extending also, it seems, to those critical of them or more generally opposed in principle to Nazi policies. He does not address the question of what if *any* actions initiated by citizens would exonerate them from political guilt for that state's actions. It seems implausible that Jaspers would have no special provision for those who stood in open opposition to a murderous regime (facing the harsh consequences that potentially would entail), but he does not even allude to instances of such opposition in Nazi Germany, although he certainly would have been aware of them — most notably the failed July 20 (1944) plot to assassinate Hitler. The most plausible explanation of this omission seems to me Jaspers' focus on the conduct of Germans *collectively* under the Nazi regime, and the tendency there, at most, of acquiescence even when accompanied by silent dissent (including in the latter group Jaspers himself).

A second and larger problem related to the category of political guilt is the distinction that Jaspers draws between it and the third category of "moral guilt." His contention here is that although political guilt, like criminal guilt, can be judged objectively and punished by others (individuals or groups), *moral guilt* in his view requires the understanding and assent of the person judged. This is an odd and difficult claim to sustain fully, although Jaspers effectively elaborates certain aspects of the distinction between political and moral guilt, principally as he considers the important question of what can be done to repair or "make good" on political guilt in its relation to individual citizens (notwithstanding the distinction from moral guilt, political guilt, too, has individual consequences). Thus: "Acceptance of political liability is hard on every individual," he writes. "What it means to us is political impotence and a poverty which will compel us for long times to live or on the fringes of hung and cold and to struggle vainly" (56). "We answer to the victors, with our labor and our working faculties, and must make such amends as are exacted from the vanquished" (72).

Jaspers' view of political guilt here seems directed mainly to the issue of reparations: the punishment exacted of a state as a measure of that guilt that may "make good" on the violation committed, beginning with the requirement of an equivalence in material goods given on behalf of the victims, drawn from what he calls the "material possibilities" of the politically guilty. The state responsible is thus obligated to find the means for righting the wrong alleged. Such judgments about political guilt or reparations are in Jaspers' view impersonal, almost as if the guilty party itself could both make the finding of guilt and assess the penalty, and would not differ significantly in these judgments from the judgments of a less "interested" source. Jaspers goes so far in this direction as to insist that in the process of repairing political guilt, "I myself, my inner self is not affected . . . at all" (68); the implication here is that the "feeling" of responsibility of the body politic differs substantively from that of an individual, "inner self."

Jaspers recognizes in the category of political guilt the need to think historically and thus beyond the present generation; following along this line, something on the order of group identity begins to surface that Jaspers' repeated references to himself *as* a German underscore. In any event, the impersonality of "political" guilt that presumably locates the object of that judgment as a governing corporation of some sort is distinguishable from the individuals comprising it, although Jaspers at the same time argues *against* the concept of collective guilt as applied to either a country or its individual citizens. The difficulty of reconciling these two impulses—on the one hand, corporate responsibility; on the other hand, avoiding collective (and inherited) guilt)—is not Jaspers' alone, but the strain it causes for his thinking is intense. So, for example, at the same time that he argues against the notion of collective guilt, he writes that "We [Germans] further feel that we not only share in what is done at present . . . but in the links of tradition. We have to bear the guilt of our fathers.

That the spiritual conditions of German life provided an opportunity for such a regime is a fact for which all of us are co-responsible" (73). Presumably, this responsibility may extend beyond the present, connecting the past "of our fathers" to the future, an extension with apparent implications of collective guilt. Even if one interprets this reach to the future as only a material responsibility—an obligation in practical terms to replace losses—the implication is of a debt that may extend beyond those directly involved or even alive at the time of the events pointed to.

Jaspers' view of political guilt here evidently conflicts with his view of criminal guilt, and through both of them with his still more general existentialist commitments to individual autonomy, freedom, and responsibility. About that foundation, he could hardly have been more explicit: "It is nonsensical . . . to charge a whole people with a crime. The criminal is always only an individual. It is nonsensical, too, to lay moral guilt to a people as a whole" (34). This insistence obviously extends beyond Germany and the Germans: "There is no such thing as a people as a whole . . . People and state do not coincide, nor do language, common fate and culture" (35). He cites in support of the same claim the stereotyped charge (especially pointed in this context), that "The Jews are guilty of the Crucifixion." For even if *some* Jews were responsible for the Crucifixion, that would not warrant the conceptual shift to a verdict of guilt with "*the* Jews" as its subject.

The dangers that Jaspers thus anticipates are indisputable; the view of collective guilt that he attacks has, furthermore, often taken on racist or genetic features, claiming the biological inheritance of moral characteristics, a view that the Nazis themselves had held of the Jews as a "race" and which Jaspers, as we have seen, opposed on a number of different grounds. Yet his own affirmation of something close to a German collective identity and of political guilt seems to run into similar and no less basic problems, *unless* one accepts as a premise the independence of political institutions from their individual members, a position that coming from the other side conflicts with Jaspers' insistence on the common responsibility of citizens for their government's actions. A model that Jaspers might be drawing on here is a commercial or industrial one: If a worker is seriously injured in an accident where his employer is liable, a monetary "equivalent" typically is awarded, although in many such cases, it would be difficult to argue that the "equivalent" fully makes good the employee's loss; in instances of mass atrocity, it becomes still more difficult to imagine what adequate reparation could be: the collective punishment that would fit the crime (or guilt). The residue left here might become a continuing burden of guilt on practical grounds, but that seems hardly to have the force or independence that Jaspers ascribes to political guilt, with its related questions of how far into the future and with what qualifications any such claim should extend.

Again, Jaspers repeatedly affirms his sense of his own identity as a German, in this connection even using the term "consanguinity" with its biological overtones—as "we feel something like a co-responsibility for the acts of members of our family" (73). "We feel ourselves not only as individuals but as Germans . . . In my innermost soul, I cannot help feeling collectively . . ." (74). To what extent such feelings entail responsibility, however, Jaspers does not say; he thus leaves the question of German responsibility—*its* political guilt—as it applies to the generations following his, actual but indefinite. Insofar as "being" German means more than only being an individual—and Jaspers clearly holds this—the impact of collective identity and thus, too, collective responsibility, is no less a matter of fact than that of individual identity. And indeed the post–World War II history of Germany in relation to "Wiedergutmachung" or reparations attests to the same problem. For although postwar Germany has indisputably made serious efforts at accepting political responsibility—guilt—for the actions of the Third Reich, it is clear that both for the aggrieved victims and to some extent for the Germans themselves, the sense of political guilt persists in a way that cannot be reduced to limited material terms. In this way, a sense persists, however vaguely defined, of a collective and continuing responsibility for the German past. Jaspers' analysis of political guilt certainly poses the problem here, but without advancing a means of resolving it *or* of reconciling it with his conception of individual moral guilt that he affirms no less emphatically.

This gap in Jaspers' reasoning has proved to be a continuing issue at the level of practice in the relationship between postwar Germany and groups or individuals who were victims of the Nazis and who regard justice in relation to that status as combining elements of the distinction insisted on by Jaspers between political and moral guilt. To some extent, this issue has been fueled by disagreements in judgment rather than in principle: by victims or their advocates who argue that more should be done by Germany than it has done (but without suggesting a limit or end to that "more"); and, on the other hand, by the conflicting view (outside as well as inside Germany) claiming that enough already has been done in the way of reparations and atonement and/or that some sort of statute of limitations should be set (in time and extent) so that the otherwise legitimate claim does not extend indefinitely, let alone infinitely.

This disagreement probably will remain a continuing source of friction, but one way of easing it would be precisely by bridging the sharp distinction that Jaspers asserts between political and moral guilt. For Jaspers, political guilt is impersonal: Every citizen of a country bears responsibility for that country's actions. (A logical implication of this view would be that political responsibility is not only universal but equal: one person [or taxpayer], one vote—and thus equal shares also of responsibility or guilt.) And since even citizens who disagree with particular actions or policies of their country nonetheless continue to remain there, to draw on and contribute to its resources, they become responsible for policies or actions that they have in principle opposed as well as for those they supported. But why, the question persists, is not such individual support and responsibility for the state *also* a moral, and not only a *political* decision?

Jaspers answers the latter question with the claim that moral guilt refers to actions that a person does entirely as an individual and for which the person must then answer not in relation to the laws of a state, but to the demands of his conscience. The prime example that Jaspers provides of this guilt is the defense commonly offered for acts committed on the grounds that they (the agents) were "just following orders" (25). Jaspers objects to this defense on the grounds that no legal or political authority absolves the individual of responsibility for his actions, for in the end it is *he* who decides whether to follow the orders or not. Jaspers recognizes mitigating circumstances that may accompany this defense (if, for example, a person acts under duress), but in many instances of actions that might have been taken or avoided under the Nazi regime but were not, no such coercion applied. And in those cases, the individual becomes *morally* guilty, but only on the additional condition (for Jaspers) that the individual judges himself guilty in retrospect.

The latter condition adds to the difficulty of following Jaspers' schematic distinction. For although it may well be that only when a person acknowledges his own wrongdoing does the concept of moral responsibility and guilt become significant *for him*, but that hardly seems a reason for precluding moral judgment of him by others. (Would, for example, an ex-Nazi official who remained convinced of the "justice" of the death camps, be guilty only on political grounds and not on moral grounds?) Here, too, it seems, the problem originates in Jaspers' insistence on a sharp distinction between political and moral guilt where a more nuanced relation applies. If, for example, we ask in what sense the individual citizen of a country is responsible for his country's actions (the condition that Jaspers accepts for political guilt), we invariably come back to individual acts that are not only "political" but also, in the term's usual sense, moral. When citizens pay income tax to a government that commits atrocities, the fact that they would be breaking the law if they refused to pay the tax is, as Jaspers himself argues, no justification for paying the tax. Surely paying or not paying one's income tax becomes at that point a *moral* decision at the same time although not in same way that it is a political one, since presumably the state could not continue to act as it (wrongfully) does if all taxes were withheld from it. This objection does not mean that there is no distinction between acting as an individual (in Jaspers' terms, morally) and acting as the citizen of a state (thus, politically), but only that the line between the two has openings in it that Jaspers does not admit. The power of Jaspers' position here is in his view that moral guilt if it comes only as the result of external judgment leaves the person responsible untouched internally, *as* a person; it does not follow from this, however, that there is *no* outside to the inside of moral guilt.

The fourth type of guilt identified by Jaspers is "metaphysical guilt," which originates, in his terms, in every person's responsibility for "every wrong and every injustice in the world" (26). A milder or reduced version of this conception of guilt would be the assertion that few people if any do as much good as they could and should do, a contention that seems close to a tautology. Jaspers also recognizes that invoking this type of guilt might work against the concept of moral guilt altogether, since, if people believe that whatever their efforts, they will still turn out to be "metaphysically" guilty, they might decide not to make even the efforts they are otherwise willing to. For the historical context in which Jaspers writes, furthermore, the notion of metaphysical or generalized guilt—since it applies to everyone all the time, not only to Germans living under Nazi rule—seems to add little to the ascriptions of guilt in the other three categories, unless it is understood as a secularized version of "Original Sin": finite man constantly challenged by demands that exceed his powers. Whatever else can be said about this view, it evidently has no special pertinence to the actions of Germans and Germany in World War II; and even if the claim that "If everyone is guilty, then no one is guilty," is itself problematic, it makes the point that there is no specific relevance of "metaphysical guilt" to judging German guilt in the Nazi war.

Jaspers openly considers himself guilty in the last three of the categories that he distinguishes—arguably also in the first category of criminal guilt as well, if one includes the violation of *natural* law. He was certainly guilty in the political sense, having lived as a citizen in a criminal state; he was guilty in a moral sense because, by his own admission, he did not act against Nazi policies or practices even in ways that might not have endangered him, a fortiori in ways that might have; he was metaphysically guilty insofar as that standard applied to all Germans and indeed to everyone else. If we ask what his characterization of these categories accomplishes, we need to recall once again that Jaspers was writing principally for a German public that had lived through the reign of the Third Reich and that had largely, even if often passively, supported it. Jaspers does not condescend to that public, since he writes also about himself; what he *is* saying is that the members of that public cannot, if ethics means anything at all, avoid looking at themselves as agents of the Nazi regime and not as its victims.

I have pointed here to certain aspects of Jaspers' account as internally inadequate for reflection and practice in the postwar, post-Holocaust period that has extended far longer than Jaspers himself was attempting to consider or account for. Even so, it seems clear that the question of German guilt and responsibility that he raised so explicitly and daringly as a question has persisted as a sharply edged constant. Not as indicating the failure of the answers he proposed to the question—although we have seen some of the objections that confront those answers—but because of difficulties in the issues themselves *and* because Jaspers' attempt that had the virtue of immediacy also seemed too personal, too close to the events themselves to find a way through them.

Could there then be for Jaspers, in his own terms, a way of responding to or of "making good" for the types of guilt he names? Jaspers' primary emphasis in his book is on guilt, not on how to undo it or get past it. In briefly considering this issue, he relies on the concept of "purification" ("Reinigung"; 112ff), suggesting that for this process, too, anything achieved must be internal to the individual, but without at all specifying the conditions that have to be met for it. Since "purification" presumably would apply differently in each of the four types of guilt, he in effect elides them, leaving his readers to make their individual ways through them. Criminal guilt, we have seen, evidently is "paid for" by punishment imposed in a court of law; political guilt is requited by material reparation made through the state, with whatever burden this imposes on its citizens; metaphysical guilt, since it is constant and inescapable, insures the "melancholy background" (113) left as a residue no matter what one does to avoid or overcome it. Even the arguably most fundamental category of moral guilt—including, one supposes, individual responsibility for the most extreme atrocities—presumably is open on his terms to "purification." However extreme and calculated the guilty actions and their consequences, it seems that, for Jaspers, history can potentially always be overcome, in a moral if not a metaphysical sense. It would follow from this that, for Jaspers, no acts are in principle morally unforgivable, *beyond* purification. This is an extreme position in the analysis or judgment of guilt and, again, one that he does not develop or defend.[9] Even if on the conception of metaphysical guilt, purification could never be complete—guilt in effect becoming part of the human condition—that does not cover the issue of moral or political guilt and, in both, the possibility of the unforgivable that seems clearly pertinent to actions of the Nazi regime.

Is Jaspers, then, too *easy* on the question of German guilt? He certainly was not "easy" in raising the question when and as he did for the audience of German readers he confronted, and there are enough edges in the findings of guilt that he does affirm to have occupied those readers. Moreover, we have seen the pressures exerted by the questions of if or how and until when Germany's responsibility for the Holocaust and the other atrocities and destruction caused in World War II continues, how that responsibility translates into practical terms of obligation for Germany and its citizens, questions that now, six decades after the Holocaust, have become more emphatic than they were in the immediate surroundings in which Jaspers wrote and to which Jaspers responds ambivalently, an understandable ambivalence, but one that nonetheless, in a post-Holocaust world, has yet to be overcome. This does not mean that the question of German guilt since Jaspers considered it has been absent or silenced but only that it has not yet been addressed to everyone's satisfaction—in certain respects, not to *anyone's* satisfaction. But it is a matter of record that the question was in a formal sense *first* raised by him, through a combination of intellectual courage and moral imagination that projected *Die Schuldfrage* onto the screen of modern German history at what seems clearly to have been its single most painful moment, at a convergence of self-discovery and immense loss. Jaspers' work thus remains a important testimonial to the potential—arguably the necessary—relationship between philosophy and history.

« » « »

I have not attempted here to locate *Die Schuldfrage* in Jaspers' philosophical thought overall, but that work's central themes are in fact closely related to themes that Jaspers elaborates in other of his writings, especially to his emphasis in both his psychology and philosophy on the central role of human freedom in defining and shaping the individual person. The term "existentialism" itself often is attributed to Jaspers, at least as the announcement of a mode of thinking; and if almost everyone identified with that "school"—including Heidegger, Sartre, Camus, and Marcel—at some time protested against being classified under its rubric, history—including the history of philosophy—does not depend on the acquiescence of its subjects. Certainly the varieties of concepts like "Angst" or "Nothingness" or even "nausée" stand themselves on the same perimeter that responsibility and guilt do, all of them presupposing and beyond that, exhibiting the individual freedom without which they would be unintelligible. To be sure, the emphasis on individual freedom or even "Existenz" prominent in the work of these thinkers is by no means restricted to them. In this sense, Jaspers' focus in *Die Schuldfrage* on a typology of guilt and the concept of responsibility foregrounds issues that had figured not only in his own and other Existentialists' thought but in most earlier writers who had addressed problems of ethics and moral responsibility. Undoubtedly, there is a specific emphasis in Jaspers' earlier work that would make his address to the "question of German guilt" and the conclusions that he arrives at in relation to it predictable, although one might also argue the converse of this: that the urgency for determining responsibility and guilt in relation to the Nazi regime adds considerable weight to any more general affirmation of individual freedom of decision and action.

Jaspers did not consider significant (arguably, he did not consider at all) the question of Nazi "uniqueness"—whether the Nazi regime was so extreme in its politics and actions as to be without precedent or equal in history. On the matter of the Nazi genocide against the Jews, it is worth noting again that the term "genocide" itself, although coined before Jaspers wrote *Die Schuldfrage*, had limited currency even at the time of his writing. (As mentioned before, it was not among the charges brought against the upper Nazi hierarchy at the Nuremberg Trials.) The term "Endlösung" ("Final Solution") itself does not appear in his book, and there remains the question, already noted, of how far Jaspers' knowledge of the Nazi genocide extended at the time of his writing. Indeed, the few references that Jaspers makes to the Nazi persecution and killing of Jews are muted, ostensibly reflecting his view of it as but one factor in the broader complex of Nazi transgressions against the countries and peoples of Europe (including Germany itself).[10]

In the by now sixty-year aftermath of the Holocaust, some readers of Jaspers' account may view these proportions as a fault or omission; but this charge, it seems to me, should be judged in the context of his conception of the "guilt question" more generally and notwithstanding the particular setting in which he addressed it. The crime of genocide arguably carries a special burden of responsibility in comparison to other crimes, but even now, with much fuller information available than what Jaspers had, the questions of how that crime is to be measured, judged, or punished—or even defined—remain disputed. And Jaspers' bold and intense, yet dispassionate account of German guilt goes far, even sixty years later, toward establishing a frame of reference for confronting the issue of guilt on a large scale: in immediate relation to Germany and the Germans, but also as bearing on other large-scale atrocities with large points of similarity, some of them committed decades after the event to which Jaspers was responding. Hegel's contention that "the one thing we learn from history is that we do not learn from history" is clearly supported by the history of national crimes and atrocities that have occurred *since* Jaspers called attention to the guilt of the German populace—and of himself—under the Nazi regime.

A compelling reason for re-reading *Die Schuldfrage* now, and again, is the hope that the genealogy of Jaspers' argument will resonate for contemporary readers who should have learned from history, notwithstanding

Hegel's astringent warning, at least *this* much: that any type of event that has happened once can also happen twice. Thus, we return to the two perspectives for reading philosophical texts that were mentioned at the beginning of this chapter: the importance of addressing such texts "there and then," in their own historical setting—joined to the importance of reading them "here and now," for what difference their presence makes at present.

II

Vs. the Unspeakable, the Unshowable, and the Unthinkable

« 5 »

Holocaust-Representation in the Genre of Silence

Isaac Babel referred to one notable period in his career as an exercise in the "genre of silence." That period marked his response to the pressure of censorship and punishment under Stalin that forced Babel, so explicit and determined a writer, into silence. Even his skill with this genre, however, did not save him from being shot, possibly at the initiative and certainly with the concurrence of Stalin, whose scrawled signature appears on the order for that "sentence." (Recognizing the brutality, it is yet no small thing that a political regime should view "committing" literature as a capital offense.)[1]

We know more generally, however, that silence, deployed as a genre in the face of persecution, has a rich history in philosophy and literature and indeed in the arts more generally, as does the related, broader phenomenon of figurative representation that "turns" words and narratives, images and shadows, in such ways that double or triple meanings emerge, designed to evade (thus also to oppose) the coercive authority of literalism. (The preciseness of coercion, after all, is one conclusion of literalism, the use of force leaving no room in its point of contact for doubt or question.) The Argentinian author, Borges, when challenged once for his political quietism, responded that *he* took action by means of irony. Indeed, the history of censorship in relation to the varieties of silence and representation inspired by it would be a way—one not yet taken—of writing a comprehensive history of both literature and philosophy; this history would reach even into the present where the received value of free speech nonetheless finds itself constrained by *self*-censorship, the self turning out to be as punitive a reader as any other. Leo Strauss's classic essay, "Persecution and the Art of Writing," thus puts a concise title to a lengthy tradition; his conception of much philosophical or religious discourse as dependent on "writing between the lines" suggests a framework for interpreting *all* texts, from the telephone book to Kant's *Critique of Pure Reason*.[2]

Silence itself, however, turns out to be a multifold genre, embodying not only political but moral, aesthetic, and conceptual elements. Together, these argue against the simpler view of silence as all-of-a-kind: merely the absence of sounded or written words. It may seem incongruous to propose an association of silence with *Holocaust*-writing, of which there has been so much, often loudly spoken, and with its bulk still growing (with this book as well). But except for some cautionary words, I will not be arguing for the ideal of silence as a displacement of Holocaust-writing; however exploitative or impoverishing Holocaust-representation at times has been, the alternate, more-threatening prospect always looms of Holocaust-silence: erasure. Rather, I mean to call attention to ways in which silence has been a causal agent in the appearances and genres of Holocaust-writing and in the visual arts as well, as they, too, often with a much wider audience, have found a subject in the Holocaust. Such representation, including its silences, has shaped not only the works in which they figure but features of the Holocaust itself, in this way serving also as a means into history.

The most dramatic and self-conscious appearance of silence in Holocaust discourse has been as a figure of speech, specifically in variations on the figure of the "aporia" that surfaces in numerous critical and theoretical reflections on the Holocaust and, more tacitly, in numerous literary or other artistic representations. As a figure of speech, the aporia characteristically asserts the ineffability, the indescribability, the place beyond words of the subject referred to. All these terms or phrases (and other synonyms) have appeared frequently in Holocaust-writing, implying as they go that no verbal (or, often, any other) representation can possibly be adequate to that subject. Such references at times explicitly say that silence itself would be a more accurate and fitting representation of the Holocaust. The logic of this initial claim might be further extended: that since attempts at verbal representation are *bound* to fail, any such attempt that pretends otherwise compounds this failure by the added violation of deceit or at least pretense.

To be sure, such implications follow only as expressions of this aporia are understood literally, not figuratively. And the fact that writers who use this aporia to assert the Holocaust's "unspeakability" often go on to write about that event at length (George Steiner and Elie Wiesel offer examples of this), suggests that they did indeed mean to speak figuratively, not literally. The figure of speech rendered in this way is common and familiar. For example: "My friend's suffering in her illness was indescribable," or "The beauty of that painting cannot be put into words," or "I can't tell you how much I love you"—all of these are figurative expressions, all designed to express intense feeling, all asserting the inadequacy of language for conveying the experience. As we understand these claims of the limits of words and (by implication) the more adequate or at least less misleading representation that silence would provide, we do not question the efforts that the speaker or writer has made to put what he describes as indescribable into words. It would be an unlikely response to someone who says "Words fail me," to suggest, "Perhaps you haven't tried hard enough; keep going." Ordinarily, we take the speaker at his word and automatically excuse him; its literal meaning is not, in any event, the point of what he said.

That some instances of figurative language are intended by their speakers to be understood literally, *not* figuratively applies to at least some instances of the aporia in Holocaust-writing. About such literal intent, two points seem relevant: first, that ostensibly literal utterances nonetheless may be figurative (as is often clear in examples that employ the term "literally" to convey their message, as in "I was so angry I was *literally* climbing the walls"). And second, that when assertions of the Holocaust's indescribability *are* meant literally (as they sometimes are), the silence implied by that usage as a preferred genre of Holocaust-discourse differs from the one noted so far, with broader and also potentially harmful consequences. To claim that there is no adequate way of speaking about the Holocaust—implying that this limitation distinguishes it from other events—suggests for the Holocaust extrahistorical status, a place outside history and thus also beyond intelligibility: the indescribable here moves into the incomprehensible.

This last step has at times been asserted more explicitly, and an argument might be made for that conclusion. But the attempt to formulate it has rarely appeared, and indeed the evidence against it comes from many directions—literary, historical, philosophical, and theological; that is, from the mass of Holocaust-discourse as a whole. Admittedly, we do not know how many potential authors have maintained the Holocaust's "unspeakability" to its (and their) end; that is, without mentioning even the claim itself. For them, the consistent ones, their silence would be actual all the way down, extending also to announcement of the aporia itself. (Primo Levi's contention, mentioned earlier, that the truest witnesses of the Holocaust are not the survivors who testified or wrote about it, but those who died in silence, is a vivid appearance of this aporia in practice.)

A second, structurally more conventional appearance of silence in Holocaust-writing is as an *internal* feature. Here silence has an explicit role in the characterization and action portrayed. The role of "silenced" characters has been much discussed in the critical literature. Holocaust writers as different as Aharon Appelfeld and Günter Grass, Jakov Lind and Bernard Schlink, have introduced literary characters who either cannot speak or who cannot be reached by speech or writing.[3] This invocation of silence is a distinctive literary trope (and limited: One can hardly imagine a fully "silent" novel), sufficiently distinctive as a literary device to bring out its expressive contribution to the context in which it appears. Here silence becomes a component of the representation of the Holocaust itself, with the impact of experience undergone in it and presented to the reader as literally dumbfounding, characterized so in representations of the event that are otherwise not silent at all.

A parallel use of silence in shaping the genres of Holocaust-writing emerges in what I have referred to elsewhere as "blurring" the genres:[4] the search in Holocaust-writing for ways to challenge and revise the "normal" conventions of genre that would suggest, in their own, more usual terms, that Holocaust-writing is like all other writing, with a subject that differs no more from others than the others differ among themselves—nothing, in any event, that would threaten the usual representational conventions. An analogy proposed by Lyotard seems applicable here: that the very instruments by which events are measured can be disrupted by an extraordinary occurrence, and that this is in fact a consequence of the Holocaust. The reflection of the Holocaust's extremity has not been incorporated universally in the conventions of genre, and much Holocaust-writing embodies the traditional lines of the novel and short story, of poetry and drama. But much of the strongest writing within these genres does challenge the conventions, searching and testing the boundaries around the space of literary silence for a means of expression that breaches and revises them. Silence thus as a component but even more as a basis for discourse, in the sense of bringing something novel into existence in a way that asserts and underscores the silence or emptiness that preceded and evoked it, and that may also follow it. Paul Celan and Dan Pagis epitomize this application in their poetry (adding, in the case of Celan, the sheer difficulty of his writing that is evidently intended as itself part of the representation; that is, literary difficulty as itself a representation of the subject-hardship). The silences that are a repeated—virtually continuous—feature of all Aharon Appelfeld's novels serve as analogues in that genre; a more unexpected use of silence as applied dramatically in historiography appears in Raul Hilberg's momentous and lengthy—but spare—masterwork, *The Destruction of the European Jews*; in his memoir, *The Politics of Memory*, Hilberg calls attention to the influence of the conciseness and use of omission in the Hebrew Bible on his own writing.

A third appearance of silence in Holocaust-writing introduces the phenomenon of silence by *self*-censorship—through the omission, whether by conscious design or not, of topics that are "unmentionable"—not because of the author's incapacity or because of fault in the language, but for external reasons reflecting cultural or psychological taboos or inhibitions. Thus, just as certain themes or tropes recur in Holocaust-writing, others topics are persistently absent, cloaked in silence, notwithstanding the fact that once brought into the open, they seem no less and at times more pertinent than others. Given the extent of Holocaust-writings, such gaps may seem unlikely, but there *have* been what amount to systematic omissions or silences, repressions, in that body of work; some of these, at least, are important both symptomatically (as ideological indicators) and in themselves, as aspects of the Holocaust itself that have not received the attention they warrant. I mention only several of these, beginning with a triad that I previously considered in an essay on Oskar Rosenfeld's Lodz Ghetto diaries subtitled: "On Sex, Shit, and Status."[5] The point of that subtitle was the unusual fact that Rosenfeld *did* write about those three topics in relation to life in the ghetto, and that even his spare references to them were more than most accounts of ghetto or camp life provided. The topics themselves, once noted, will seem both obvious and self-explanatory as factors in the "everyday life" of the ghettoes (outside them as well, albeit in different terms), as also in their absence from the large number of Holocaust memoirs and "fictions." The issue of status within the ghettoes, for instance—*class differences*, however vaguely formulated or disguised the dividing lines were (perhaps, as Dalia Ofer has suggested, to be measured and compared by the number of calories ingested daily)—was only too often a determinant of life and death, in selections for work or for "resettlement," even in preferential treatment for obtaining more food. But the severe forms of discrimination that ensued from this source and their relationship to it have been little, and certainly not systematically, analyzed. If, as seems likely, the reasons for this absence involve shame or guilt or even continued perplexity, those reasons also would have to face history's analysis and judgment, a conclusion that applies to the other topics of the title as well: "sex" and "shit," in their presence in the ghetto. (The stench from corpses, human waste, and garbage was constant and unavoidable, one of the elements from which nobody in the area could escape; it has been noted that birds avoided the areas around the ghettoes and still more the death camps.)[6]

Again, a largely "silent" topic, notably absent not only from memoirs but from discursive accounts as well, is that of revenge, a phenomenon that, from evidence that *has* come into the open, was far from uncommon, especially during the period of the liberation or immediate postwar period, but before that as well. Buried still farther beneath the surface except in a few boldly unconventional works (such as Grossman's *Life and Fate*) are the accounts of brutality or even murder inflicted by the victims themselves on other victims (in the ghettoes and camps and even in hiding).[7] Such accounts undoubtedly have been silenced at least in part to avoid inflicting further pain on the victims who, after all and whatever their actions, paid a terrible price. But this is not necessarily the most fitting response to such actions or a reason for suppressing them. As Primo Levi points out in relation to the instances of internecine brutality that he observed in Auschwitz, the soundest understanding of such acts is to be found in a grasp of the extremity to which the victims were driven and of the agency responsible for it, not the moral character or failings of those who fell before it. In any event, all these instances of silence as repression share a common two-fold meaning: the phenomenon passed over in silence, and then the reasons for those omissions, as this can be inferred; for once recognized *as* silences, these too speak out loud. (Certain topics may remain unmentioned in Holocaust texts, of course, because they are, by any standard, trivial or irrelevant to the course of events; but one would not know this much except as those unmentioned that *are* significant come to be addressed.)

The Holocaust-texts cited so far are found mainly in literature, not in philosophy (putting aside for the moment the questionable grounds for regarding philosophical texts at somehow "extraliterary"). But if we set out from that conventional division of the professional world, a parallel analysis of silence in relation to philosophical texts seems no less pertinent than for the "literary" texts alluded to. Aspects of this philosophical silence have been discussed in chapters 1 and 2, and I would rehearse here only briefly the conclusions reached there, beginning with the fact that notwithstanding the mass and diversity of writing about the Holocaust, the place of philosophers in that work has been barely noticeable (or noticed). What *has* appeared, furthermore, has had to make its way out of the mainstreams of both philosophy and Holocaust-studies. Evidence of this absence, as noted in chapter 1, is apparent in the small number of philosophers who have addressed the subject of the Holocaust as more than a passing example, in contrast to the number of philosophers writing in cognate fields of ethics and political philosophy. It is worth emphasizing, again, that this silence should not be understood as accidental or inadvertent; its sources in an attitude of antihistoricism reinforced by the drive of philosophical method for generalization at the expense of the particular have persisted in the history of philosophy (in which the consciousness of its own history as history has also been markedly thin).

These features, too, can be identified in relation to the role of silence, if only to mark the challenge of incorporating silence into the process of analysis: bridging the vacant, unspeaking space between the particular and the general and attempting to articulate there something akin to the concrete universal that Hegel built on (and that Saul Friedländer's conception of an "integrated" or "interactive" history of the Holocaust evidently aims at in the domain of historiography).[8] The earlier discussion in chapter 1 of a related matter turned to Arendt's *Eichmann in Jerusalem* as exemplary of its philosophical confrontation with a specific historical occurrence (Eichmann serving as a metonymy for the Holocaust). Again, the immediate issues there did not include the adequacy of Arendt's account of evil but her criticism of the role of the Judenräte, the legal process of the Eichmann trial itself, and Arendt's own Jewish identity (recall Gershom Scholem's accusation that she lacked "*ahavath yisroel*" [love of Israel]. Such discussion as there has been of the topic of "banality" has been centered largely on the charge that, with that concept, Arendt let Eichmann "off the hook," which is at once far from what she intended and diversionary from the underlying distinction between "banal" and "radical" evil. To be sure, philosophers themselves have at times conceded a role to silence, perhaps the most frequently quoted such reference being the last sentence of Wittgenstein's *Tractatus:* "Whereof one cannot speak, thereof one must be silent," which later found a companion gesture in his statement that "My work consists of two parts—that which I have written and that which remains unwritten." One might add in the same spirit that there may have been more of a basis in these words of Wittgenstein's than he himself recognized.

Silence, to be sure, is understood most literally as an auditory quality (even in its absence: consider the epitome in John Cage's piece titled 4'33"; that is, four minutes and thirty three seconds of silence [written for the piano, of course]). But it has a direct visual analogue in absence or emptiness, and with an additional analogue to what has been mentioned as the (literary) unspeakable or indescribable in the visually "unshowable" or, slightly more abstractly, the "unimaginable." For at all these levels, visual representations *do* omit, avoid, repress, extending hints at *what* is omitted: seascapes that fade into the horizon don't imply that the ocean ends where the painting does—quite the contrary, in fact—and so on. In principle, it might be argued that anything that can be imagined can be represented visually, extending to complex discursive or literary tropes like irony or satire or even jokes, all of which get their point only by implication. (No "irony marks" provide assurance of irony's occurrence, although that indeed has been proposed; if a corresponding visual marker could be found, that might well make its visual representation more common.) Perhaps omission or absence is more notable literarily, but the same pressures and instruments of concealment reflecting taboo and repression have been both available and applied in the visual arts. Certainly ideologies and orthodoxies have been influences there as well—and if one makes allowance for the special political danger that mass circulation propelled by the printing press has posed but for which no equivalent has yet been found for the visual arts, the presence of absence arguably would be equal in the two. Consider the both literal and symbolic epitome of artistic concealment: in the visual history of the fig leaf, and what sculptor and painters were able to omit by becoming expert in *that* representation (which remains familiar to most viewers only by this depiction).

And then also—to bring the discussion back to omission and absence in Holocaust-representation—there is the large body of tacit knowledge of the Holocaust that both writers and visual artists assume in their audience but do not articulate themselves. How do readers *know* that a Holocaust novel or poem is a "Holocaust-work"—that is, *about* the Holocaust? At times, to be sure, the text itself says this, although even then it invariably assumes *some* independent knowledge of the event in the reader. (So, for example, Leslie Epstein's *King of the Jews* or Primo Levi's *If Not Now, When.*) But for many literary works, including a disproportionate number of central ones, the connection is left largely for the reader to make. Why, for example, is Celan's "Todesfuge" read as a *Holocaust-poem* (a response that Celan himself came to resent)? A reader who knew nothing of the Holocaust might be puzzled by some of that poem's lines or images and yet appreciate its force overall, the latter impression not very different from that of readers who know much about both Celan and the

Holocaust. Similarly for readers of Appelfeld's *Badenheim 1939* (especially for those who set out from its original Hebrew title, *Badenheim the Health-Resort (Ir Nofesh)* or the title given its German translation which was just *Badenheim*—the omission of "1939" patently intended to avoid the association that that date might evoke). This problem becomes still more pressing in attaching a "Holocaust-marker" to visual representations, especially in spatial arts like painting or sculpture. Unless certain stereotyped images are invoked (swastikas or railroad tracks leading into a barbed-wire opening or goose-stepping soldiers), the question becomes more difficult of why a viewer should recognize any particular work as related to the Holocaust. If the subject of a painting is people who are suffering or dying, even as victims of violence as portrayed, the specific context may be vague or ambiguous without detracting from its effect. Edvard Munch's archetypal work, *The Scream* (1893), often is cited for its expressiveness of agony, although it is also known to be part of an essentially domestic series. Or again, unless one imports the external history of military dress and weaponry, Goya's series, *The Disasters of War* (1810–1820), might refer to any time, any place, as indeed, without knowledge of the Spanish Civil War and his relation to it, would Picasso's *Guernica*. That titles or legends assigned to a painting or knowledge of the artist's biography may affect the viewer's response is perhaps unavoidable, but the information they provide may have little to do with what the work itself shows or means, either deliberately (as in Mark Rothko's *No. 18* [1948]) or because of the title's apparent arbitrariness in relation to the painting it is assigned to (as in Robert Motherwell's *Elegy to the Spanish Revolution* [1971]).

Again, such subtexts of "absence" apply to literary representation, but the phenomenon has a larger proportionate presence in visual representation, partly because the range of articulation in individual visual works is more limited than it is in works of the major literary genres; partly because the presence of what *is* visually represented has a transcultural immediacy that the written word does not (and so also when something is missing). The Biblical prohibition against "graven images" was *first* a prohibition against the visual representation of God (or would-be gods), initially directed against three-dimensional idols but later extended to visual representations of all other "subjects," including photographs ("abstract" painting thus had a legacy of Biblical authority long before the New York School provided its own version). To be sure, a similar prohibition banned the utterance of the name of God, the tetragrammaton; but references to that name at one remove proved to be acceptable, figuring largely in the Biblical narrative and subsequently in religious prayers.

Is the biblical prohibition against "graven images" ethical as well as religious in its force? The question itself implies a distinction between moral and religious principles that is alien to understanding those practices, at least as they appear in the biblical text. This is not the place to attempt to place these distinctions, but the way in which visual representations of the Holocaust have incorporated omission or absence warrant consideration apart from that. (All this, in addition to the fact that for most of those caught up in the Holocaust, the brutality and suffering endured was individual, *not* experienced as what only later became known as genocide or "the Holocaust"—an instance of "back-shadowing" or, more simply, of anachronism; this is to be discussed in more detail in chapter 6.

A decisive instance of the un- or nonvisual in relation to Holocaust representation occurs in the medium of film, accentuated there insofar as film, because of the range of film's technical possibilities, pushes the limits of visual representation virtually to the limits of visual experience itself. A recent count of Holocaust-films in all languages since 1945 has estimated the number at 900. Predictably, these films vary widely in their points of view as well as in quality, but a common denominator among them is their representation of at least some instance(s) of the Holocaust's brutalities. Given that purpose, furthermore, one would suppose that nothing known of those brutalities would be regarded as visually off-limits, beyond the reach of representation, a consideration that gains added weight from the institutional move of cinematography toward blatancy, even (or arguably especially) in relation to violence. And in this connection, just as the term "Auschwitz" has become a metonymy for the complex event of the Holocaust, so the gas chambers (in the six "death camps" but also in certain concentration camps) have come to stand for the extremity of transgression, epitomizing the conjunction of mass, "impersonal" murder and the imaginative depth of the Nazi project. What is notable, however, is that this same extreme marks an unspoken (and unshown) boundary that the visual representation in film evidently has refused to cross. In the 900 Holocaust-films cited, a few show the victims on their way to the gas chambers; only two, to my knowledge, go *inside* them—(Nelson's *The Grey Zone* [2002] and Deitch's TV film, *The Devil's Arithmetic* [1999]—and these cloak what occurred in the gas chambers under various shifting covers. That event has in effect been blocked from representation. (An egregious *anti*representation of the gas chambers—which has the effect of underscoring this point—occurs in *Schindler's List*, as the film's viewers wait for the gassing of a group of women assembled in the camp's "shower room"; viewers are, and are meant to be, startled when the apparent "showers" turn out to be real ones.)[9]

The absence of this subject of film representation cannot be due to cinematographic problems, since the technical means required are relatively simple. There must be another reason, and especially at a time when cinematic "special effects" depict violence in extraordinary detail, the boundary observed here seems to reflect not a limit on violence so much as recognition that, unlike the projection of most cinematic violence (which has no particular historical ground), the weight of the actual historical reference added to the brutality of the gas chamber crosses an ethical boundary: it is "too much"—"too much" for viewers to watch, and in explanation of that, "too much" in the way of ethical repugnance, approaching a point at which the visual representation might itself count as an ethical violation; that is, as showing what is unshowable, not because it cannot be shown, but because it should not.

The explanation proposed is not a proof; but the omission described requires *some* such explanation. (I do not claim that the omission is unique to Holocaust-representation.) On a smaller scale, consider Samuel Johnson's refusal, after he had seen *King Lear* for the first time, to read or see it "ever again," because for all the play's greatness, its ending, he suggested, was "too cruel." A very different but pertinent example occurs in relation to capital punishment in the United States, also, after all, an expressive "representation." For although a principal defense of that punishment is its alleged deterrent effect, executions nonetheless are not carried out in public, with the unstated reason for that evidently reflecting an ethical scruple that presumably is distinguishable from the justification for capital punishment itself. By contrast, there is no avoidance of the gas chambers in literary representations of the Shoah (fictional *or* nonfictional). Arguably, the most compelling and direct representation of the gas chambers in film appears in Claude Lanzmann's *Shoah* in its largely linguistic narratives, in the telling much more than in the showing. If this difference among the arts reflects differences in their media or genres, the role of ethical limits in visual representation that is claimed here seems part of the more general relation between the aesthetic and the ethical, the beautiful and the good.

I referred earlier in this chapter to silences or absences in Holocaust-writing that appeared under the subtitle of an essay as "Sex, Shit, and Status." Those same absences (together with others) carry over into the realm of the visual, in Holocaust-films and no less notably in the nontemporal visual arts of painting and sculpture. Admittedly, thematic representation is intrinsically more difficult to achieve in the latter; we may recognize cross-sections of complex narratives—as in the many compositions of "The Last Supper"—but those frozen sections assume an understanding that both precedes and goes beyond the works themselves. As mentioned before, visual representations of scenes of the Holocaust often have relied on external (nonvisual and nonartistic) markers drawn from the artist's biography or from stereotyped images (Nazi emblems, etc.). But these function as signs rather than symbols; they seem as distinct from the *artistic* features of the works as historical information is about the identities and histories of the Dutch *burghers* who sat for their portraits to Frans Hals or Rembrandt. And then the question becomes increasingly more pressing of what or how much remains of the expressive content of the Holocaust itself *after* the external markers or signs bracketed. As one restricted aspect of this, odors pose a particular difficulty for visual representation; they certainly can be written about, as can taste and touch; but are there any examples—outside of advertisements—of the visual representation of smells, whether repellant or fragrant?

What has been said here about the boundaries of visual Holocaust-representation requires balancing on a slippery slope, for it would seem that to be consistent, part of what is omitted or nonvisual in the visual turns out to be excluded not on ethical grounds but on artistic grounds. For if didacticism in art is a fault, then art *should* omit it, which the markers or signs referred intentionally deny or at any rate hope to be able to compensate for. And here I would compare the work of Samuel Bak—himself a survivor—in his large painting titled *The Family* (1974) to a work taken from the Jewish Museum Exhibition in 2002 on "Mirroring Evil: Nazi Imagery/Recent Art": Zbigniew Libera's *Lego Concentration Camp Set* (1996): a series of Lego constructions "mirroring" the layout of a concentration camp. The immediate issue in this comparison is not the comparative artistic value of the two works, but the way in which they handle the matter of omission. And on this, it seems clear that counter to Libera's attempt to represent visually as much as can possibly be visualized through the refractory lens of the Lego set, Bak goes to great lengths to pare away, to limit, to omit—to the point where a viewer unaware of Bak's biography or the external history of this painting (but generally knowledgeable about the Holocaust) would not necessarily make the association at all but might nonetheless appreciate the power of the work anyway. Bak, as a painter, seems to be following Aharon Appelfeld's explanation of *his* writerly understatement: "One doesn't look directly at the sun." That impulse suggests a convergence of the ethical and the aesthetic, arguing *on behalf of* omission in the visual; that is, for asserting a role for the nonvisual in the visual.

More can and should be said about silence as a figure, theme, or genre in Holocaust-representation. But the account here is meant as an overture, not a conclusion, and for a mediating point between these, a further suggestion might be added. In an opening comment of this chapter, I alluded to the danger of silence as a dominant or preferred genre of Holocaust-representation even if the price paid for avoiding that danger makes room in writings and visual representations that have the Holocaust as a subject for exploitation, sentimentalizing, diminution, and in the end straightforward *mis*representation. But there is also another and weightier side to this danger for the individual artist attempting to craft a representation related to the Holocaust—a version of Charybdis joining Scylla in the face of the still-larger catastrophe of the Holocaust itself. All art, but especially art involving a subject with the moral weight of the Holocaust is a presumption on silence, implying that what it "says" adds value to the subject that the silence or absence it displaces would not have. We do not usually think of silence as a criterion or standard in this sense; words or shapes that are the expressive means of art are such common currency that we *assume* their legitimacy to begin with—much like the oxygen we breathe—and as a separate question from that of judging their existence. But to think against the grain here, viewing silence as an alternative—even, at a harsh extreme, judging that it would be better if certain works had not been created at all—is surely also a way, a decisive way, of asserting the presence of silence in the texts we encounter (arguably still more in those for which we ourselves are responsible). To be consistent, this principle, the challenge of silence, would apply to all artifacts if it applies to any, although even within that more general standard, certain events or issues pose a greater challenge than others. The Holocaust is surely among these, for which the danger of silence is equal to the importance of making its presence actual and known.

« 6 »

Representation and *Mis*representation

On or about the Holocaust

In the *Republic*, Plato speaks of first applauding Homer and then leading him up to—and across—the model state's border. Homer thus would be honored mainly in exile, with the ideal republic more secure in this arrangement, more *just*: for everybody, including the critics who earlier had been willing to expose themselves to Homer's poetry in order to judge its dangers. The fault that Plato identifies in such broad strokes was not Homer's *specific* misrepresentations (although Plato names a number of these) but the act of "committing" representation itself and as such. Representation, more concisely, *is* misrepresentation: distortion, dissembling, diminishing.

Plato's basis for this ascetic view becomes more evident when "mimesis" is translated as "imitation" rather than "representation." (Why the former's pejorative, "faux" semblance does not apply to the latter, whether in art or politics—"No taxation without representation"—warrants separate discussion.) But the defects of imitation as (at most) second-best generally are recognized even when they are not judged the hanging crime of Plato's metaphysics. For there, imitation not only articulates a second and lesser order of being (i.e., Being), but presents itself *as* real, engaging emotions at the expense of reason, the more easily to lead art's audience down its illusory garden path. Art's artifacts, in other words, are ingredient with deception, the pretense of truthfulness; they pose as real but aim in effect to displace it. By contrast, what *is* true or real employs no such blandishments. (What, after all, would they add? Should they speak of themselves as "really real"?) But this restraint means also that the true or real may be lost in the crush, and indeed, Plato's reaction against the displacement of reason—the denial that there is any truth to be discovered—that, according to him, had spread through the influence of the arts and artists, those central educators in Athenian culture, was crucial in shaping Plato's extreme reaction. Plato's own (artistic) parable in the *Republic* of the inhabitants of the cave, who do not realize they *are* in the cave, vividly depicts this displacement. Even if the public cannot exactly be blamed for falling victim to art's seductive power, that result might in any event be averted, and so, for Plato, it should be; hence, the prominent place reserved in the Republic for the state censors (a.k.a. the true educators, a.k.a. philosophers).

If Plato had left behind only this verdict on art and the artists, he probably would have remained a footnote to the history of philosophy instead of (as Alfred North Whitehead's elegiac phrase had it) the other way round. Yet it is noteworthy, although too little noted, that this cranky, seemingly idiosyncratic view of art's menace has had an influential and persistent afterlife, in some instances drawn on Plato himself, at other times reinvented, whether for his or for other reasons. In one of these expressions, it converged on the nascent Western religions' taboo that proscribed figurative representation of the newly one God—a specific prohibition that on some interpretations then broadened into a prohibition on figurative representation as such, literarily as well as visually. ("Scripture" in this context is not exclusively *literary*). If we scan the history of the visual arts backward from their present position of cultural authority and commercial weight, it is easy to forget the efforts required at their medieval origins to set them in motion. More categorically: The modernist celebration of the visual arts for their originality and novelty, their capacity for articulating new forms, subjects, and idioms, and for their growing popular currency (in contrast to the ever-narrower "professional" norms emerging at the same time in the natural and humane sciences)—all these have conduced to what was (is) an exceptional moment in the role of the arts in Western cultural history.

The latter generalization, however crude, is meant as an historical summary, no more an *assessment* of art's current standing than of the apparently inverse decline of religious belief. (The coincidence of those two processes recalls Dostoyevsky's prediction that "Incredible as it may seem, the day will come when men will quarrel more fiercely about art than about God." Prophets themselves, it seems, might not wish their predictions so quickly realized.) That the flourishing of the arts in the nineteenth century would run head-on into Hegel's also Romantic pronouncement of the "end of art" served only to immunize the arts; for better or worse, the arts and artists continued to look not to philosophy, but inward, for their prospects.[1]

And yet. When we come now to consider the threat of art's *mis*representations, this historical (let me label it "Platonist") back-shadowing is sobering and clarifying. For despite art's current authority, judgments within or about the arts still identify and distinguish the relative value of individual works, applying criteria in these judgments that often reflect the same stringencies found in their Platonist prehistory. Artistic faults, for example, of implausibility or inconsistency, bias or overgeneralization, inauthenticity or factitiousness, superficiality or vulgarity, melodrama or sentimentality—all these are at their basis charges of misrepresentation, claiming that the representation questioned has in some way failed its subject, distorted it for purposes related to the agent's interests in contrast to the subject's. These charges, moreover, become increasingly forceful, the weightier (intellectually, morally, practically) the subject is that is "represented" (or, in the event, *mis*represented). The outcome of this judgment may at times be so extreme as to call for an aesthetic version of capital punishment: that on balance it would be better if the particular misrepresentation did not exist at all (the actions called for by that conclusion would be a separate issue).

Thus far is the beginning of an outline of the binary relation of *Holocaust*-representation and misrepresentation that I consider here in a sequence of three stages, in part but not always cumulative and in any event disclosing how distortions may (and at times have) occurred in Holocaust-representations and (consequently) in what they are meant to "represent." To be sure, any specific charge of misrepresentation will be open to disagreement, with no systematic means even in principle of either avoiding or settling such disputes. Such disagreement, however, does not constitute an objection to the claim of a distinction between representation and misrepresentation; the possibility seems intrinsic to the concept of representation, as well as an incentive for its analysis. What lurks on the borders here, as it does elsewhere for other "offenses," is the possibility of gradations, perhaps through the conceit of a table of degrees of misrepresentation (misrepresentation in the first degree, in the second degree, and so on).

Apart from this speculative prospect, two premises seem to me to underlie the concept of misrepresentation itself. First, that representation is differentiated, various, and sufficiently so as to require analysis of how it works (thus also of how it may fail) both for specific cases and more generally. In other words, representation and misrepresentation are interlaced conceptually: there is no running into the one without running into at least the possibility of the other. To this extent, the Platonist position on that relationship seems fully warranted, which does not in itself substantiate the next step in Plato's account that *equates* the two sides, representation then merging with misrepresentation.

The second premise also bears on the logic of representation: that any account of representation presupposes the existence of a "thing" that is represented and that can be specified apart from the representation. Representation is in this sense a three-place relation, involving the artist or viewer, the representation, and then the latter's source or referent, which, again, is in some measure independent of both the representation and the artist or viewer. This formulation may seem needlessly abstract, but its exemplifications are close at hand: a Chardin still-life is "of" a bowl of fruit; *Bartleby the Scrivener* is "about" a man who "would prefer not to"; Michaelangelo's *David* is of, well, David. Holocaust-representations (whatever their medium and whatever other subjects they touch on) are of or about "the Holocaust." And so, too, of course, would be any *mis*representations of these or other subjects—the one necessary condition for the latter being that even in distortion enough of the referent exists so that *something* of the relation between that and the misrepresentation is recognizable. In this sense, too, no misrepresentation without representation.

Again, the referents in these relations do not live only in or by their representations. This is not to claim that literary characters or painterly depictions "really" exist (the status of "fictional" existence or subsistence is a large but separate issue), but that the basis of what appears representationally has independent standing with the fact of that standing evident in the representations themselves. Think, for example, of the extensive historical and factual detail that the examples just mentioned simply assume as understood: the "normal" forms of human bodies (as in Michaelangelo's David); the referential character of language as a medium in the Melville story; for the Chardin still-life, the rudimentary shapes and colors of "real" fruit; and then, no less basically, the causal links that hold and move all of these. The audiences of art rarely reflect on such rudimentary assumptions, undoubtedly because they *are* so commonplace; but the assumptions nonetheless are present, active, and necessary. (How often, after all, inside or outside art, does anyone—artist or audience—pause to reflect on the assumed presence in their experience of something as elementary and constant as the law of gravity?) If we try to imagine encounters with art in the absence of such assumptions, however, the importance and relevance of the latter quickly become evident.[2]

Admittedly, the numerous assumptions of this sort, drawn from beyond the pronounced boundaries of art, are a great deal to "take for granted" practically and still more so in their theoretical reach. For they entail in effect a realist view of history and experience and thus a full-blown (albeit unfashionable) philosophy of history: The thing or quality or event that a representation represents must be or have been more than only a representation. I have said something more about this broad claim in chapter 2, and in any event stop here with the assertion that if ever a prima facie case can be made for historical realism, representations of the Holocaust do that. What more, after all, than that event's bare chronicle—dates, actions, numbers—could historical or epistemic realism (as in the assertion that "it"—the Holocaust—happened) require? And what more than the denial of that chronicle would be needed in order to assert the presence, in concept or practice, of misrepresentation?

LEVEL 1: TECHNICAL MISREPRESENTATION

I now turn back to the general, and also (initially) to the trivial, in the first stage of "technical" misrepresentation. Aristotle noted in the *Poetics* that the painter who wrongly depicts a horse's gait in the combinations of his legs as they hit the ground is at fault, but at a lesser fault for having painted what he mistakenly thought to be correct than if he had known that (for example) the two right legs don't land at the same time but was for some reason unable to paint that. The latter failing would be "artistic"; the former is "technical." (Aristotle does not consider which of these categories would apply to Flaubert's "misrepresentation" in describing Emma Bovary's eyes first as brown and later in the novel as black, a discrepancy that involves more than only a criterion of consistency, since that criterion's application in this context presupposes empirical knowledge of how human eye-color characteristically changes or does not.)[3] Such errors, when few and localized, are inconsequential for whatever it is that is being represented, little more than annoyances (much like the person in the next seat at a concert who continually coughs). But insofar as they recur or form a pattern, they become more obtrusive and would at some point move to one of the "higher" levels of misrepresentation (more about this below). Intentional artistic misrepresentations, as in expressionist or surrealist painting, or literarily, as in *Alice in Wonderland* or *Gulliver's Travels*, must be judged on different grounds; their effectiveness, in any event, clearly assumes their audience's recognition of the norms or conventions they deliberately set out to violate (for reasons that may then result in still other conventions).

Admittedly the technical misrepresentations mentioned are viewed here in the context of art, not history, where the weight of the valences would shift. A merely "technical" mistake about a horse's gait in a painting becomes more significant in a book on dressage. Analogously, the greater the moral or intellectual weight of the artist's subject, the more importance attaches to even the historical or "merely" technical elements of the ensuing work, with even rudimentary and obvious instances likely to have a larger impact on the other levels of misrepresentation. So, for example, the disputes about the accuracy of the portrayal of Pius XII in Rolf Hochhuth's *The Deputy* were (are) less focused on that drama's aesthetic features than on its historical/technical elements: what Pius XII did or did not do or say as the events of the Holocaust unfolded, and then, at a further step, what Hochhuth's design was, as he does or does not recount that history accurately. The technical issues in this case are so serious, in themselves and for the work, that related charges of misrepresentation cannot depend on artistic license to mitigate them; their historical standing, in other words, makes so large a difference for the other levels of artistic representation (as seen below) that those potential connections must be anticipated even when the focus of analysis is on individual "technical" details.

Again, in a somewhat different example: Holocaust-representation often has run up against the issue of technical misrepresentation in the borderline artistic genres of testimony and memoir, where the intervention of memory and its artifices or lapses at times may be challenged by history and/or the criterion of consistency. Elie Wiesel, for instance, has made what amounts to a claim for historical immunity in such accounts, as in his angry objection to Alfred Kazin's expression of doubt about a particular survivor-witness's account of his experience in the Holocaust. (Wiesel criticized both Kazin's specific question and the legitimacy of skepticism about *any* survivor testimony.[4]) In reference to the Holocaust (as in similar cases), eyewitness testimony undoubtedly adds weight to the historical as well as to the related moral considerations that apply; but this is far from granting it historical immunity in the face of analysis or judgment. (Any such claim of immunity would be self-defeating: If the *fact* of witnessing is a condition of testimonial accounts, it would be arbitrary to limit the role of historical evidence to that one "moment" and to deny the relevance of such evidence beyond that.)

LEVEL 2: NARRATIVE MISREPRESENTATION

Technical or historical misrepresentations have in common (i) an internal or external "mistake" as judged by normal rules of evidence; and (ii) the relative isolation of these mistakes from the overall structure of the work of which they are part. Viewed from another side, these misrepresentations, even when corrected, ordinarily would not affect the understanding of the work overall in any substantial way. If the number of such faults is large or the same fault often repeated, they no doubt would begin to obtrude on the response, but such cumulative instances are unlikely; where the occurrence of technical misrepresentation is flagrant, it may become the focus of attention that otherwise would attach to the work as a whole, but even this would not alter their character as technical or empirical. In Holocaust-representation, the controversy over the historical role of Pius XII or, to imagine a more extreme example, a work that cited the "several hundred thousand Jews who died as Nazi victims" as an echo of Holocaust-denial, would be examples of this. But discussions of Holocaust-representation and misrepresentation have not focused on this first stage of the progression if only because the issues in such cases are readily verifiable or refutable (or at least opinions about those issues treat them as if they were) and to that extent separate from the overall judgment of the works.

The issues at stake become quite different, however, at the second stage, of "narrative misrepresentation," as that draws the individual technical elements into the design of the overall narrative. At this level, interpretation *of the whole* becomes the basis of assessment, a process necessarily more complex (thus more open to disagreement) than reactions at the first level to the work's individual elements. In the event, the presence of misrepresentation at this level would threaten—less nicely, impugn—the work as a whole. Here, too, judgments—now of the whole—may conflict, but the claim of narrative misrepresentation moves the discussion up to a level of judgment in which the individual technical or historical misrepresentations are viewed in a larger context, intruding there as extrapolated from the individual faults noted at the first level.

An example of this narrative misrepresentation in relation to the Holocaust appears in Roberto Benigni's film *Life Is Beautiful*, which has been both attacked and acclaimed on a variety of other grounds, although the charge of what I am calling its narrative misrepresentation seems to me basic. The depiction in the film of the "camp" to which the father and son (Guido and Giosue) are deported—where the father eventually is killed—is unmistakably (thus, one infers, intentionally) a sanitized version of the Nazi death-camps and even of the "lesser" concentration camps set up by the Nazis across the countries they had occupied. This representation of the camp as relatively orderly and clean, habitable, akin to a standard Western prison, viewed by itself, would be a "technical" or historical misrepresentation like others in the first category outlined above. Even in these terms, it would be significant as a misrepresentation because the camps in their naked brutality were historically so central to the process of the "Final Solution." But the role of Benigni's camp in shaping the narrative-misrepresentation here is more extensive than that, since its depiction turns out to be the pivot around which the film as a whole, that is, the representation, revolves. This becomes evident as the film makes it *necessary* that the camp should be humanly livable, "possible," since otherwise the games that Guido plays with Giosue as a means of shielding him from the camp's reality (again, with that reality already much diminished) would be impossible. Also at least highly improbable would be the process of Giosue's survival, his being reunited with his mother, and his concluding (offensive) and celebratory words that carry the game to its conclusion, as he happily yells out, "We've won!" That last shout is heard against the background of his father's murder; it goes against the grain of even the sanitized grimness of the concentration camp world as portrayed.

The issue thus raised in reference to the film is *not* whether a place can be found for the comic in Holocaust representation. There exists, we know, a genre of Holocaust-jokes: bittersweet and yet, for some instances, genuinely funny. In the literary canon at large, moreover, the most compelling writers of tragedy have demonstrated how wit and the comic, far from being alien, may sharpen the tragic edge, with *Hamlet* and *King Lear* especially vivid examples in this group, further exemplifying what Plato in the *Symposium* explicitly cited as the intimate relation between the comic and the tragic. It is not, then, the intended humor in *Life Is Beautiful* that supports the claim of its narrative misrepresentation, but the center around which the film as a whole revolves: the structure that represents the particular camp in which the narrative is set as humanly habitable, sufficiently so to support the "games" depicted, thus also, as the film would have it, to transform or at least to neutralize the other aspects of the camp as it must have been and of which viewers are given only slight intimations. Technical or historical representation at this point turns into something larger, affecting the broader character of the work, and then (so I have been arguing) distorting the work as a whole. This is narrative misrepresentation.

It might be objected that to create or find a Holocaust-narrative that concludes on an "up-beat" note like that projected in *Life Is Beautiful* necessarily would require some instances of technical misrepresentation. But this objection begs the question of whether individuated up-beat themes or points of view would ever be warranted in the context of a Holocaust-narrative. The classic trope and understanding of comedy underscores this reservation, as we recall the classic features (as in Shakespearean comedy) of ultimate reconciliation in a "green world" in which everybody, at least everybody who deserves to, lives happily ever after. Certainly in this classic sense, the argument seems compelling that the context of the Holocaust is *not* a subject for comedy, that any attempt to find the fact or even the possibility of reconciliation or redemption in that event must be a misrepresentation. And indeed defenses of *Life Is Beautiful* that argue for the compatibility of the comic with even the most terrible sides or moments of human experience typically do not consider the comic in this generic sense; they focus rather on individual interventions of a sort that do occur in the film. What such defenses ignore is the price that the film pays for those moments in its basic structure, what makes such individual comic moments possible: the structure that on the argument here exemplifies the film's narrative misrepresentation. If the claim is made, nonetheless, that the film's humorous moments outweigh its misrepresentational faults (singly or collectively), the issue becomes a matter for interpretive judgment on which, after all, evaluation inevitably (here or elsewhere) depends. The film's defenders evidently would be willing to sacrifice enough in the way of technical misrepresentation (which they might well recognize as such) in order to realize what they find valuable in its narrative whole. That the disagreement here becomes a matter of practical as well as of aesthetic judgment must be itself a factor in the discussion.

STAGE 3: MORAL MISREPRESENTATION

As narrative misrepresentation involves interpretive judgment of the art work as a whole—with increasing likelihood of discordant views—the prospect of "moral misrepresentation" opens the way for still further contention. Even if one grants the relevance in general of moral or ethical value to the assessment of art, the dependence of such judgment on the two levels of misrepresentation previously mentioned, with *their* complications, indicate the likely complexities in anything built on them. Not all representational subjects impel the progress of such judgment with the same urgency, and one factor that clearly makes a difference in this progression is the moral weight of the artistic subjects themselves outside of art; that is, as such. The reason for this is evident: The more significant a moral issue, the more care ought to be given its address (whether in art or any other context); and of course, the more ways or nuances in which that address can go wrong (as in misrepresentation).

I cannot provide here a systematic conceptual account of the connection between the aesthetic and moral or ethical aspects of representation, or of the relation between that connection and art's historical or technical aspects; the histories of aesthetics and of metaphysics more generally attest to the complexity of the relational triad of the Good, the True, and the Beautiful. A case can be made, however, by example, which although itself open to dispute, may yet identify both the form and relevance of this third level of "moral misrepresentation."

A specific example of this type of misrepresentation has itself been much discussed, although not for the reasons elaborated here. William Styron's *Sophie's Choice*—the novel and then the film—revolves around the decision eponymously designated in the title: in the context of the Nazi occupation of Poland, Sophie is given a choice of life for one of her two children, the other to be killed. The narrative out of which this coerced decision emerges is subsidiary to that climactic event; everything else in the novel (and film) revolves around it. Partly because of this, the issue of narrative misrepresentation does not seem to me central for judging the work, although Cynthia Ozick has argued (in terms related to those in the two stages of misrepresentation previously outlined) that Styron's creation of Sophie as a Polish Catholic in the context of the Holocaust is a serious flaw in the representation (as a matter of historical disproportion or implausibility). Whether one agrees with this criticism or not, at the level of moral representation—a point in the texts, in fact, where the aesthetic and the moral narratives converge—a more fundamental misrepresentation stands at the very crux of the narrative. This is the author's (own) choice of the decision forced on Sophie, the decision with which she is confronted between the life of one child and the life of another (a decision that can be considered quite apart from the issue of Sophie's religious/ethnic identity to which Ozick calls attention). I am not claiming that the decision—or even the sort of decision—that Styron places at the center of his work in this way is implausible, that it could not or did not occur; and few would argue that the kind or measure of cruelty in that coercion is inconsistent with what else is known about the calculated brutality of Nazi policies.

What does become an issue of moral misrepresentation in Styron's work, however, is the articulation of that "instance" as a means or key to a representation of the Holocaust as such. I mean by this something that in its own terms is quite simple. Even under the Nazis' own standards, the episode that Styron places at the center of his work would have been exceptional, if only because of the set of circumstances out of which it necessarily would have to come (the role of the Nazi officer, his relation to Sophie, the situation in which she and he and the two children appear, and so on). But still more basically than this: The effect of Styron's "crux" is to call attention to an extraordinary "moment," when it was—on the contrary—an extensive array of much less dramatic moments occurring at the same time and in the same context that made up the core character of barbarism in the Nazi genocide, with no more than that required to demonstrate or represent it.

More concisely still: the melodrama of Sophie's "choice" diverts attention from, and to that extent diminishes, the millions of—more commonplace?—murders that were being committed at the same time, of children and also of adults, with the scope and extent of that design (or "Solution") larger and heavier in weight (*much* more so if one ventures the comparison at all) than the extraordinary event to which Styron calls his audience's attention. The latter is a representation, in other words, that in its effect places "under erasure" the key elements of the very event that Styron's own framework of discourse asserts to be responsible for it. But those elements require no intensification or exaggeration; indeed, attempts to enlarge them in order to intensify or to highlight the process or consequences of the Holocaust, seem bound to produce exactly the opposite effect, of detracting from or diminishing them, which is, I should argue, what they do in *Sophie's Choice*.

To be sure, a contrary reading might be given of the same evidence, proposing that as Styron epitomizes Nazi barbarism through Sophie's "choice," he provides a perspective for confronting and understanding whatever other reports we come upon of Nazi atrocity: no matter how extensive or cruel such others might be, it could be claimed after seeing that choice, nothing further would be needed to enlarge or to frame the scope of moral enormity. But this rejoinder might serve as an apologia for *any* hyperbole or melodrama; the fact that it may be convincing in certain contexts is no warrant for its application in others, let alone in all. Furthermore, if it is the systematic extent of Nazi murder with all the efforts of imagination and will distinguishing that atrocity, the extremity of the particular case that Styron depicts works against rather than for such recognition. A broader, more sustained and more brutal history is buried when it is precisely that deeper history that is supposed (on internal grounds) to provide the novel with its subject.

This reading is a particular judgment of a specific work and its setting, and there can be reasonable disagreement about its conclusion (as well as its premises). The formal issue here, however, is the *kind* of misrepresentation being alleged rather than the particular example cited; that is, the possibility of moral misrepresentation and the difference that it would—and should—make in public responses to the work in which it appears. In other words, going beyond *Sophie's Choice* to the possibility of moral misrepresentation as such: to the way in which technical or historical detail becomes cumulatively incorporated in the next stage of narrative representation, as those in turn converge on moral judgment that may affirm or object to the representation. At each of those stages (so the cumulative claim here goes), the corresponding possibility arises of *mis*representation. And where the subject has the heightened significance of the Holocaust, the latter possibility has the same heightened dimensions—and risks.[5]

« » « »

Various objections can be raised to the position outlined, with its focus at once on the possibility and dangers of Holocaust-misrepresentation. Let me anticipate two such objections.

QUESTION 1: Why, given the intrinsic inventiveness of art and the license this presupposes, does the charge of artistic misrepresentation, even when warranted, *matter*?

RESPONSE: It doesn't, if one views originality or imagination or even genius as a blank check, with its specific amounts then to be "drawn" by the bearer. In one sense, of course, this is indeed how the arts work: There are no rules to be followed, any more than there are proofs for beauty (or wit).

For artistic creation, everything in principle is possible (although as Heinrich Wölfflin famously pointed out in his *Principles of Art History*, however devoted aesthetic theory is to this principle, it clearly does not apply to artistic practice, where *not* everything is possible at any given moment). In any event, this claim about creativity, even broadly formulated, does not mean that aesthetic responses or judgments are similarly unfettered. The issue here is not necessarily based on moral intervention, but on the measure of responses more generally: Did it make a difference to responses to his Holocaust "memoir," *Fragments,* when it was discovered that "Benjamin Wilkomirski," the author, far from having been born in Riga and having suffered through the concentration camps (as his book claims), grew up as a non-Jew in the fastness of neutral Switzerland? Would it make no difference to our reading of him if we learned that Primo Levi had spent the war years in an alpine village, and only upon returning to Turin imagined a year in Auschwitz and the episodes he then recounted?

To be sure, these are "external" questions to the works mentioned; some actual or potential readers, furthermore, might claim (indeed, *have* claimed) that the displacements conjured make no difference, or that whatever difference they make is trivial. Disagreement among readers on this point calls into question other, more fundamental differences about the definition and status of truth (at the most immediate level of this disagreement, there seems nothing more to be said: the two opposing judgments must go their own ways); but this does bring into the open what is at stake here. For the issue on which the relevance of any claim of misrepresentation draws is the issue of truth itself, whether as an external judgment on aspects of the art work, or as truth or referentiality are seen to figure internally, in terms of the work's coherence. And unless one argues (in praise or blame) that feeling or emotion are disconnected from cognition — as Plato does, against himself, in his expulsion of the poets from the Republic — the continuum on which truths appear ensures their constant relevance.

QUESTION 2: Does not *all* Holocaust-representation — even in simplified or exaggerated or misleading forms — have value insofar as it calls attention to that important subject, sometimes in ways accessible to audiences who would not respond to more sophisticated or exact or imaginative or subtler accounts?

RESPONSE: Possibly. And perhaps the argument would be made on the same ground for giving license to representations of Holocaust-denial (at the very least, not to banning them legally, although other principles then enter the fray). Furthermore, even if the general point of this question were granted, it would not imply equality among the varied expressions of Holocaust-art. Undoubtedly, there is something to be said for the assertion implicit in the question. One has only to consider the very different numbers represented by the respective audiences for Claude Lanzmann's classic *Shoah* and for Gerald Green's water-thin but much more widely viewed *Holocaust*. That different audiences respond most willingly or strongly to quite different types of representation (and at times, also of misrepresentation) comes as no surprise; nor is there reason why anyone should expect this to apply less to art with the Holocaust as a subject than to art with other subjects or means. But this is also not in itself an argument against discriminating among instances of Holocaust-representation, or in the articulation of criteria for analyzing or comparatively evaluating them. What draws the attention of the largest audiences may do so for good or bad reasons, and these need to be sorted out: perhaps the more so for a subject of weighty moral dimensions than others, but in any event. A strong argument could be made that the more people who know something about the Holocaust, the better, and that in order to accomplish this, quite different representations will be more effective (as more "inviting") for some audiences than for others. Except by applying a simplistic numerical criterion, however, accepting this contention does not mean that the representations themselves are equal in the adequacy or value of their representation. To argue *for* that thesis would be to preclude the possibility of any aesthetic or moral distinctions whatever.

In conclusion to this outline of certain modalities of representation and misrepresentation in their bearing on Holocaust-representation, I would add some comments about the category of "Holocaust-representation" itself. These in part recall the Platonic view discussed earlier, concluding, however, not that misrepresentation is intrinsic to representation but that, and how, the concept of "Holocaust-representation" (or its synonyms) has itself been a source of misrepresentation. One expression of this is in interpretations of the phrase "the Holocaust" itself. To be sure, the usual connotation of the phrase directs attention to individual events or characters "*in*" the Holocaust—whether they purport to be faithfully historical (as in the novel and film *Schindler's List*) or not (as in Aharon Appelfeld's novel *Badenheim, 1939*). No more than slight familiarity with the context of the

Holocaust by a prospective audience is assumed in relation to these texts, and similarly weak assumptions are common in analogous settings, as, for example, in the nomenclature of a "Civil War" novel or a "Late Renaissance" painting.

Beyond this restricted marking function, however, a tension becomes evident in responses to the phrase "Holocaust-representation" that Holocaust-artists and Holocaust-audiences have often noted and almost as often found problematic: the implication that any work subsumed under that rubric had undertaken to represent a consciousness of that event as a whole rather than (for example) only the narrative of a single person's life or death. The framework of the Holocaust as such, in other words, is represented as the subject or reference of "Holocaust-writing" or of Holocaust art more generally. To be sure, for some writers, that framework is deliberately assumed and is assigned an important role in the response of the "implied reader" (Appelfeld especially relies on this tacit basis, as in novels like *Tzili* and *The Age of Wonders*). But for other authors, it appears as a function imposed externally, one, furthermore, that narrows the artists' own professional scope (as they then become "*Holocaust*-novelists/poets/painters") in a way that they themselves often have objected to. The creators of art need not and arguably should not have the last word on how their work is to be assessed or interpreted; it could be argued that designations like "Holocaust poet" or "Holocaust-novel" are no more than conventional place-markers, to be taken no more seriously than many other such conventional labels (an "Irish" author, or a "Renaissance" painter). But those characterizations at times strike more deeply than this, reflecting substantive understandings or assessments of the artists' works, and to this extent, the rubric itself becomes a source of potential misinterpretation. A distinctive example of this possibility (already mentioned) was Paul Celan's strong objection to characterizations that viewed him as a "Holocaust-poet" and of his poetry—including the widely cited "Todesfuge"—as "Holocaust-poetry." It is not only because of the unusual stature of Celan as a poet or because of the character of his poetry as open to appreciation even without specific reference to the Holocaust, that his reaction should be taken seriously; clearly it points to a more general issue than his personal aversion.[6]

A second, deeper possibility of misrepresentation in the phrase sets out from the history of its own terms, specifically from the fact that "the

Holocaust" did not become a common designation—the definite article followed by the uppercase substantive—until a lengthy period of time had elapsed after the end of "the Holocaust" itself. (The first entry for "Holocaust" in the *New York Times* Index, for example, occurs in 1960). This does not prove lack of concern or attention to the events constituting the Holocaust before then (although this was to some extent true); but names add more than only a public face to whatever it is that they identify, and the increasing reflective and representational focus on that event since the 1960s has both depended on and reinforced the name by which it generally has come to be known. (This period includes a struggle over the nomenclature itself, as "the Holocaust" competed with references like "Shoah" or the "Nazi genocide" or the Nazis' own "Final Solution.")

Again, "the Holocaust" hardly differs in these semantic respects from analogous phrases like "the Cold War" or the "Victorian Age." In "Holocaust-representation," however, a significant factor related to its formation ensues in two questions that hardly apply to those other, or similar, examples. First, the historical question of what consciousness there was of "the Holocaust" (as such) among its victims; and second, the aesthetic question of the extent to which this awareness is assumed in Holocaust-representations *of* the people who appear in them.

The first of these issues can be put in straightforward historical terms: On the generally accepted estimate that by the end of 1942, at least half the total number of Jews ultimately murdered in the Holocaust had been killed; and again, on the evidence that the intent of Nazi genocide was not generally known even in outline and was certainly not generally acknowledged among its potential or even its actual victims until well into 1943 or later: It could not have been awareness of "the Holocaust" that weighed on the victims prior to that time or on many of them even after that. (Primo Levi reports that when he learned, at the beginning of 1944, that his transport from Italy was headed for "Auschwitz," the name meant nothing to him; indeed, he describes a sense of relief in learning that there was now a definite place to which he and the others were going.) Of course, these victims of the Nazis suffered brutality and murder *as* Jews, and most of them would have been aware of that causal connection, although even on that point, there is the exception of young children and the incapable elderly without such awareness who constituted a not-insignificant percentage of those killed. Would it have made a difference to the victims capable of such awareness if they *had* understood that beyond the consciousness of their individual plight or that of their immediate group (family, village, etc.), the act directed against them was also genocidal? that the Nazi intention was the destruction of the Jews, to make that people "disappear from the earth"?

There is no way to answer this question by anything more than conjecture, but it is worth noting that the issue it raises would be irrelevant in many analogous cases. Representations of the American Civil War, for example, incorporate the assumption that those affected—soldiers or their supporters on either side—were aware of the purposes and antagonisms of the war, however vague they might have been on the details underlying them. The few public proclamations within Jewish communities that did attempt to persuade their members of the Nazi intent to destroy the people as a whole did make *some* difference in communal attitudes (e.g., the declaration in Vilna initiated by Abba Kovner at the end of 1941), as did the same conclusion arrived at less publicly or collectively by a considerable number of German Jews immediately after Kristallnacht. For some of the European Jewish populace, this awareness, when it came, led to resistance or flight; for others, it expressed itself in the need to record the events. For most, however, including even such heroic figures as Immanuel Ringelblum, evidence of the Nazi intentions was so extraordinary as to meet first a barrier of incredulity and only later gave way to acknowledgement, with many never reaching the latter conclusion. Even for those immediately experiencing Nazi murder, as they focused attention and desperation on their own fates, a consciousness of the total destruction of the people in addition to that of their selves and families might have made some difference. But then, too, awareness that what was happening was genocide was notably limited: understandably in part because of the constrained sources of information, more harmfully but even then understandably, because of psychological defense mechanisms of avoidance or disbelief.

On the other hand: increasingly, as the Holocaust appears in Holocaust-representations articulated farther and farther from the event itself, the aura of the Holocaust as a whole has come to shadow and shape those representations. As mentioned above, virtually all Holocaust-authors depend to some extent on such assumed knowledge, with some of them more reliant on that source than others. Imagine the difference, for example, between the reactions of two readers of Appelfeld's *Badenheim, 1939*, one of whom brings to the reading some knowledge of the Holocaust, the other of whom knows nothing about it at all: the two, it seems, could well be reading two different texts. There is the twist here, of course, that Appelfeld's novel builds—critically—on the obliviousness of the Jewish "guests" in the spa to the events going on around them that they *should* have been aware of and reacting to.

A second aspect of this presumptive awareness goes beyond the knowledge brought to the work by the audience by making assumptions about the internal consciousness of the Holocaust-figures who appear in the representations, that is, as their motivation and understanding are depicted in the representations. In certain Holocaust-works (for example, in Borowski's *This Way for the Gas, Ladies and Gentlemen*), the accounts are spare and restricted to the (then) "here and now." But it is worth noting that Borowski's writings came early in the evolving history of Holocaust-representation—and that what becomes much more common over time is the projection into the victims' minds of a consciousness of the Holocaust as a "whole." This projection appears, I would argue, in a wide sampling of Holocaust-writing, from such relatively early works as Wiesel's *Night* to the various revisions of Anne Frank's diary to D. M. Thomas's *The White Hotel* and then to more recent representations such as Cynthia Ozick's "The Shawl" or Thane Rosenbaum's *Second-Hand Smoke*: all these, I should argue, include an overlay that not only assumes knowledge in the audience of the intent and outcome of the Holocaust (which in some sense enters each of the levels of misrepresentation that have been distinguished). Most significantly, this assumption projects into the consciousness of the individual characters depicted and so into the plot as a whole that same awareness: the recognition of a cataclysm that goes beyond their own immediate condition, dire as that was.

And this, it seems clear, is a fundamental misrepresentation, combining the elements of "technical" or historical and "narrative" and "moral" misrepresentation. For—at least so I have been claiming—it was virtually never "*the Holocaust*" that its victims experienced. And this means that so far as the fullness of that event is made part of the consciousness or agency of figures depicted in Holocaust-representation, that representation becomes a *mis*representation at the level of the genre, a form of overdetermination that although understandable in origin, is yet a distortion.

In strictly historical terms, it would be an anachronism, one with potentially more serious consequences than most instances of anachronism, since any judgment of Jewish reactions to the Nazi threat about which there has been continuing controversy depends on how much was known about the nature of that threat (and by whom and when). In the narrative and moral terms of representation that have been outlined, the danger of misrepresentation thus extends also to them: The arts construct the "plots" of Holocaust-narratives and of any issues of moral agency included in them from the many variables among which the artist has to choose. These obviously include artistic factors in addition to historical, narrative, or moral ones. We have seen examples of how what starts out as a historical or technical element of Holocaust-representation may verge on or over the borders of narrative and moral representation, conveying the possibility in those areas of misrepresentation as well. The consciousness of characters in works of art is arguably the most essential element in their construction as well as the one most difficult to delimit or mark off. This suggests both the cause and the source of misrepresentation in the concept of "Holocaust-representation"—potentially but also, as has become evident, actually.

« 7 »

Applied Ethics, Post-Holocaust

THE RHETORIC OF PROFITS

Odd as it may seem, the analysis of ethical issues in relation to the Holocaust has not gone very far or struck very deeply. Why this should be the case warrants scrutiny in its own right, and I do not attempt that here, although certain contributory reasons seem obvious. The most striking of these appears in the line between perpetrators and victims of the Holocaust, a line at its basis so clear and decisive that to speak of "analyzing" or "discussing" it would seem blatantly beside the point, certainly beside the main point: What, in ethical terms, is there to discuss? And then, too, related to this first response, there is the ready distinction between those *historical* discoveries that seem continually to come to the surface of Holocaust studies and warrant scrutiny as straightforward matters of fact and, on the other hand, the stumbling forays of ethics that, when their conclusions are not simply obvious, seem undecidable and relentlessy vague. And then, too, even beyond these, we hear the conventional nostrum: that for the many difficult or problematic decisions and acts that figured in the Holocaust (on all sides: among the victims as well as the bystanders, at various levels and degrees even for the perpetrators), the conditions of the time were so fraught and complex that nobody reviewing them now could possibly be in a position to judge actions or decisions taken *then*. Only those who were there at the time have that authority. And then, finally, still rising in pitch and with specific reference to Jewish conduct or reactions in the camps and the ghettoes: Since at the end of those days, millions were killed, and killed irrespective of whether they had acted nobly or not, selflessly or selfishly, the very effort now to judge or analyze what they did and how, to weigh against that what they *might* have done that they didn't do (or might not have done that they did do), seems itself a violation. What more could anyone have then asked of them that would justify asking more of them now?

All these reasons singly and the more so together have considerable weight, even if one argues in response (as I would) that even this weight does not justify the conclusion that analysis of ethical issues within the context of the Holocaust is either self-evident or, if murkier than that, itself a moral violation. (That such objections are typically raised selectively is a secondary reason for skepticism about them). To be sure, many of the ethical issues that warrant reflection are complex and difficult in the abstract as well as in their immediate settings. So, for example, the analysis above, in chapter 4, of Jaspers' attempt to consider the collective responsibility of the Germans in the history of Nazi Germany pointed to the continuing force of that question for the Germany of 2008 as well as for his own, then-contemporary German readers. Jaspers' response to that question seemed caught between contradictory principles: on the one hand, recognition that a country and culture (so also, its citizenry) bear a continuing responsibility for the heritage from the past incorporated in them: It *was* Germany and the Germans, after all, who stood behind Hitler. On the other hand, it also seems reasonable—just—that at *some* point, there should (on moral as well as practical grounds) be closure, an application here too of the "statute of limitations," the more so, since most of the individuals bearing the burden at present of any alleged responsibility had themselves no direct part in the policies or actions stigmatized; they were not alive at the time.

The range of such issues in ethical theory and practice extends broadly, over the multiplicity of events and acts that constituted the Holocaust. For example, the concept of the "righteous Gentiles," or as that category has at times been designated less invidiously, the "heroic rescuers": Is the implication here, in examining the role during the Holocaust of the hundreds of millions of "bystanders" not directly threatened by the Nazis and not now included in the select group of the "righteous," that it had been their duty to act as those others had—also risking their lives? And that no analogous assessment is relevant for judging Jewish (that is, non-Gentile) conduct?[1]

And then there are the myriad concrete, practical decisions—matters of ethical judgment—that arose on all sides in the midst of the Holocaust: the obligations of the German citizenry in relation to the Nazi regime insofar as individually they opposed its policies, to act even in silence or passively; the obligations of "bystanders"—whether under Nazi occupation or free of it—to demur without hazarding open resistance from what was known to be occurring; the decisions within the ghettoes for the Judenräte (the Jewish Councils) on whether to accede to Nazi demands for "selecting" deportees; and then, following agreement to that first demand, on how to determine the selection (there is no evidence that the system of a lottery—the fairest means that could have been used, on the premise of the equal value of lives—was ever applied to that process). The objection that any judgment made in hindsight about such decisions must be intrinsically flawed or misbegotten, if accepted as a principle, would disrupt every system of conventional justice, since they all involve retrospective judgments about decisions and actions initiated by other people in contexts quite different from those in which the judges or juries sit to consider them. *Of course*, hindsight is easier, more readily given to sharp distinctions, than was likely at the time. But that may be as much an advantage as a liability. And in any event, the alternative to judging in this way, retrospectively, would be to forfeit the process of judgment not only in those instances but in any; how otherwise are even the most deliberate or disinterested judgments arrived at? That conclusions or verdicts reached in this way may be divided by dissent or by hung juries, with reason on each side, is itself informative; it is not a justification for rejecting the process, and not only because no alternative presents itself.

The same reasoning at a lesser level holds for articulating and facing ethical questions in the *post*-Holocaust period—now—in settings much less fraught. For here, too, issues of various sorts occur that also are underscored in their relation to the Holocaust, if less dramatically. And although less is at stake in them than characterizes the questions referred to the Holocaust itself, their bearing on ethical issues as related to the Holocaust is nonetheless evident. Events from the Holocaust have amply demonstrated how small-scale decisions have ways of leading into and shaping much larger ones.

And so, too, I call attention here to two issues, both in minor keys, but which, also because of that status, can be addressed locally; that is, in the persons of individual readers. The first of these concerns the use of terms derived from the Holocaust as metaphors or similes, a form of usage that has become so commonplace as to be applied at times to almost any act or person for almost any wrongdoing. The number of alleged Hitlers, or Eichmanns, or S.S. men who have been pinned with those labels seems as large as the number of the original figures within the Holocaust itself; virtually any act of violence or oppression in any social or political context may now turn out to have its "Nazi" sources. And if one adds to this individuated misrepresentation, the milder but still exploitative use of the phrase, "the Holocaust," itself in lectures, sermons, and even academic works ostensibly focused on other topics but that, in the view of the pundit or clergyman or professor would benefit from an extra kick of emotive intensity, we arrive at a full house of Holocaust references and allusions in contexts that have little to do with that event, except for the disclosure that the speaker stands heartfeltly against it, and that whatever subject he *is* speaking or writing about is in need of an edge or a point otherwise missing.

But the effect of this promiscuity is debasement or devaluation, a form of exploitation often accompanied by straightforward historical and conceptual misrepresentation. It is true, obviously, that the Nazis were racists. But it is not true, or even close to that, that anyone who is a racist—objectionable as that is in its variations—by that fact favors, let alone practices, genocide. And if it is genocide in the Holocaust that definitively marked the Nazi "project," then how could "racist" and "Nazi" come to be used synonymously, as one is substituted for the other? Eichmann himself was certainly "an Eichmann," but on the evidence of his Nazi career, it seems more than only hyperbole to speak of or even to imagine the varied populace of the World Trade Towers on 9/11 also as "Eichmanns." Admittedly, that reference was an extreme example of what at a lesser level would still be extreme; the point here is, however, that for a subject with the magnitude of the Holocaust, inflation of the rhetorical register serves not to increase but to reduce the force of its terms. And to misrepresent the terms themselves.

Even agreement on this criticism leaves open the question of what possibly could be done about these abuses of language, thinking, and the Holocaust itself. Censorship from above is not an option if only because there is no "above." Refusing to listen to linguistic turns of the sort described or refusing to read the books or periodicals in which they appear might be an option, except that by the time we decide not to read or listen to them, we usually will have already done so. One solution, however, does occur to me, a (very) modest proposal. It would be difficult to bring into practice, but its Dantesque overtones—in that sense, not modest at all—may compensate for that. The concept of "use taxes" is a familiar one, in many instances more congenial to those paying them than most others forms of taxation where the monies paid have no visible or human-sized outcome. "Use taxes" thus are levied at parks, on toll roads, at beaches or museums, and so on, wherever a public utility charges those who use it a fee beyond their normal taxes for the particular service provided: the hike in the park, the highway with no stop-lights, the dip in the ocean. But the more severe analogy here seems fitting: Anyone (politician, clergyman, professor) may employ metaphors or similes or emotive free-associations that invoke the Holocaust or Nazis when those are at most a sidebar for what they are saying, but for this they pay a use tax (per mention)—a levy with both educational and economic value. Educational in emphasizing that metaphors or similes have historical responsibilities, that considerable thought and effort has been given to establish their meanings; economic, as the funds gathered from the use tax payments might then support research and education on the Holocaust, that is, for efforts that are *not* figurative or associative. (An alternate rubric might invoke the category of "sin taxes" like those on alcohol or tobacco; but it might be excessive to prejudice the standing of this particular tax more than the act it is applied to already does.)

The second, related issue strikes closer to home for anyone who writes or talks, professes or preaches, about the Holocaust in professional life. Much has been said (much of it tendentious and itself inflated) about the "Shoah Business" or "Holocaust Industry": the exploitation of aspects or themes of the Holocaust for self-interested or political purposes that often begin and end with personal advancement and profit or ideological persuasion, by the common means of drawing on a variety of emotional strings found in the fabric of the Holocaust. That those expressions have at times been exploitative is undeniable, and one hardly requires the tendentious evidence in Peter Novick's *The Holocaust in American Life*, let alone the caricature of Norman Finkelstein's *The Holocaust Industry*, to become aware of this.[2] Even when such exploitation occurs for ostensibly "high-minded" reasons—in the interests of communal solidarity or for educational purposes—objections might be raised and often have been; no area open to criticism directed at exploitation seems to have passed unremarked in this scrutiny.

Except, it seems, for one—or at least for *this* one. A considerable number of scholars, writers, artists have profited financially from their professional work related to the Holocaust. For some of this number, the gains received have been substantial, even very large; for others, they have at least been actual. I do not refer here to regular employment (as in the ordinary roles of journalist or attorney or teacher) but to profits beyond that, as in public lectures, book royalties, films, conference honoraria, and so on. And the moral issue set in those terms seems straightforward: Is it not a serious ethical question whether anyone who was not himself directly in the Holocaust should profit from its events, most concretely, from the suffering and loss undergone by others?

A number of the best-known figures who address the Holocaust in their work have acknowledged the force of this question by setting up personal foundations. Few "workers" come close to having gains on that order, and of course there could be no way of compelling compliance for even much lesser terms. But this need not impede a minimalist response to the *prin-*

ciple in which at least a percentage of the profits accrued—perhaps by tithing, or more or less than that "tenth"—would not be used for one's own personal affairs but voluntarily given up, set aside. For surely (I would argue), the gains from such accomplishments ought also *in some measure* to recognize the nature of their source. And what likelier way to do that, than to build the fund previously mentioned in support of Holocaust research and education? ("Profits with Honor," the fund might be named.)

The practical difficulties here seem negligible. The fund could be overseen by any of the established institutions involved in Holocaust study or research; the contributions to it would be determined, in percentage or amount, by the contributors themselves. The crucial issue here, it seems, is the *principle* on which such contributions would be based, a principle related to, but more specific than the general justification for charitable giving. In what is still the immediacy of the Holocaust for those who turn their energies and talents to it—as distinct from the many other historical atrocities that are the subjects of other historical and creative narratives—recognition of the source on which they build reflects moral considerations beyond those asserted in the compass of "normal" professional principles. The Holocaust remains a live issue in a way that such events as wrenching and consequential as the American Civil War do not. It is not only that survivors of the Holocaust—groups and individuals—still speak in their own voices, but that the causes or elements that led to it and now also away from it are very much still present.

It could be argued, it seems to me, that the proposal made here would be defensible even if these specific circumstances did not hold, and indeed the impulse for thinking along these lines arose for me from two very different contexts. The first was the Rabbinic tradition that stipulates that since the teaching of holy texts is a religious commandment, those who do such teaching should not be paid for that: Commandments are done for their own sake. But how then should teachers support themselves? They may be paid, in fact, but not for the work they do, only for the work they might have been doing if they were not teaching.

The second context was a performance of Mozart's *Don Giovanni* at the Metropolitan Opera in New York City, where what struck me, in the "frame" of the evening around the production, was the sharp contrast between the glitter of the audience, the warmth and glow in its appreciation of the performance and performers—singers, conductor, orchestra, on the one hand—and the easy, unmentioned neglect of Mozart himself, still (perhaps?) in an unknown grave in Vienna's St. Marx cemetery: the neglect of whatever it was in him and the history after him that had had made possible the evening's warmth and pleasure and glitter. Should not *some* of what appeared in that glow be committed, once again, to its means? And is not that an ethical issue?

Comparisons are always invidious, but the point here, it seems to me, is clear. The present can block out the past, and to some extent, it must do this, if only because of the most basic truism about the past—that there is so much of it. The question then becomes what of the past should be admitted into the present, taken seriously, consciously, and reacted to. *That's* the question that those who in the most literal and concrete way profit from the Holocaust ought to ask themselves, joining it to the broader question of what the moral imperative is that holds at any time for voluntary giving or charity. Is there such an imperative? One has to listen very hard in Holocaust conferences or other Holocaust ambiences to hear even a whisper of this, and it seems doubtful that the reason for this absence is because talk about money is vulgar or crass. Perhaps at some point, as the post-Holocaust period stretches out farther, the issue thus raised will lose its force, the presence of the Holocaust having faded. But that time is not yet.

Two concluding comments about this provocation in ethical practice: First, in response to the reflexive question, yes, I have myself been doing what I propose, and I would be surprised if numerous other people engaged professionally with the Holocaust were also not already doing this. But a public fund would have a greater impact than any individual, private depository. Second: Six years ago, during a year I spent at the Holocaust Museum, I circulated a memo urging a proposal of this sort among the museum's fellows and staff. It met then with glacial silence. Not rejection, but silence. Where should the proposal go now?

THREE DEGREES OF DIFFICULTY IN WRITING DIFFICULT HISTORY

The first difficulty in the writing of history—all history—stems from the fact that what history is "*of*" is over: past, irretrievable.[3] This may not seem to pose a difficulty when contrasted with writing about the present or future, since, unlike these, the past, just because it *is* over, is settled, ready to be pronounced and in that sense, easy, accessible. (It could be claimed that in these terms, death, the paradigm of all endings, turns out to be the single, thus universal subject of historical discourse.) The awareness of that passage and its irretrievability, however, often evoke feelings of pain, sometimes of guilt, invariably of associations, personal or ideological. This first difficulty of difficult history thus expresses itself in the "historian's flinch" — the reflexive move first away from and then back to confront the discovery that the past, which in addition to being his subject also has incorporated his own history, unavoidably impinges on his line of vision. What appears in his view as even superficially clear and distinct remains, then, open to question. And so, too, even in his own terms, always contestable.

This first difficulty is obvious because it appears on the surface of historical texts: It *is* their surface. In this, however, it contrasts with a second, less apparent difficulty that (only in part because of that) is more difficult still: the dissonance between historical fact and historical contingency. Here we find the historian, now attempting to take account of the lens through which he looks, of the effects of its curvature and thus, more generally, of the fallibility built in to whatever he "sees," yet responding insistently, faithfully to the question of "What happened?" and its premise that some thing, event, quality — substantial and well-defined — warrants his attention. *And* that this "thing" is marked clearly and fully enough to be articulated in thought and expression, provided that the historian finds a way through the thickets of the first difficulty, mediating there between evidence and interpretation, and also judging degrees of relevance and separation. But then the second, less apparent difficulty — harsher because it is covert — struggles to the surface, pushing past the earlier focus on the actual to disclose the no lesser "fact" of contingency: the evidence in any historical moment of unrealized possibilities that stand ghost-like, yet side by side with the contrasting possibilities that became actual, those that have entered and shaped the latter by their very exclusion. This evidence, in other words, articulates the presence of absence. And if history and historians can hardly be faulted for the positivist dictates that incline them to give precedence to the actual over the possible, this precedence, history itself attests, remains a matter of degree: The Actual is always, only, 100 percent, but the Possible (still more, the Probable) even when not actualized, has or had its own possibilities. Actual ones.

And further: If death by metaphoric extension is the universal subject or at least the medium of history, that same subject may also at times be murder in a narrower, more literal sense: physical, personal. And with this "advance," the difficulty of history in the two aspects just noted becomes still more acute, since here, it seems, the two aspects converge in a third. For the composition of history now struggles not only with the constraint of the historical past as past and with the second difficulty of contingency's "normal" undermining of history's hard, factual representations, but here, in the third degree, also with the separate denial of contingency within past individual and group lives—not just to those lives (and deaths) as part of history's external movements, but from the inside out, in the probability of what those lives, had they endured, might have become: a feature of native possibility standing as close to the center of the human presence, and thus to all the tenses of its history, as any other that defines them. Historians themselves typically take this feature for granted without acknowledging what it commits them to. They thus move from the drama of history affecting the persons walking its stage to the larger-scale, external history of nations and other groups without leaving a place for the individuation that makes the larger whole possible at any (and each) moment, all the way through, until the point of its conclusion. Historians who follow this pattern in effect deny the origins from which they had set out; theirs is a willingness to restrict the writing of human history to an internal life of their subjects identical to what they would find in tracking the history of a rock or a lake. To be sure, this is rarely the way they *do* write. The more reason, then, that we should be looking at history for what it does still more than for what it says it intends to do, or even for its own judgment of what it *has* done.

Would it be so difficult for the historian to find enough space to bring the actual and the possible together, to see what these have to say to each other, indeed to view them joined, side by side? The imagination, after all, does not stop at history's borders any more than it does for the boundaries of physics; indeed it would be foolhardy, here or anywhere, to predict limits for the imagination (how would we go about imagining them?) But even the imagination is subject to judgment after the fact, and *then* the question of possibility turns into one of aptness or fit, in the relation between form and content. To record the historical occurrences of massacre or genocide with the same measures or weights used in writing about weather patterns or the dating of fossils would surely distort the one even if it adequately represented the other. And the surest means of understanding this dissonance is in the difference between fact and contingency—a difference that may not affect the historical representation of weather conditions or fossils but is crucial for human history—the more emphatically so for murder in its varieties. For there, except in the rarely and truly random act, the fact of contingency casts a long shadow for its recorder as distinctly as for the act's agents and victims. Our recognition that an act (any act) *need* not have happened implies the need for constructing alternate histories: those that did not occur but might have. And here the difficulties of difficult history become most intense, reaching the point at which historical and moral discourse intersect: where the supposed gap between historical or scientific fact, on one side, and moral value, on the other, collapses or, at times, explodes. Subjunctive history—what could or would or should have occurred—is authentic history; "indicative" history, the history of the actual, would remain empty without it, literally vacuous, in a vacuum.

« » « »

To reflect on Polish-Jewish relations in the context of World War II or the Holocaust, the Nazi genocide against the Jews, also will be to recognize the various, and especially the more covert "degrees" of difficulty I have mentioned. There is a compelling, arguably flagrant need to view what occurred in that relationship during those years under the quite different modalities of what did not occur and what might have. Not only because of personal histories or associations between individual Poles and Jews that proved exceptions to the general patterns, but because of the harsh dissonance between fact and contingency that the outbreak of the war, in the Nazi invasion of Poland, heralded. That effect, we now recognize, concluded with the severing of the relationship between these two groups. On one side, the original assembly, in 1939, of more than three million Polish Jews—10 percent of the total populace; on the other side, less than six years later, the 10 percent of that number (300,000) who remained alive, some of these having remained or returned to Poland, some outside the country. So, too, the names of the "Death Camps" that had been placed so deliberately in Poland by the Nazi occupiers, with the names enduring now as synonyms and symbols for murder or genocide: "Auschwitz" as the standard among them — but not because Belzec, Chelmno, Treblinka, Majdanek, or Sobibor would not do: familiar names to so many people able to identify no other place-names in Poland.

To be sure, neither those camps nor the more numerous "lesser" ones were "Polish": It is as certain as any counterfactual historical claim can be that without the Nazis' will, decisions, and systematic efforts, no camps would have existed. But the fact also remains that it is there, in Poland, that they arose, then to be nourished further — here an element within the difficulties mentioned occurs — by ambivalences in the history of Poland toward its many-centuries-old Jewish settlement. And here, too, the difficult challenge intensifies of fact versus contingency: What did happen versus what might have happened or might not have happened. The latter is burdened by the weight of the historical past of church antisemitism, of nationalist and economic and cultural attacks on Jews, not only in the war period itself but — more startling still — even *after* the war "officially" had ended. (Between five and six hundred died in post-Holocaust killing, of which the 1946 Kielce pogrom was the most notable but not the only one.[4]) Brought together, these facets of difficulty shape a disfiguring, even if not predominant lens, one that must be looked through from both sides if the difficult history displayed there is to be understood, let alone countered.

What became actual in the Holocaust with the denial by the Nazis of contingency in the double lives of the Jews, individually and as a group — the group that was "to be made to disappear from the face of the earth" — also set in motion what would then be the actuality that both Poles and Jews now continue to absorb. It marked — there is no way to dispute or avoid this conclusion — the end of Jewish settlement in Poland. And if this were not a large enough actuality for historians and other observers to address, there remains the related and hardly less evident concern of contingency: What might have been the case if what did occur had not occurred — this, on the large scale of nationhood and peoplehood. And then, too, what might have ensued if individual actions that could have been taken (but were not) had been taken. Rather than remaining possibilities that we now look back on only as possible (although in that role as actual; that is, actual possibilities).

Again, the essential contours of this disruption and its particular layers of difficulty originated with Nazi decisions. But these seeped outward into

Polish history and geography, encountering there currents that moved to meet them, sometimes to stand against them, sometimes to accommodate them. Writers and readers of history *should* find themselves caught here, between the fact of what did occur and the possibilities outdone—or undone—by that fact: not as a plea in hindsight for heroism or self-sacrifice (which would be everywhere, always in short supply), but for a commonplace humanity that would balk at collaboration, balk even at benefits gained from others' losses, even (or especially) without having a direct hand in causing those losses. Consider only the personal possessions left behind in the disappearance of three million people: Did those possessions also disappear into the air?

There seems no more striking measure of the difficulty of writing difficult history than by imagining the life of Poland now but with its Jewish populace of the past intact: life in the country, its cities and villages, if the Holocaust had not occurred. This prospect as prospect is, after all, no less real than what became actual remains actual: the conclusive difficulty.

Historical accounts that ignore or avoid contingency's shadow presence are, of course, easier to write and pleasanter to read than their (possible) counterparts. The reach of possibility into the present and the future is much shorter and promises greater, albeit vaguer reward than the reach into the past. But those accounts are also, as we see in looking at them, blind. And by their own hands. It is not a matter here of seeking or inventing difficulties: History itself is the source.

« 8 »

The Jewish Declaration of War against the Nazis

In addition to the large decisions and actions that drove the Nazi genocide, the history of the Holocaust includes numerous small-scale "episodes"—initiatives, transactions, scenarios, confluences—that although sounding now in a minor key, reflect in their combination of improbability, cruelty, and (often) irony, the harsh and arbitrary edges of the larger atrocity of which they are part. Both improbability and irony figure in the episode described here that is still generally unknown, and about which even those aware of its occurrence usually know few of the details involved in it. For good reason. At the beginning of the events in which he had a part, Theodore N. Kaufman, the principal actor in them—as much an anti-hero as any fictional character of literature—was unknown outside his immediate circle (which was also unknown); when the sequence of events he set in motion ended, a little more than two years later, he disappeared from public sight as completely as he had been invisible before. Nor did the events he initiated—through his unlikely role in them as author—affect in a significant, let alone decisive measure the "Final Solution" that was itself being set in motion at about the same time, beginning in 1941, reaching its greatest intensity in 1942, and continuing until the end of the war.

And yet, Kaufman's writings made their way quickly from slight and local origins, the effort of an amateur author and a vanity press in Newark, New Jersey, to the highest echelons of the Nazi regime in Berlin, thence to the German army and the German public, illuminated for a moment at these crossings in the spotlight not of local but of world history. More than sixty years later, with Kaufman's writings now scattered and rare (rarely sought *or* found), the way in which his private, clumsily formulated declaration of war against Germany underwent a transformation into a public, quasi-official declaration, regarded seriously by some the most prominent agents in a conflict that remains itself distinctive in the history of war, warrants consideration at least for *that* part of its history. At the very least, the Kaufman affair highlights the startling combination of contingency and arbitrariness that conspired with more predictable elements of historical causality to mark the procession of the Third Reich as a whole.

The very idea of a Jewish "Declaration of War" against the Nazis conveys its own improbability. How could a relatively small group of people without a country or army, its few members scattered across countries and continents, "declare war" as anything more than a metaphor, or even more probably, hyperbole? And how could one member of that group with no special standing within it speak as representing the community even metaphorically, when those *with* standing could promise little agreement even on the most pressing and one-sided issues? But against these reservations, as against other appeals to reason or evidence, the history and social dynamics of Nazi ideology would go its own way. Thus, a recurrent motif in Nazi rhetoric pre-dating Kaufman's appearance on the scene emerged still more strongly with the Nazi accession to power in January 1933: first, with Jewish disenfranchisement inside Germany, soon evolving into sporadic killings and other physical abuse, the growing network of concentration camps, the pogrom of Kristallnacht; thence, beginning in 1941, the full-scale genocide both within and outside Germany's borders. *All* this was, in the Nazi portrayal of it, not an assault on the Jews, but a *counter*-attack, recourse to self-defense against the war-by-other-means that the Jews had been successfully waging in the world and particularly against Germany at least since the debacle (for Germany) of World War I.

It was the Jews, Hitler prophesied in his annual address on January 30, 1939, as he marked the sixth anniversary of his accession to power, who would be responsible for any more conventionally recognizable world war that might yet occur, and which he then made certain *would* occur in September of that same year. Did he or anyone else need a stronger or more accurate term than "war" for the corruption of culture, the undermining of the national consciousness, of economic justice, and of racial purity that the Jews, as Nazi ideology looked dolefully through its social magnifying glass, had so deliberately inflicted on Germany?

How widely or deeply these beliefs were held and how heavily they weighed in Nazi motivation persist as questions on which historians' assessments still differ. But certainly the conception of the Jew as alien, still more dramatically as on the attack, had a clear and common presence; and certainly, albeit with varying emphasis, the Nazi hierarchy believed that public expressions of this view would be useful in sustaining the nation's support for the regime and the nascent war. It was in this context that early in 1941, in Newark, New Jersey, a small book—in effect, a pamphlet or screed, about a hundred half-pages long—appeared under the title of *Germany Must Perish*, with Theodore N. Kaufman named as author. Kaufman himself, as would have been readily discovered by anyone troubling to inquire about him, was otherwise the small business owner of a theater-ticket agency in Newark; similarly, the press that published the pamphlet, mentioned on its title page as the "Argyle Press," would have been disclosed as Kaufman's creation: not only a vanity press, but his very own. So far as I have been able to determine, the entire publications list of the press consisted, in addition to *Germany Must Perish*, of one earlier pamphlet (1939) and a later one (1942)—all of them written and issued by Kaufman himself.[1]

Yet despite this dubious genealogy, *Germany Must Perish* found its way into the review columns of American periodicals "of record" like the *New York Times*, the *Washington Post*, and *Time* magazine; it then somehow catapulted across the Atlantic to the Nazi Ministry of Propaganda, there to be promoted by the minister himself, Joseph Goebbels, who had the book excerpted and translated into German with an afterword that he wrote and who then saw to the publication and distribution of the "partial" edition of the book, with commentary interspersed, in more than a million copies.[2] (The translated edition was excerpted, Goebbels noted in his diaries, because of his concern at being charged with infringement of international copyright laws if his ministry were to translate and publish the whole book: *copyright infringement*!) All this was occurring, we now understand, in the months of 1941 when the decisions for implementing the plan of genocide that would become "the Holocaust" and the early stages of its implementation were in process.

Kaufman, the book's author, became himself part of its "translation" into German. His middle name—"Newman"—appeared in the German translation and subsequent public references as "Nathan." And Kaufman himself, the Nazi Propaganda Ministry proclaimed—with echoes to follow in the national German press—was part of the Jewish cabal surrounding President Roosevelt (a Foreign Ministry spokesman would allege that Roosevelt himself had been the author of several of the book's chapters). In Kaufman's text, the German commentary to the translation claimed, the true designs of the Jewish-Bolshevik conspiracy, including now the intended destruction of Germany, came clear: the naked truth, in contrast to its more often veiled or deceptive appearances. So Goebbels would write in his diary (with or without tongue in cheek: It's difficult to tell): "Even the dumbest person will understand from this brochure what danger we face if we weaken." [August 28, 1941]. To be sure—and here the circle of Nazi hermeneutics begins to close—the extremity and blatancy of Kaufman's proposals were not all to the bad so far as Goebbels' propaganda ministry was concerned; far from it, in fact, as they could be brought to bear on Nazi efforts to strengthen the will of the German people for fighting and suffering. Thus Goebbels would write soon afterwards: "If this book had been written by a member of the Propaganda Ministry, it couldn't have been more favorable for us." [October 10, 1941].

These prefatory comments may seem to leave Kaufman's book itself as almost an anticlimax: *almost*, because the plan proposed in it may bring a chill to its post-Holocaust readers in a way that its author or its original audience could not have imagined. Unsystematic and fragmented as Kaufman's writing is, its pace at least is leisurely, deliberate; he makes his readers wade through six chapters before letting them in on his solution to the "German Question." In those six chapters, he traces the history of what he names "Germanism": the persistent German will for war and domination for which he finds evidence extending back to the earliest "folk" roots of German history. Germany's transgressions in Europe during the nineteenth and early twentieth centuries thus appear as adding weight to a consistently belligerent past. The source of this will to aggression, in Kaufman's view, with its expression intensifying in World War I and then growing even stronger with the rise of Nazism, is so deeply rooted in Germany and the Germans that cultural or historical or political factors alone can neither explain nor counter them. The crimes of German history in its past and its probable future, he concludes, could only have a biological or genetic source, thus requiring a biological or genetic "solution" if their future consequences are to be avoided.

The line of reasoning beyond this point becomes almost predictable: "Quite naturally, massacre and wholesale execution must be ruled out. . . . There remains then but one mode of ridding the world forever of Germanism — and that is by preventing the people of Germany from ever again reproducing their kind. This modern method, known to science as Eugenic Sterilization, is at once practical, humane, and thorough" (86). Once this conclusive pronouncement appears, Kaufman moves quickly to detail the mathematics of the sterilization process and its intended outcome: With the exemption of German women over 45 and men over 60, 48 million people (of Germany's 70 million) would require sterilization; an international team of twenty thousand surgeons could complete the process (he estimates) in three months for the men, in three years for the women. After the sterilization campaign is completed, on the assumption of an annual mortality rate in Germany of 2 percent, within two generations Germany and Germans would be no more. Thus, the Kaufman Solution: "practical, humane, and thorough."

The grotesque and the comic, we know, often meet; their convergence in this setting requires little commentary. More difficult to grasp than Kaufman's plan itself, however, is the question of why it was taken as seriously as it was when he proposed it, on both sides of the Atlantic and among people and agencies that were themselves taken seriously. To be sure, even for Goebbels and the Nazi Propaganda Ministry, for whom the rationale for war against Germany's enemies stood to gain from the threat of Kaufman's polemic, a question remains of how literally they took that threat, not because of its substance but because of who its creator was or, more precisely, wasn't. No less puzzling is the question of why his book received the attention it did in the United States *before* the Nazis elevated it to international political prominence. For what in the editorial or publishing world would seem impossible now was also improbable in 1941: that *Time* or the *New York Times* or the *Washington Post* would find space for reviewing a book by an unknown author published by a vanity (and unknown) press. Kaufman's efforts at self-advertisement were perhaps a factor; there was something in the way of an emotional consistency between them and the solution he was proposing: Before sending review copies of his book to the media, he sent a preliminary mailing to each periodical. This mailing was a cardboard model of a black coffin with a hinged lid, inside which was a simple message: "Read *Germany Must Perish*. Tomorrow you will receive your copy." (Kaufman first attempted to have these coffins delivered by Western Union, the usual transmitter at the time of urgent communiqués; when Western Union refused to make the deliveries, he settled for the U.S. Post Office.)

This macabre self-advertisement by itself probably would not have sufficed to produce the unlikely amount of attention that the book received; the principal reason for that was undoubtedly the radical "solution" it proposed for Germany, against the background of the growing threat that Germany seemed to represent beyond its own borders and to more than only its Jewish inhabitants. Even so, the tone of the American reviews (and of later news columns about Kaufman and his book) reflected an odd combination of straight reporting and skepticism. Thus, for example, the review in *Time* (March 24, 1941) appeared under the heading of "A Modest Proposal," aligning Kaufman with Jonathan Swift's suggestion that the Irish solve the problem of the famine by eating their children (a suggestion whose irony was missed by many of *its* original audience). With an almost straight face, moreover, the reviewer for *Time* includes in his account details of an interview with Kaufman (also an unusual step for a reviewer, then or now), details that sound now as madcap as the plan itself. Sterilization of the Germans, Kaufman is quoted by the reviewer, could be implemented easily: "It would be just like registering for Social Security" (96).

Once transmitted to Germany, however, the book's reception met with no such equivocation. (I have been unable to trace the book's journey across the Atlantic; one source might have been the German embassy in Washington that was still in place in the spring 1941, but the book also might have been spotted by industrious eyes in Goebbels' Propaganda Ministry itself.) Nazi rhetoric had before this laid the ground for explicit proclamations of a "Jewish War against Germany." Some of that ground was narrowly focused and directed against the Jews as one group among others; so, for example, the "backstabbing" charge against those responsible for the German defeat in World War I—a charge that began while that war was still being fought—gained strength in the postwar (and post-Versailles) period (as in Hitler's own *Mein Kampf*), and then became received doctrine when the Nazis took power in 1933. The same path to German victimization in the equivalent of a war otherwise would be nourished by the metaphors of disease, which identified the Jews as a cancer or tubercular bacillus, acting to destroy their German host. (Elaborating this metaphor, Hitler once likened himself to Koch, the German discoverer—and of course, potential eradicator—of the tubercular bacillus.) The growing threat of war prior to its outbreak in September 1939 (also after that but especially before) had brought with it both inside and outside Germany (including in the United States) the charge that the Nazi threat to the Jews had been exaggerated by Jewish sources, which meant that if nations of the world did go to war against Germany, they would in effect be fighting a "Jewish War." The causal reasoning in this last argument was clear and dubious: The fact of Jewish persecution by the Nazis would have made *any* resistance to the Nazis a Jewish cause.

These charges, added to traditional antisemitic themes of economic exploitation by "the" Jews, of their divided national loyalties, and of their infectious moral degradation provided a basis for Nazi claims about their own anti-Jewish policies as *defensive*: reactions warranted in self-defense, and thus no different from other reactions in face of other (national or individual) threats. From that basis, it would be a small step to speaking of the Jewish "attack" on Germany and thence to the Jewish "*war*" against Germany. The move to the last of these appeared quickly and early in the Nazi rule; so, for example, the German press reacted in these terms to the widespread but largely uncoordinated Jewish boycott in Europe and the United States of German goods that was initiated and then quickly abandoned in March 1933. What the consequences of that boycott would have been had it been sustained is uncertain, but the Nazi hierarchy was at least sufficiently concerned about even its early days to protest inside and outside Germany, threatening reprisals against German Jews if it continued and indeed organizing a counter-boycott of Jewish businesses in Germany at the beginning of April. That initiatives like this in Jewish communities outside of Germany were seen not only as reactive but aggressive was, furthermore, not exclusively a Nazi "interpretation." The British *Daily Express* (March 24, 1933), for example, gave a front-page headline to the international Jewish boycott of German goods: "Judea Declares War on Germany."

Boycotts and other economic or cultural forms of attack arguably amount to war "by other means," but an actual battlefield requires no such mediating terms, and *that*, too, followed with the German invasion of Poland on September 1, 1939. Among other reactions, that invasion elicited one response clearly identified with the Jewish community, arguably slight in its own terms, that was seized on by the Nazi government and enlarged. On September 6, three days after the British declaration of war against Germany, the London *Times* published a letter that Chaim Weizmann, then head of the Jewish Agency and president of the World Zionist Organization, had written to the British Prime Minister Chamberlain. However one understands Weizmann's intentions in writing the letter, his words were unequivocal: "I wish to confirm, in the most explicit manner, the declarations which I and my colleagues have made during the last month, and especially in the last week, that the Jews stand by Great Britain and will fight on the side of the democracies." This was represented by the Nazis as a still more explicit and authoritative declaration of war that would then be reinforced more than a year later by Kaufman's cruder but more detailed pamphlet.

To be sure, nobody familiar with the sparse resources of the Jewish Agency at the time of Weizmann's statement or with the miniscule membership of the World Zionist Organization or with the sharply divided religious, cultural, and political opinions of the worldwide Jewish community, would regard Weizmann's declaration as more than symbolic: an expression of hope more than fact. But as his own reference to "*the* Jews" conveyed the sense of a corporate decision or will, much like the stereotypes in myths of Jewish power and conspiracy, and with an actual war ongoing, Goebbels and his Propaganda Ministry found in Weizmann's statement the explicit threat of an attack on Germany that they then could employ to justify Germany's own anti-Jewish legislation and actions. How else to interpret this open declaration of war by Weizmann? And why *not* see it as another, now public step in a progression that began earlier with others less overt but pointed in the same direction?

Kaufman was unknown in person or name to Weizmann; he was similarly unknown to Churchill or Roosevelt; no reference to him appears in any of these figures' papers. But that this fact would have been apparent at the time made no difference to those who seized on Kaufman's plan for propaganda purposes. The proposal of national sterilization—in effect, of genocide (although that term itself came into the language only later)—was an enormity, at least when the Germans saw that *they* were threatened with it. That sterilization already had been practiced as part of the Nazis' plan of eugenics, directed against non-Jewish German citizens ("asocials," the mentally ill) even more than German Jews, undoubtedly would have been a factor in the German reaction to Kaufman's proposal (the number "treated" in the sterilization campaign within Germany is estimated at about 400,000). More basically, however, the proposal was quickly associated in Nazi rhetoric with the war in which Germany was engaged: specifically with the role of the Jews as the war's alleged initiators, and then also to the Allies' leadership, which, by imaginative transference, now came to include Kaufman himself. The Newark, New Jersey, ticket-broker became, in the Nazi edition of his book, a member of the Roosevelt "Brains Trust," together with the Jews Felix Frankfurter, Bernard Baruch, and Henry Morgenthau (to none of whom was Kaufman's name known). That the menace of Kaufman's polemic extended beyond the war, to what would happen *after* it, fanned the propaganda flames still more vigorously; the threat of what Germany could look forward to if it were defeated would be an added incentive for supporting the Nazi regime, even for members of the German public otherwise skeptical of or even opposed to Nazi policies and the war.

Beyond the inflammatory rhetoric it provoked, what were the substantive consequences of Kaufman's book? Certain of these are known, suggesting that there may have been others as well, and, still more, that the book had a general currency beyond its actual readership and even if not many specific acts can be directly traced to it. But there were indeed instances of the latter. A *New York Times* story (September 9, 1941) describes the eviction of the Jews of Hanover from their homes, which were then to be sold off, an act that the mayor of Hanover justified by referring to Allied bombing of the city in a war "forced upon Germany by the Jewry of other countries" and then *also* to the book by "the Jew Kaufman in New York [sic] demanding sterilization of all Germans." (In the same news story, the *Times* also reported Kaufman's banal response to the latter charge: "The Nazis are merely finding a scapegoat for their barbarities.") Goebbels is alleged to have shown Hitler himself the German edition of Kaufman's book—Goebbels' own doing—an occasion later claimed to have occasioned the law ordering German Jews to wear the Yellow Star (issued on September 1, 1941, notably later than similar orders in the occupied territories of Eastern Europe). Ludwig Fischer, the Nazi District Governor of Warsaw, alludes to the Kaufman plan as having been part of the "justification" (his term) for a policy of starvation in that ghetto, a policy he himself was at the time attempting to ameliorate (October 15, 1941).[3] And Adolf Eichmann refers in his "memoirs" to Kaufman's plan of "total sterilization" as "possible" provocation used by Heydrich and Himmler to justify the genocide against the Jews.

It is difficult to know exactly how much weight to attach to these scattered and unsystematic references, or to decide whether they are symptoms or causes, but their diversity suggests a currency for Kaufman's plan among the Nazi upper echelons that then filtered downward and sideward. The life of *Germany Must Perish*, furthermore, did not end with the end of the war itself: Editions of the book have been published and the book itself cited since the war by Holocaust-deniers (e.g., Paul Rassinier and Heinz Roth) as well as by neo-Nazi groups who not only admit the Holocaust's occurrence but continue to affirm its justification. These groups have received less attention than the "deniers," although there is a substantial difference, on historical and arguably also on moral grounds, between someone who denies that the Holocaust occurred and someone who agrees that it occurred and continues to justify it. At any rate, the two groups together are the main sources for whatever currency Kaufman's name, writings, and history still have.[4]

Kaufman himself, after publishing through his Argyle Press another screed in 1942, titled *No More German Wars*—a more reserved version of the earlier book that seems to have been largely ignored by both American and German observers and publications—disappeared from sight. Newark city records have no later reference to him, and nobody yet has traced his family origins or relations in New York City where, supposedly, he was born in 1910 or 1911. This sharply truncated history has raised the possibility that Kaufman was a German "plant" or provocateur, put in place by the Nazis themselves. It may be impossible to disprove this conspiracy theory (like most others); but both large and small details in the "Kaufman Affair" argue against it. (How would one explain, for example, that his allegedly Nazi sponsors would come up with the unlikely middle name for him of "Newman," and then consistently mistake that for "Nathan" in their own references to him?) Although possible, then, it seems unlikely that anything that may still be discovered about Kaufman will alter significantly the improbability—or match the distinctiveness—of the brief period during which he appeared and then disappeared on the world stage.

On that stage and against the background of Holocaust enormity, Kaufman's was obviously a minor role. But the fact that he came to have a role at all poses a more general question about the causal history of the Holocaust, a question that begins with the contingency of that momentous event, which, notwithstanding all the evidence and explanations that have been gathered as bearing on its origins, still and quite clearly *need* not have occurred. The large question thus posed remains: Why, when it did not have to occur, it *did*, with the improbable figure of Theodore Kaufman making his own small and unlikely contribution to it. How seriously—that is, literally—did the Nazi hierarchy or Goebbels himself take Kaufman or even their own claims about the reach of his influence in the highest levels of Allied (specifically, American) policymaking? The latter remains a question with broad ramifications. Goebbels, the chief Nazi propagandist, however blinded by his devotion to Hitler, was nobody's fool; his extensive diaries (themselves an extraordinary accomplishment) demonstrate that he recognized quite precisely the line between fact and fiction, including many of the fictions for which he himself was responsible.[5] But when propaganda becomes itself *a*, or even *the*, motivating cause of discourse, the location of that line becomes less obvious, from the inside hardly less than from the outside: what is useful for propaganda, with use the sole criterion for the purpose, can come to be regarded as true in *that* sense, and then, quickly, as simply *true*. Certain passages in Goebbels' diaries describe his consciousness of his role as propagandist in just those terms. But even his own consciousness of the danger would not necessarily immunize him against it. More than anyone else in Hitler's inner circle, Goebbels was a true believer; if a stronger phrase for dedication and commitment were available, it would apply to a man who, in the shadow of his Führer's death, would initiate the poisoning of his six children (by his wife) and then, together with her, commit suicide himself.

"Backshadowing" from that to his exploitation of Theodore Kaufman's plan for genocide makes the literal acceptance of Goebbels' account of it—and virtually anything else that he might have believed—plausible, although even so it does not resolve the more general question of the degree of commitment to Nazi ideology in members of the Nazi upper hierarchy. What seems clear is that one effect of Kaufman's plan and his writing was to allow the Nazis to strike out more forcefully or at least less circumspectly than they would have without them. To be sure, this was not Kaufman's intention, but then it also remains unclear exactly what his intentions were, as it is also unclear what his expectations for his proposal were. Perhaps he was more practical in predicting the future than in prescribing for it, although it is difficult to see evidence of practical judgment of any sort in his writings. (Arguably, the closest comparable proposal for postwar Germany was the later Morgenthau Plan, which, only slightly less improbably, envisioned permanent ruralization and de-industrialization: a pastoral Germany.)

It is certainly unlikely that Kaufman, notwithstanding his extreme view of earlier German history, imagined that the essential features of genocide that he recommended for implementation against the Germans would instead be put into practice *by them*, and with a conscious and systematic brutality that his own account had mentioned as unimaginable. In this sense, Kaufman's own improbability extended to prophecy: the act of genocide that he got approximately right, except for the single, very largest detail of confusing its victims and its perpetrators. A similar improbability extends to the spectral shadow cast forward even now by his writing, more than sixty years after both the Holocaust and his book supposedly had been fixed and settled, completed, in history.

III

The Presence as Future

« 9 »

From the Holocaust to Group Rights

Minorities in a Majority World

This chapter has two aims: first, to outline the development during the second half of the twentieth century in reaction to the atrocity of the Holocaust of the idea and practice of "group rights": rights that belong to groups as groups and only on *that* basis to the groups' individual members. Then, secondly and building on the results of the first, to show how that development represents not only a display of history in its course, but a valuable addition to our thinking about justice and moral judgment in our present and, almost certainly, our future society. The conceptualization and public awareness of genocide and group rights thus add significantly to the reach of moral consciousness and imagination in contemporary ethical and political discourse. *And* to a deeper understanding of the structure of the Holocaust.

The historical development referred to unfolded in what can be characterized as three stages. The first of these was the Holocaust itself—in the Nazis' euphemistic and coded phrase, the *Endlösung*, the "Final Solution of the Jewish Question"—their campaign, again in Himmler's infamous words, to make the Jews as a group "disappear from the face of the earth." The second stage of the process came in reaction to the first; this was the identification of the general concept (and then, too, of the *term*) of genocide, a theoretical turn that itself served as the basis for a body of international legislation and judicial review marking genocide as a distinctive crime. The third stage, implicit in the first two and, like the second, still evolving, is the concept or principle of "group rights" that has come to be recognized as applying not only to genocide (as violating one such right), but also to other rights entailed if the primary right to group-existence is to be realized.

This sequence, condensed and simplified as it is, seems nonetheless an accurate representation of a historical sequence. With the dots causally connected among its parts, moreover, it provides a fuller understanding of the three "moments" it singles out than would be possible if those moments were viewed separately: Holocaust, genocide, group rights. I do not mean to suggest that the causal line thus asserted was exclusive or sufficient; there had been earlier gestures in the twentieth and even the nineteenth centuries, for example, to a role for group rights (I elaborate on these below). And it is clear that substantial issues remain unresolved relative to the concepts of genocide and group rights, beginning with the claims made of their distinctiveness for each of them (and indeed, for the Holocaust as well). But the genealogy cited is fully grounded historically, a contention independent of any judgment of conceptual or moral *value* ascribed to the several stages, whether by advocates or critics.

That then turns into my second purpose, as evaluative and in the end commendatory, arguing that the historical development noted has been not only consequential but valuable in what it has added to contemporary moral and political discourse; in this respect, it also has made explicit some of what had been omissions or gaps in earlier appearances of that discourse. The principal addition identified here is that of *group* rights in its supplement to the longer-standing tradition and analysis of rights as such, which had focused almost exclusively on *individual* rights, with group rights, when mentioned at all, held to be reducible to the other. But that is precisely what group rights, in the sequence outlined here, are *not*. In relation to their "bearer," in other words, group rights are as autonomous and irreducible for the contexts in which they apply as individual rights are in their contexts.

Before elaborating on these two claims, however, it will be well to consider a peripheral issue that might easily usurp the discussion. For it might be inferred from what has been said that I am suggesting that even as horrific an event as the Holocaust turns out to have had some good emerging from it, since it did lead to the formulation of such new ethical and legal principles as the concepts of genocide and group rights. This conclusion would be an ethical variation on the cliché that "Every cloud has a silver lining," arguing that somehow the "post-Holocaust" period has advanced morally beyond earlier historical moments by turning an aspect of that evil event into enlightenment and in this way advancing another step in the long and difficult course of moral development.

But I *do not* mean to imply this. It should go without saying (although I say it anyway) that nothing would "make good," even in part, the occurrence of the Holocaust or the phenomenon of genocide. Indeed, what undercuts the observation proposed should be familiar from many other moments in the history of ethical practice, since in that history ethical rules invariably appear in reaction to the committing of the wrongs identified and proscribed. The wrongs govern the rules, with their common source, the smoking gun of moral legislation, the violations that precede it. No prohibitions against murder except after its occurrence, no prohibitions against robbery, assault, torture, except in reaction to them. No harm, no law: a less-than-golden rule for interpreting the cultural history of ethics, and a sobering reminder of how much "better" the domain of even the loftiest moral code would be if there had been no need at all for it. In this respect, the very prospect of moral or ethical progress—and as part of it, any inclination to find good even in evil—turns into cant.[1]

The first two stages of the development mentioned are so clearly related that they need to be viewed together; that is, as the Holocaust and the reaction to it converge in the conceptualization of genocide. On the Holocaust itself, I mention here only two points as especially salient to this account. The first is the understanding now generally accepted that by late summer 1941, Nazi policy—determined as for all crucial decisions from the top down—had settled on the murder, the genocide, of the Jews. The second (and related) point is that this "solution" had emerged as the conclusion of a process that had not set out with genocide initially as a goal. This does not mean that the Nazis were more kindly disposed toward Jews in the 1920s or early 1930s than they were later, but that the conception of killing them all—in contrast, for example, to the policy of forced emigration that held officially within Germany until 1941—represented a novum even for them; it required in effect the Nazi discovery of genocide. Again, this does not mean that they would not have articulated that goal earlier if they had seen it as a realistic possibility, but, more simply, that they had not viewed it that way.[2]

The reflective articulation of the concept of genocide—the second stage in the historical sequence outlined here—came largely in reaction to its specific implementation by the Nazis. As is generally known, the term itself was coined by the Polish-Jewish jurist, Rafael Lemkin, in the context of World War II and the Holocaust (in which more than forty members of his own family were killed). Lemkin himself escaped from Poland; after traveling via Lithuania, Sweden, Russia, and India, he reached the United States in 1941 where, until his death in 1959, he lived the patchwork existence of many refugees, especially fraught for him because of what became his solitary mission to bring the concept of genocide into public consciousness and conscience. The book in which he introduced the term was published in 1944, under the superficially neutral title of *Axis Rule in Occupied Europe*, but Lemkin had been concerned with the status of minority groups and rights well before World War II.[3] In his analysis of international law during the early 1930s, he concluded that international law had been literally just that: laws governing relations among *nations*, with slight protection for groups other than nations who also might be attacked (by their own countrymen or by others). These minority groups, he saw, had no legal standing as groups, even if their members who were citizens of a nation might have individual standing in *that* group; and even though, in and following the Versailles Treaty after World War I, scattered discussions of the status of "minority rights" or protections had begun to appear. In other words, Lemkin saw the need for a broader category than those centered on the nation-state, one that would focus on "groups" in or across nations that as yet had no legal standing but that *also* warranted protection against persecution or (at an extreme) destruction. Hence the fittingly transnational linguistic roots of the hybrid term "genocide": "genos" from the Greek, "cide" from the Latin.

The onset of the Nazi genocide against the Jews understandably intensified Lemkin's concern with the history and structure—thus the *concept*—of genocide as such. While World War II was still being fought, he began his own campaign through writing and public advocacy to have genocide recognized as a crime in international law, distinct from individual but also (more contentiously) from mass murder. It was to be a category more precise in reference—thus also, he hoped, in enforceability—than, for example, the concept of 'crime against humanity' that had gained currency. (The latter figured largely, for example, as a charge in the Nuremberg Trials of Nazi officials that began in November 1945 and from which the charge of genocide was still absent).[4] Lemkin himself, even in the shadow of the Holocaust, took a broader view of the applicability to that event of the charge of genocide than other observers who began to speak of that occurrence as unique even before the terms "Holocaust" or "Shoah" were affixed to it. In the 1944 book, he identified what he held to be early instances of genocide in the Hebrew Bible and in Greek and Roman antiquity. He does distinguish among certain types of genocide (versions of some of them were later incorporated in the U.N. Convention on the Prevention and Punishment of the Crime of Genocide), but he does not elaborate differences of degree or wrongfulness among them. Genocide *in itself and as such* was the giant step his thinking took—a step all the more remarkable considering the term's status now, little more than sixty years later, as a staple verging often on cliché, in political and ethical discussion. How, we might ask, could such discussions have managed for so long *without* it?

To be sure, the difficulties of specifying what exactly the crime of genocide *is* were matched early on by the difficulties of persuading the public to recognize it as a distinctive crime. This became increasingly evident in the early postwar years, as Lemkin devoted his efforts to the newly convened United Nations, which he saw as the likeliest hope for international governance. Retrospectively, the success of those efforts seems no less improbable now than it did at the time. For what Lemkin succeeded in accomplishing, against the background of general destruction and political disarray left from World War II that demanded the United Nations' attention—on top of its own organizational birth pangs—was to persuade that body to pass in the General Assembly, first in 1945 as an expression of sentiment, and then in 1948, as the substantive U.N. Convention on the Prevention and Punishment of the Crime of Genocide, a brief statement that defines the act itself and remains unamended to the present, for all the unanswered questions it raises.[5] Nowhere in this document is the Nazi genocide against the Jews mentioned. But the shadow of that occurrence, the continued uncovering of new information about its implementation together with constant question of how that could have taken place in a great center of Western culture and under the eyes of other such centers, was all too visible. Moral history had an extraordinary agent in Lemkin, but only in response to the extraordinary actions of the Nazi regime itself.

This much-condensed background to the immediate history of the concept of genocide opens onto the subsequent development of that history: the reaction to the conceptualization. The implications that began to rise to the surface should be evident even from the brief details that have been presented. Step one of the process, again, went from Holocaust to genocide—the occurrence of the former crystallizing recognition of the general category—a difficult and uncertain move, legally and politically, but also imaginatively and conceptually. Those same features characterize the movement to the third stage of the progression as well: from the identification of genocide to a growing recognition of the importance of group rights. Again, the structure of the sequence as a whole, in three stages, with the two steps connecting them: from the Holocaust to genocide, and from genocide to group rights.

So, now, to historical and conceptual details of the two steps. The most compelling evidence for the causal connection that has been claimed appears in the chronology of the phenomena themselves: evidence of the planning and of Hitler's authorization of the "Final Solution"; the "liberation" and uncovering of evidence in the death and concentration camps during the last year and a half of the war; establishment of the International War Crimes Tribunal, planning for which had begun in 1943 and which, through the trials beginning at Nuremberg in November 1945, provided legally scrutinized evidence of the crimes committed; the convening of the United Nations in the immediate aftermath of the "World" War; the Lemkin campaign *in* the United Nations, and then, among other early legislative acts by that body, the Convention on Genocide. The causal connections in this genealogy are more complex than the sequence of these references by itself indicates, and of course, a chronological sequence does not entail a parallel causal sequence. (Nor does the narrative imply that the novel recognition of genocide reflected a "first-time" occurrence for the *act* of genocide, the latter raising issues quite distinct from the former.) But again, if we think of the development of a conceptual *core*, it is in the conjunction here that we see the underpinning, the notional base, of what has since been understood as genocide. In this phase, the Nazis themselves had first to imagine genocide and then to implement it. They accomplished both these aims, and if they failed in their ultimate design, that failure contributed a feature to the eventual conceptualization of genocide, including its conflation of "attempted genocide" with "genocide": The whole of a group does not have to be "made to disappear" in order to justify the charge of genocide, in contrast to the accepted legal distinction between (e.g.) murder and *attempted* murder. ("Failure" is an awkward term to use in relation to the Holocaust, but it is nonetheless relevant to keep in mind that the Nazis did in the end fail in their war against the Jews, as they did in their larger project of which that was part.) Lemkin then articulated the Nazi intention and practice in its formal conceptual design, and it is that concept, with all its loose ends, that remains the focus of contemporary discussions of genocide.

However, it is the movement from the second to the third stage in the progression cited—from genocide to group rights—that warrants consideration here in greater detail, mainly because its connection to, or more precisely its dependence on, the first stage has gone largely unremarked. The articulation of the concept and relevance of group rights, furthermore, sheds light retrospectively on the phenomenon of genocide and, in turn, on the Holocaust itself. It may be objected in anticipation here that *so much* has been written and said about each of these terms or stages that nothing new is likely to be added about them. But the problems in analyzing them have been as persistent as the allegedly unproblematic claims made and conventionally assumed about many of them. (I was at one point tempted to title an essay, "What's So Bad about Genocide, Anyway?" In the end, for obvious reasons, I settled on a different title, but that first rudely elementary question remains far from settled.)

On to the implication proposed from the concept of genocide to group rights. One notable obstacle to basing that connection either historically or conceptually on the U.N. Convention on Genocide is that the convention itself does not mention it; indeed, the Convention makes no reference to rights of any sort. Nor, apart from this, is the meaning of the phrase "group rights" itself clear, let alone self-evident, the more strikingly so because, as already mentioned, the history of philosophical discussions of rights, usually traced in origin to medieval political theory (or more contentiously, to Aristotle), has had a consistent emphasis on *individual* rights, not group rights at all.[6] The distinctive and most generally influential modern formulations of the individualist conception of rights appeared during the Enlightenment, in the work of figures such as Hobbes and Locke, more publicly in eighteenth-century political manifestoes like the U.S. Declaration of Independence (1776) and the French Declaration of the Universal Rights of Man and Citizen (1789). In these sources, *natural* rights—"unalienable," as the Declaration of Independence terms them: innate rights that cannot be taken or given away—are at once assumed and asserted. The rights are variously specified, for example, to life, liberty, happiness, property: all of them, however, are ascribed to individual persons not through their membership in any group, but *as* individuals. Even the right of revolution among the rights named (most pointedly in the American Declaration), which is activated when other rights are violated, also sets out from the individual, however improbable it would be for a single person to effect a revolution. (The U.S. Declaration's statement of the right of a "*people*" to revolt seems clearly reducible to the rights of the individuals constituting the people.) In the post–World War II period, the phrase "natural rights" has gone out of fashion, replaced with probably deliberate ambiguity by "*human* rights"; why and how that displacement came about warrants its own discussion.

The question thus rises to the surface of political and ethical theory of what the concept of "group rights" adds to that of individual rights. And here I come back—or in my thinking, forward—to the U.N. Convention on Genocide. For although that document nowhere mentions "group rights" or indeed rights at all, the focus of its attention is clearly on group existence: setting out from the fact that groups, *like* individuals, are subject to destruction, and that when this happens, not only the group's individual members may be destroyed but, more decisively from its perspective on genocide, the values embodied in *the group* are threatened. The distinction here between individual and group as bearers of rights is thus crucial. The readiest way of seeing this appears in the convention's stipulation that genocide can be initiated not only by acts of physical killing but also by transfer or deportation, the forced assimilation of one populace in another, or by the prevention of births within a group (as in forced mass sterilization; see articles IId and IIe in the convention). What is crucial in the latter two articles is that the acts cited, if carried out, would ensure a group's disappearance without the blatant violence of physical murder; this brings out clearly that the issue here addressed in the concept of genocide is the existence of the group as group—in *this* sense and respect as distinct from the fate of individuals as individuals..

Genocide thus *may* at times involve killing at the levels of both individuals and group; in my reference earlier to the Holocaust as epitomizing genocide, it was just such "double murder," systematically implemented in the Nazi "Final Solution," that warranted the designation. But more restrictively (and for the definition of genocide, more tellingly), genocide involves the intention to destroy the group, *its* erasure, whether this involves killing or not. And insofar as the group's destruction is the act at issue, identifying that as a crime would follow, it seems, only as the existence of the group is recognized as having its own (group) value. Here the link begins to emerge between genocide and group rights, with the "group killing" of genocide appearing as distinctive a crime in relation to the group as individual killing is in warranting the more common charge of murder. That is, genocide's violation of a "right" to group existence is comparable to the violation in murder of the victim's right to individual existence.

Admittedly, this inference to the conception of a group right is a substantial leap to ascribe to a document that does not mention rights at all. But here we do well to consider the specific groups whose destruction is alleged by the convention to trigger the charge of genocide—the "eligible" groups as they appear. Four such groups are mentioned (article II), presumably not only as examples but as exhaustive: "national, ethnical, racial or religious" groups. This collection is obviously a hodgepodge:

racial groups are designated apparently as if biologically given, a contentious assumption even at the time of the convention's drafting and still more so now, when the few biologists who consider race biologically significant yet disagree about both the markers defining race and how many races there are; *most* biologists reject the scientific distinctiveness of supposedly racial features altogether (more about this issue in chapter 10). Religious groups appear on the U.N. list, overriding the vagaries in conflicting definitions of religion and ignoring the serious disagreements in their histories about who is or is not a member of which group. The category of national groups assumes the existence of the nation-state, very much a time-bound development of the eighteenth and nineteenth centuries; and the concept of ethnicity as elaborated by the social sciences has if anything, proved vaguer and more contestable in its application than nationality. Furthermore, *other* collectives that appear to be no less important for shaping group or individual identity are missing from the list, for example, political or linguistic groups. (A good deal is known about the deliberate omission of political groups, through records of the proceedings at the United Nations prior to the convention's passage, specifically as the then-U.S.S.R raised political objections to including them as a fifth type). And so on.

On the other hand, one compelling implication does emerge from the list as given, in the contrast between the groups mentioned and the much larger number of groups that are *not* named. Bridge clubs, redheads, dentists, Phi Beta Kappas, and teenagers are not among the groups protected, with the differences between them and those that are mentioned evidently more pertinent for the convention's purposes than any similarities. Again, we are forced to infer the rationale for this part of the U.N. Convention, but if we follow that inference, the four groups cited do point to a common premise (as well as having been the victims of prior attempts at genocide): that in the contemporary world of social practice, certain group-sources of identity figure more importantly than others, as arguably crucial for the fabric of social organization and the development of individuals within it. In these terms, even if convincing arguments can be made for adding groups to the list, surely the groups already on it have earned their places (if any at all should be there) as having figured significantly in the shaping of identities in contemporary (also in many past) cultures. The strongest evidence of this comes if we try to imagine how such identities would have emerged *without* the influence of those groups: a difficult prospect. In this sense, it was no exaggeration, arguably not even a metaphor, to describe the destruction of those groups as a form of killing or murder, nor should it be surprising that the emotive force of the term "genocide" has since its formulation become so intense. The charge of genocide serves now at times as a synonym for atrocities as such, often designating acts only marginally related to the term's core meaning; genocide now has the status, arguably, of being the worst of all political crimes, perhaps of *all* crimes.

The key issue for the discussion here is not the adequacy of the U.N. list of groups so much as the premise underlying the list that among current social and cultural structures, certain of them figure more largely in shaping human lives than others. This does not settle the question of *which* groups these are, and clearly there have been and may yet be shifts historically in the character and roles of any groups that have been or might be named. But insofar as group-identity of *some* sort is recognized as crucial in shaping social (and by implication, individual) existence, the rationale for the convention would have at least that much weight, as designed to protect the groups closest to the center of such influence that are otherwise, in legal terms, "extraterritorial": outside the protection of standard national and international law. And of protecting them *as* groups, not in the person of their individual members, since, although the groups are sustained by individuals, the group-formations themselves do not exist in, or at least not only in, individuals.

Even agreement to everything that has been claimed said so far would not establish the actuality of group rights, beginning with the most immediate question of what the source of their (alleged) authority is and moving on to the question of what the specific group rights are. Here we come to a "tipping point" in the present discussion, although I hope that the point of that point will by now be apparent. If the act of genocide, as its definition claims, is a *group wrong*, then the violation committed will be the violation of a group right, the most fundamental of any such rights; that is, the violation of the group's right to exist. The right to existence or life, in other words, would have been posited here not for individuals, not even for individual members of the protected group as individuals, but for the group as group.

This is the conclusion I am in fact urging, arguing from the phenomenon of genocide and its consequences to the conceptual basis of that finding in group rights, at least in one such right. This may seem less an argument than a stipulation or fiat, and the fraught history of rights as such—*any* rights, group or individual—may seem to promise slight support for adding to their number or kinds. Once one goes beyond "legal" or "civil" rights to *their* grounds in rights, even their most compelling formulations as powers or entitlements or claims (all terms used variously in definitions of rights) resist immediate inspection: Where do they come from? How does one determine what rights there are? And so on. To speak of them as "natural"—as in the locution of "natural rights"—suggests that they appear in the natural world as do its other features; but that claim seems impossible to make good on, and it was just such vagary that led Jeremy Bentham, the Godfather of Utilitarianism, to criticize the idea even of individual rights as "nonsense upon stilts" and his successor, John Stuart Mill, to disparage all talk of rights at the same time that he was defending individual liberty as the most basic political value. (Utilitarianism, more generally, has formulated its ethical and political theories without recognizing a basis for them in a doctrine of rights, an advantage from its point of view that for most of its critics remains a serious liability.) One can only imagine the invective Bentham or Mill would have reserved for a claim of *group* rights.

I cannot consider here in any detail these difficult issues at the general level of rights-talk, but briefly offer about them one stipulation and one observation. The stipulation is that, as perplexing and basic as these questions are, they apply across the board to individual and not only to group rights; in other words, that the problems run in tandem between the two types of right. (This claim will be elaborated further below.) The observation is that notwithstanding the difficulties cited, declarations *of* rights and the sheer number of rights asserted, individual and group, have increased steadily in the post–World War II period, with both the legitimacy and importance of rights-talk very much taken for granted. So, for just a few examples from the U.N. Universal Declaration of Human Rights (also adopted by the United Nations in 1948): the right to "education," to a "standard of living adequate for . . . health and well being," the right to "work," the right even to "periodic holidays with pay."

To be sure, the proliferation of rights-talk is not a justification for it, and the difficulties related to group rights may still seem more intractable than the problems associated with assertions of individual rights. Numerous such problems have been raised and confronted in current discussions of group rights.[7] If, for instance, the "right" of group existence is a function of the value of the group, the question immediately arises of what obligation this imposes on group members for sustaining that existence. More bluntly: Do group members have a responsibility for remaining in the group, or is there a "right of *exit*" even if the exercise of that right would contribute to the group's demise? (Such a "right of exit" would presumably be an individual right.) Or again: How, in general, are other conflicts between a group and an individual right to be resolved (for example, as a group's right to determine the education of its members conflicts with a member's right to realize his individual potentialities). And then, too, there is the basic "sorting out" difficulty: deciding how individual group members are to be identified, especially in the common cases when they are members of more than one of the "essential" groups, which may at times find themselves in conflict.

These or other problems may seem sufficiently fundamental to undercut any claim for group rights. But here, I would argue, the balance should go in the opposite direction, starting out again from the source of group-rights recognized (on the claim made here) in the act and crime of genocide. In that context at least, group-identity and thus group-existence are irreducible to individual rights, and there too we see a notable element of the contemporary political and moral landscape, for various reasons more prominent than it had been previously, and demonstrating that history is for the future as well as for the past. In effect, we find ourselves forced to a choice between the problems confronting the concept of group rights and those that would confront political and social theory in a multicultural world without them: a majority world increasingly populated by minorities, with no defense of their group existence. To be sure, dilemmas of this sort are not novel: Few if any ethical or political theories come "cost-free," with no systemic gaps. This concession is cold comfort, but it makes explicit the unavoidable choice between the problems we are more—and less—willing to live with.

The proposal surfaced earlier in this chapter that the problems affecting group rights are analogous to but no more severe than those confronting individual rights, and this claim, too, weighs in the balance. So, for example, the difficulty of finding a criterion for determining which groups are entitled to "group rights" has a parallel in the domain of individual rights, in the definition presupposed in the latter of what or who counts as a person or individual. The controversy over when somebody *becomes* a person, with all the latter's rights, is part of the problem here and the source of related and also difficult questions (the legitimacy of abortion, the "right" of a person to his or her own body). Or again: the conflicts between competing individual rights (for example, between the right of free expression and the right not be harmed by words uttered or written by somebody else) have been a continuing source of contention in jurisprudence. In these terms, disputes between competing group rights or between a group right and an individual right add nothing new formally or systematically. Recognition of these parallels does not solve or even diminish the problems on either side, but it undercuts the objection that issues related to group rights are so severe and distinctive that they outweigh any conceptual or practical advantages the concept might provide.

A significant step in the history of group rights—balancing from the starting point of a group right (creation) what genocide does at an endpoint (death)—is the principle of national self-determination most forcefully asserted in Woodrow Wilson's post–World War I "14 Points Declaration." Wilson's premise was that insofar as the nation-state was (and, it seems, still is) the primary unit of political structure, its formation has embodied a right as well as a fact, one that any group sufficiently cohesive and self-sufficient (however these are measured) is entitled to claim. The Versailles Treaty that put the final stamp on the end of World War I spoke of the protection to be accorded minority groups within nations. These early stipulations stopped short of a full conceptualization of group rights; however, they were intimations of what else would need to be done to advance the general principle underlying them that the violation manifested in the Holocaust brought into view so dramatically and explicitly.

It was this gap that the Convention on the Prevention and Punishment of the Crime of Genocide confronted and that other formulations of the United Nations would later reinforce. Thus, the International Covenant on Civil and Political Rights (of 1966) asserts the right of "all peoples" to "self-determination," insisting also that "minorities shall not be denied the right . . . to enjoy their own culture, to profess and practice their own religion, or to use their own language." The connection here to the concept of group rights is clear even if not explicitly stated, since (again) national self-determination necessarily involves more than an individual right; clearly, group self-determination is not something that individuals *can* do, no matter how individual rights are defined; nor is it reducible to a particular individual right such as the right to personal liberty or to self-realization.

The various legislative references that have been cited may seem to give undue weight to statements of the United Nations which has often been criticized as a largely symbolic organization, given to unenforceable pieties. This objection obviously has some basis, but taken by itself it also underestimates the institutions and mechanisms that the United Nations has created or fostered that have made a significant difference even without having the power of enforcement associated with national governance. Aside from the Convention on Genocide itself, probably the single most significant development related to the historical sequence outlined here was the establishment in 2002 of the International Criminal Court (ICC) that was charged specifically with prosecuting the act and perpetrators of genocide (as well as "crimes against humanity" and war crimes). This court, sitting in the Hague, has been carrying on this work, although that has been complicated by concurrent processes under the jurisdiction of the separate International Court of Justice and several individual criminal tribunals (such as the one sitting in "the former Yugoslavia") with (varied) relationships to the United Nations. But the trajectory here is clear: that extra-national crimes also will be subject to world judgment—an extraordinary, arguably revolutionary development, with autonomous nations supporting and submitting to a world court for acts against groups other than nations or individuals that the countries involved could not or would not confront themselves. The United States and a few other nations have still refused to ratify the ICC legislation. This opposition is a troubling reminder of the five attempts and forty years (until 1988) before the U.S. Senate ratified the Convention on Genocide, and even then with riders attached to it that seriously limit its applicability.

The influence of group rights as a principle, furthermore, already has extended more widely than is sometimes realized, going beyond the right to group-existence to include measures needed to sustain existence or to repair harm. There has been much controversy, for example, about the justification for "Affirmative Action" programs that have been criticized as discriminating against certain individuals in favor of others. But the target of criticism here—if objections are raised at all—should be not the claims of certain individual rights against others, but the claim of one group right against a competing group right and/or the question of whether group rights can *ever* trump individual rights. Affirmative Action is indeed the assertion of a group right: the right of certain groups to preferential treatment on the basis of previous group wrongs.[8] Admittedly, Affirmative Action programs were conceived exclusively as a temporary remedy, but the standing of the concept of group rights underlying their claims is no more to be judged by that temporary status than would hold for an analogously time-specific application of any particular individual right. Similar policies based on group rights (although usually without being identified as that) have extended in the United States to policies concerning education curricula in primary and secondary schools, linguistic rights, medical practice in the context of religious belief, and so on. The spread and impact of group rights as a principle of public policy have been still more evident in other countries, notably in Canada and Australia. As minorities increase and extend their presence in the process of globalization, the majority-worlds in which they seek places for themselves will have to think harder and farther about the claims of minority groups as groups. The likelihood that those who are now majorities will at some point themselves become minorities might serve as an incentive here, although not exactly a morally uplifting one.

« » « »

I have described, as both a historical and conceptual sequence, these three stages: Holocaust, genocide, group rights. I alluded earlier to my skepticism about any view of this sequence as evidence of moral progress, and perhaps more evidence for that disclaimer has emerged than is advantageous for the thesis that I have asserted. But I hope to have shown that to analyze contemporary political realities *without* reference to group rights runs into as many problems (and arguably more serious ones) as the claim for the existence of those rights does. As one such consequence, I have argued, rejection of group rights would entail the dismissal of genocide as a violation, leaving no way either of explaining or otherwise positioning the moral weight that the concept now carries. Admittedly, the question remains of how the historical and conceptual sequence outlined fits into the overall history of ethics, of whether that sequence bears in any way on what is so often referred to (what we seem to *want* to think of) as moral progress or enlightenment. We have seen, however, how the concept of group rights is linked in its origins to an extraordinary historical instance of a "group *wrong*" and its subsequent conceptualization, but with no suggestion that what has been built on that base in any way erases or redeems its occasion. Significant as the principle of group rights unquestionably has become for protecting minorities in a majority world, on the question of whether the sequence of events and analysis leading to that principle's current significance represents progress—whether in moral or social or legal terms—the most responsible answer now seems at best equivocal. That is, "Yes and No." Or more precisely, "No and Yes."

Is a metaphysics of race more or less serious
than a . . . biologism of race?
JACQUES DERRIDA

« 10 »

Metaphysical Racism
(Or: Biological Warfare by Other Means)

In the sense of the British expression, that "So-and-so had a good war," metaphysics, undeniably, has had a bad (last) century. Battered in its cradle by the cash values of pragmatism; squeezed in young adulthood between the narrows of logical positivism and all-seeing phenomenology; torn in midlife by the inflationary spur of existentialism and the deflationary asceticism of ordinary language; forced in decline to read its own obituaries, poststructuralists and modernists competing to have the last word (again and again): the multiple combination points to a more lurid past than could be gleaned from standard histories of philosophy.

And now, evidently, the title of this chapter may suggest that the charge of racism is to be added to the collection of metaphysical sins or blunders. Well, perhaps. But I certainly do not intend "metaphysical racism" as redundant, to imply that racism is necessarily metaphysical or that metaphysics is necessarily racist. Rather, I mean the conjunction—racism as metaphysical—to contrast with two other versions of racism, although apparently independent, for which metaphysical racism turns out to be a common source, the base for their superstructure. This ground identifies group difference not in allegedly genetic traits or cultural homogeneity—the sources, respectively, for the two other (biological and cultural) varieties of racism—but in certain essential, that is, metabiological and metacultural, features. The latter—what could they be, then, other than metaphysical?—are presented as intrinsic, and value-laden, attributes "found" in the group's individual members and thus invidiously distinguishing them and the group of which they are part from others.

Metaphysical racism here takes on the pejorative connotation of "racism" itself, and it might be objected that this move to criticize *racism* has gone too quickly; that wherever we wind up, we have to speak first—conceptually, historically—about race itself. So, Anthony Appiah, in *My Father's House*, distinguishes between the invidious use of racial traits or categories and the prior identification (more precisely, the nomination) of those traits or categories. These are, evidently, two distinct projects, perhaps newly named but by no means newly recognized. So, for example, Louis Agassiz, the prominent nineteenth-century biologist, makes the distinction in what sounds close to an apology: "We disclaim . . . all connection with any question involving political matters. It is simply with reference to the possibility of appreciating the differences existing between different men, and of eventually determining whether they have originated all over the world, and under what circumstances, that we have tried to trace some facts respecting the human races."[1] Thus, too, Appiah distinguishes between "racialism"—which identifies characteristic, allegedly biological features of a group in evaluatively neutral terms—and "racism," which finds in that first level of biological features a warrant for the ranking of groups, a ranking that may in principle refer to moral or cognitive capacities or to any other capacity with an allegedly biological basis that can be measured in comparative terms.[2]

This distinction is useful in certain ways, but I focus here on its "racism" side, mainly because however reasonable and reasoned the dualism seems when displayed in this (presumptive) chronological order, its actual history has been quite different. Much evidence shows that what Appiah's distinction between "racialism" and "racism" posits as an historical sequence—the former as a condition of the latter—has in fact appeared in its reverse order. In other words (and contrary to Agassiz's statement), the search for categories of racialism typically has been motivated by racism—the attachment of invidious weight to racial characteristics—rather than the other way around.

It might be argued that this ad hominem argument is irrelevant in its conceptual genealogy to what is legitimate or not in the conceptualization and empirical grounds (whatever they be) of race. Nonetheless, even if the genealogical claim does not itself undermine the foundations of the concept of race, it illuminates that concept's structure and presuppositions that (I propose to show) hover between incoherence and ideology, a not uncommon combination, but one that even currently is not usually associated with definitions of race (that is, with "racialism"). This conclusion may be clearer from observing the contrast between two versions of racism: biological or scientific racism, on the one hand, and (on the other hand) cultural or ethnic racism, as both appear, in the account here, as derivatives of metaphysical racism.

About biological or scientific racism certain obvious features must be mentioned as a basis for turning to others that are less obvious. Clearly, scientific racism has been the preeminent public form of racism for the past two centuries, partly because of the general hegemony achieved by science in the modern Kulturkampf for intellectual authority; partly because of developments in nineteenth-century biology and linguistics that provided an inviting metaphorical ground for describing (more accurately, *in*scribing) racial differentiation. I refer to that ground as metaphorical because one way of understanding the supposedly scientific category of race is as the product of a covert conceptual displacement, with distinctions by race first taken to be *like* distinctions among biological species (lacking only the latter's distinguishing mark, the barrier to interspecies reproduction), with that analogy then followed by a literalist shift that asserted race to be as biologically determinant of the individual as its species.

With or without this rhetorical genealogy, the supposedly scientific concept of race, even detached from *racism*, turns out to be problematic on the very grounds it claims. Only consider, for example, the conflicting numbers of races identified by the relatively small number of biologists or social scientists who continue to affirm the concept of race as empirically significant. The numbers here—among the researchers most closely involved with the gathering and analysis of the relevant evidence—range from a minimalist two (the smallest number logically intelligible: what would a "universal" race amount to?) to a conventional three or four or five (manageable and interesting numbers), to an increasingly stressful fifty, and then on to a deconstructive sum in the thousands.[3] Discrepancies of this order represent more than "normal" scientific differences of interpretation or opinion; quite aside from the details of the differences, their number and magnitude raise suspicions about the very issue from which they set out.

Admittedly, the criticism that allegedly "scientific" racism is questionable scientifically is hardly novel; so too, the skeptical claim that the ordering or even the distinction among races has at most the force of convention and, less benignly, the force of force. It is almost always possible, in any large natural population, to identify subspecies. *Which* subspecies are identified—that is, which traits are selected for classification below the level of species—may be explained psychologically or functionally, but hardly in terms of the intrinsic importance of the traits identified for selection. (Even the distinctions among *species* are not always so evident, as we hear Darwin himself complaining: "After describing a set of [biological] forms as [two] distinct species, tearing up my MS., and making them one again . . . I have gnashed my teeth, cursed species, and asked what sin I had committed to be so punished.")[4]

Evidence for the claim of this tendentious relation between racialism and racism is thus plentiful, what amounts methodologically to the nonfalsifiability of that supposed sequence or, in nonfalsifiablity's moral equivalent, its "shamelessness." The Nazi efforts to identify a scientific basis for distinguishing the "Jewish" race provide a full-scale view of this alleged relation, including elements that even in that context might qualify as farcical. These range from the establishment in Nazi Germany of research institutes measuring nose lengths and chin shapes to the growth industry of genealogical shops employed to exempt clients' family-trees from any Jewish connections. For S.S. volunteers, the requirement extended back in time, for the volunteer and his wife if he was married, to 1750, ideally to 1650. As Himmler himself soberly explained: "I will not go any further back than that . . . There is no point—for 1648, the end of the Thirty Years War, is mostly the limit . . . [of] parish records");[5] to the bizarre decisions of the Nazis to solve the issue of racial identity posed by their Japanese allies by designating them "honorary Aryans," or to exempt the Karaites (a community who professed to be not only Jews but the authentic Jews since they accept *only* Biblical texts as authoritative), from being classified as Jews (basing this decision, in further irony, on a [non-Karaite] Rabbinic decision).

Beyond this arbitrariness in the application of racial categories, of course, there remains the more basic issue of the specific racial definition, and here the historical ground of the category's tendentiousness is no less evident. In April 1933, soon after the Nazis came to power, the "Aryan-Paragraph" was promulgated that required the "retirement" of "non-Aryan" civil servants—"non-Aryan" then being defined (in a separate document, dated April 11, 1933) as anybody having one "non-Aryan" parent or grandparent (there were other sufficient conditions as well, but this was the "biological" condition). Two years later, in the specifications attached to the 1935 Nuremberg Laws, the condition of Jewish identity—the euphemism of "non-Aryan" had disappeared—was suddenly narrowed to three Jewish grandparents. Contemporary records show that the Nuremberg Laws were drafted hastily as part of a grand finale projected for the 1935 Party rally at Nuremberg, but the pressure of time alone does not explain the significant change in the racial criterion. Quite simply, the earlier specification had proven too broad, its reach including an unduly large number of "Germans" or "Aryan material" whose "Jewish" roots were far behind them, an extent that made the repressive legislation in place as well as future restrictions more contentious and difficult to implement.

The Nazi racial definition of "who is a Jew?" was thus narrowed not because of biological evidence concerning racial identity, but for social and political reasons closely tied to the reasons for the racial stigmatizing of Jews in the first place. This change brings out still more emphatically the arbitrariness of even the narrowest definition of that particular "racial" category: Exactly what genetic line is crossed by a single grandparent that is not crossed by a single great-grandparent? The supposedly scientific distinction that later would mean the difference between life and death was nonfalsifiable—shameless—just insofar as it misrepresented a convention as nature. Even this objection does not take into account the more obviously nongenetic opening asserted by Jewish law of the possibility of conversion *into* Judaism: hardly an option consistent with biological determinism.

In comparison to the arbitrariness of the Nazi definition of Jews as a race, the traditional "one-drop" rule applied in the past by various states in the United States for determining who was to be counted as Black seems a model of consistency, if no more plausible empirically. On that definition (invoked in laws against miscegenation and assumed in the context of inheritance law as recently as in a 1986 Supreme Court ruling), *any* evidence of Black ancestry, no matter how remote in generations, would suffice to identify a person as Black (hence the "one-drop" designation).[6] Admittedly, as soon as more than one "drop" is considered determinant (as in the difference between one grandparent or three), that slippery slope brings the arbitrariness of the definition still more clearly into the open, but this practical emphasis further underscores the arbitrariness of the "one-drop" rule as well: grounded not in biology, but in social disposition, symbolism, and hierarchy.

The strongest evidence for the dissociation of racism from biological racialism is to be found in the history of racism itself, specifically the forms of nonbiological racism that both preceded the nineteenth-century analysis of speciation and persisted after its discovery. This claim is supported by evidence in both Jewish and Black history, among others. The justifications for Black slavery in the United States from the seventeenth to the early nineteenth centuries (including some by America's "Founding Fathers") indifferently mingle cultural and quasibiological grounds, with the latter no more attentive to "scientific" evidence than the former. Stanley Elkins summarizes a standard syllogism of argument: "All slaves are black; slaves are degraded and contemptible. Therefore blacks are degraded and contemptible and should be kept in the state of slavery."[7] Some version of this argument, with its logical and biological gaps, was found nonetheless compatible with proclaiming "liberty throughout the land" (a Biblical proclamation that in its context heralded the Jubilee emancipation of slaves [Leviticus 25:10]). To be sure, skin color of itself is evidently a biological trait. But in the long and transcultural history of slavery, skin color itself has been an inconstant, often negligible factor. And indeed the defenders of Black slavery did not wait for evidence that would test that defense, with the claims they made for the quasibiological defense of slavery as a "natural" institution related to skin color not only preceding the work of Darwin and Mendel, but proceeding independently and largely unaffected after it.

Still more obviously, antisemitism predated nineteenth-century biology. Although there is weight to the contention that antisemitism of the early or medieval church, for example, was not racist because the church always extended the option of conversion, the discourse of racism appears not far below the surface in the form of constant, at times intractable alienation, most familiarly in institutional forms like the Inquisition, which began to contest the affirmation by individual Jews of their conversion to Christianity (that is, to refuse to take Yes for an answer). Often the *conversos* remained under suspicion irrespective of their professions of faith; this reflected an understandable skepticism about the trustworthiness of coerced conversions, with that doubt about sincerity (obviously difficult to measure) then moving over the boundary into a version of "natural" group intransigence on the part of the Jews: if not a full-blown racial distinction, something close to it.[8]

Much more openly and conclusively, however, the secular history of antisemitism in the last two centuries, although often employing the rhetoric of science, includes important strands that are not even superficially scientific. Admittedly, the term "antisemitism" itself, introduced by Wilhelm Marr in the late nineteenth century with his founding of the "Anti-Semitic League," was chosen specifically for its biologically racial—and *racist*—connotation. (In this sense, current use of the term "antisemitism" reinscribes a racist designation; attempts to replace it by alternatives like "anti-Jewish" or "Judophobic" have at least this starting point in their favor.) Marr himself emphasized that his antisemitism was not about religious belief but about biology, a putatively scientific ground that became an essential element in the later, more virulent expressions of Nazi antisemitism.[9]

It is important, however, to recognize that even for the Nazis, their supposedly biological or scientific antisemitism never achieved priority among their conceptual commitments over the political and social basis that remained central. Whatever advances Nazi science claimed toward defining the racial features of Jews, it hardly demonstrated the connection between those features or even among the often-contradictory cultural characteristics ascribed to Jews in the standard antisemitic representations of them: Jews were represented there as avaricious and wealthy, but also as parasitic, dependent; deracinee and cosmopolitan, but also parochial and clannish; sexually potent and seductive (both men and women), but physically weak and repulsive. How to explain such contradictions belongs to the general study of ideology in which the very notion of contradiction takes on special, revisionary features; in any event, the conglomerate of features cited in the litany of antisemitism clearly fall under the category of social or cultural, not genetic, identity. This does not mean that those features *also* may not be alleged to be (or even *be*) natural functions, as Nazi racist theory claimed. But biological claims here no less than elsewhere presumably are subject to testing by "normal" standards of scientific evidence, and by that standard, Nazi science—in even starker contrast to the distinguished prior history of biological studies in pre-Nazi Germany—was a travesty. Why it was not seen in these terms by the "scientists" who contributed to it attests to a sometime relation between science and ideology that has begun to be discussed in the history and sociology of science.[10]

An especially dramatic example of the distinction between biological and nonbiological racism appears in relation to the charge of antisemitism in the "question" of Martin Heidegger's history. In his own most direct response to the charge that he was himself antisemitic—the response appearing in a letter (November 4, 1945) requesting reinstatement to the faculty at Freiburg after a "De-Nazification" commission had denied him the right to teach there—Heidegger calls attention to what he claims had been his consistent opposition to Nazi biological racism. In this connection, he cites the statement in his Rectoral Address (of May 27, 1933) that "The greatness of a Volk is guaranteed by its spiritual world values." "For those who know and think," he then elaborates in his letter of appeal, "these sentences express my opposition to [Alfred] Rosenberg's conception, according to which, conversely, spirit and the world of spirit are merely an 'expression' . . . of racial facts and of the physical constitution of man."[11]

However one judges the turn that Heidegger retrospectively gives to his own words, what is striking about that apologia is its premise that Nazi racism and antisemitism stand or fall on their biological bases, that rejecting those grounds is itself sufficient proof against any such charge. That Heidegger feels able to cite in his own defense an assertion linking the "greatness of Volk" to its "spirit," moreover, underscores the concept of metaphysical racism on which this discussion focuses; one side of the distinction that Derrida mentions in the epigraph quoted at the beginning of the chapter and according to which biological racism emerges as a subordinate, not even the most consequential form of racism. Heidegger evidently would have had judges believe that Nazi antisemitism rested *entirely* on a conception of biological racial differences, arguing that since he did not give much or any weight to *those* differences, he could not be accused of antisemitism or of any responsibility for policies of the Nazi government based on that doctrine. To determine whether Heidegger himself believed this about the basis of Nazi policy or about his own attitude toward the Jews may be impossible to determine, but even giving him the benefit of doubt on both points leaves him a remarkably (implausibly?) naïve participant and observer of the social and cultural elements integral to the antisemitism of his milieu. That form of blindness evidently extended to features of his own thought related to, but not themselves immediately open to the charge of antisemitism. For example, the reference in the quotation cited to the role of the "Volk" as itself *non*biological seems to reify on other grounds the lines then asserted as distinguishing "peoples" from each other, at least as among those who qualify as "Volk" (thus also, presumably, between the Jews and others), with the reification here, since it is not, on Heidegger's word, biological, someplace in the realm of the metaphysical.

Biological racism is thus not only a relative latecomer in the history of racism, but when it does appear, far from displacing racism's other varieties, it has served often as a cover for them. First, by invoking the authority of science for racist practice based on other grounds (if the Jews were a biological threat—a disease, in the common Nazi metaphor—the extreme measures taken against them become plausible; if Blacks were innately morally degenerate, slavery and laws against miscegenation have an arguable ground; and so on); but then, also, in providing a cover for racism that is *not* biological, through its implication that anyone who rejects the latter basis could not be a racist. Not many people who seek this second means of cover are as open about it as the English diplomat and author Harold Nicolson when he writes that "Although I loathe antisemitism, I do dislike Jews." No doubt the number of those "practicing" this second form of racism (cultural racism) is larger than those applying the first. This is the case because the second category includes many (arguably all) members of the first one, but also because its near-random specification of cultural markers lends itself even more readily than the specification of allegedly genetic traits to the nonfalsifiability of its distinctions.

Cultural racism has been at the center of so many recent discussions that I mention it here mainly in passing from biological racism on one side to metaphysical racism on the other. If anything, the shamelessness of distinctions asserted in cultural racism is more flagrant than that of biological racism. For example, it is difficult to know where one would begin to argue with the words of Senator Vardaman, as recalled by W. E. B. Du Bois in his *Autobiography*, who on the floor of the United States Senate (February 6, 1914) could assert with a flourish: "[The negro] has never risen above the government of a club. He has never written a language. His achievements in architecture are limited to thatched-roof hut or a hole in the ground. No monuments have been builded by him to . . . perpetuate in the memory of posterity the virtues of his ancestors. For countless ages he has looked upon the rolling sea and never dreamed of a sail."[13] And what exactly would one say (even now) to Chauncy Tinker, the distinguished professor of English Literature who, during his tenure at Yale that lasted until 1945, successfully opposed the appointment of any Jew to the Department of English because of "cultural incompatibility . . . He [Tinker] did not believe that a Jew could be understanding of the English literary tradition."[14] "Polite antisemitism" thus turns out to be as little concerned about the falsifiability of its claims as it often was unconcerned to be polite; and even *that* rarely has been attached to the typically more blatant forms of anti-Black racism in the United States, which says much about *its* history.

In systematic terms, it is at this point, responding to the persistence of both biological and cultural racism in the face of counterevidence—how many "master races" can there be, after all?—that the category of metaphysical racism emerges as a covert premise underlying the two other forms of racism referred to, in effect setting the parameters within which they appear. In my claim for this sequence—finding behind biological racism the hand of cultural racism, and then behind that the hand (or head) of metaphysical racism—it may seem that other possible explanations of scapegoating or prejudice are simply ignored. But few biological racists have claimed that racist *beliefs* are biological and innate, and in the absence of evidence to that effect, the presumption must be that even "simple" prejudice is not self-defining, that also its agency and character, the forms of its expression, are part of history and culture.[15]

How then, or where, does metaphysical racism appear? As biological racism has been alleged here to be dependent on cultural racism, an analogous relation exists between cultural and metaphysical racism. As it underwrites the claims of social hierarchy and classification by which cultural racism incites *biological* racist categories, the same metaphysical ground serves the comparable function for cultural differentiation. Directed proleptically toward these of its "applied" expressions, metaphysical racism asserts a basis for group difference not in genetic traits shared by members of a group or in group cultural features open to empirical discovery and generalization, but in essential (that is, extragenetic and extracultural) features of a group (greed or dishonesty are typical examples cited) that, in one direction, are transmitted to individual group members; and that, in the other direction, mark a place for the group relative to other groups within a common ontological and evaluational framework. Group-identity thus becomes destiny, with the identity itself a metaphysical attribute.

The sequence of argument here can be put in transcendental terms, responding to the question of how biological and cultural racism are "possible." Three main principles seem implicated in the response to that question. The first is that human identity and activity are the function first of a group and only then of an individual, that is, the group is prior to the individual. (Think here—although with sharply different implications drawn from it—of Aristotle's conception in the *Politics* of the relation between the individual and the polis, and of the analogy he cites there of the relation between the hand and the body, with the hand's function obscure except in relation to the body.)[16] The second principle is that human group identities (and then the identities of individuals within the groups) vary not only accidentally (as in customs of dress), but essentially, in their access to or grasp of reality, moral and/or epistemic. In other words, group identities differ in respect to intrinsic moral and cognitive capacity, in their personhood. The presupposition of this claim is that these differences occur within a single overall framework that then allows for measurable gradations and distinctions. And finally, the third principle holds that the group identities so realized are "naturally" ordered hierarchically and evaluatively, with their various capacities corresponding to differentiated and essential values. In other words, the rights and entitlements of groups are hierarchical. What results is arguably not a "great" but a "lesser" chain of being—more precisely, a chain of lesser beings. Not by virtue of biology or nature, and not, except symptomatically, in terms of comparative cultures, but as a reflection of the *essences* of groups and then of their members for which invidious claims of biological or cultural differences can be made and arranged hierarchically, but which derive finally from some other, ultimately nonempirical foundation.

These three principles require more elaboration than I can provide here in relation to their assumptions and the evidence to which they purport to answer. But the point about them that already has been stressed is crucial to any such further investigation; namely, that much if not all biological and cultural racism assumes—more than that, *requires*—these metaphysical principles or conditions in order to sustain the hierarchies they are claimed to support. A commitment to the two subordinate versions of racism outlined, in other words, is also a commitment to the metaphysical conditions cited, although not necessarily the other way around. (The latter asymmetry opens the possibility of metaphysical racism distinct from biological or cultural racism, although it would be—and has been—unlikely to find the first without either or both of the others.)

An analogous logical and substantive relation undoubtedly stands behind the practices of gender discrimination, although I can here only sketch briefly the terms of this analogy. That the biological differences between the sexes are both more basic and more evident than the differences related to skin color seems evident. But no more than the latter do the former differences in themselves translate into cultural, let alone into metaphysical distinctions. In this sense, cultural ideology has been as much responsible for the construction of gender (as a concept and then in the distinctions based on it) as it has been for the construction of race and *its* distinctions. The common formulation in which those two hierarchical patterns are embodied, then, is metaphysical insofar as the hierarchy does not simply display or logically derive from the ostensible biological or cultural properties cited but essentializes them, first as properties and then in their evaluative standing with respect to their bearers' respective capacities and worth.

Admittedly, it is awkward to subsume the metaphysical gender-hierarchy under the rubric of racism that has been discussed more extensively here. But the analogy between the genealogies of the two constructions is evident, as based on the metaphysical foundation presupposed in both. No common designation applies as yet to these two versions of the metaphysico-social hierarchy, but this is a semantic problem, not a conceptual one, nor is it a matter of disagreement about the evidence. There may even be some advantage to the lack of such a "portmanteau" term, since although it leaves the way open to the ingenuity of prejudice for adding new objects, it also leaves the way open for innovation in shaping the reaction against them.

It may be illuminating in conclusion to relate the foregoing critique of metaphysical racism to a practical issue now dramatically present in the United States. The issue is this: Even if one supposes that racism in the forms mentioned is both conceptually and morally questionable, the concept of race underlying them undeniably has been a significant factor in shaping group identities in the current American social structure—a principal influence on the identities of individuals living together (or more often, apart) within that structure. Furthermore, as the oppression and discrimination that figure in the collective memories of the groups have begun to diminish, in recollecting the past and as actual in the present, an impulse in the groups themselves has emerged for joining the past to the present, affirming that past as a means in part of overcoming it but also as a means of honoring it. What this effort to sustain continuity in an identity that originally was defined racially entails, however, is the reinscription of the same racial categories that founded the collective memory. For indeed, however misbegotten those grounds, those grounds *have* shaped a continuing history and still-present identity.

The irony of this reinscription becomes still more intense in relation to specific issues of social policy. Consider, for example, the status of Civil Rights legislation and programs of Affirmative Action in the United States that have been designed to address a combination of social—racial, gender—injustices and disparities. However one judges that goal, a necessary condition for the implementation of such programs is a means of *identifying* the groups to whom the policies are addressed: primarily—unavoidably and however vaguely defined—groups defined in terms of race. For *all* Affirmative Action programs and for most other programs under the broad heading of Civil Rights (like the Voting Rights Act of 1965), the basis for deciding when and what action to take depends on the concept of race and the differences asserted in its terms between the groups of persons who are intended to benefit directly from the policies and other groups who are not. In order to repair or "make good" on prior social injustice, in other words, categories are applied that in their historical causality are at best question-begging—if not incoherent, then tendentious—and at minimum, trivial and mischievous.

The problem here is epitomized in the complications accompanying what would seem to be the relatively straightforward matter of the national U.S. census. For it is on the basis of the census that funding of certain social programs are made and that civil actions (concerning voter registration, for example) are initiated, once again, as based on the racial categories by which respondents to the census classify themselves (one of the questions that respondents are asked to address). The conceptual problems raised by the concept of race clearly surfaced in vagaries built into the racial "choices" given respondents to the U.S. census in 2000. In addition to an initial five choices (White, Black or African American, American Indian or Alaska Native, Asian, Native Hawaiian or Other Pacific Islanders), two other possible responses were "Some Other Race" or "Two or More Races." The indeterminacy here, moreover, is not a problem to be solved only by substituting or adding more narrowly defined racial categories, and this, together with more basic issues about the conception of race referred to above might seem a serious objection against introducing race as a category at all.[17] Yet it is also clear that some Civil Rights and all Affirmative Action legislation and programs that address issues of group discrimination (including those of race) assume as a premise that certain racial disabilities are identifiable and warrant social action if they are to be repaired. (This issue as raised is independent of the question of whether such programs are constitutional or ethically justified or not.) It poses the ironic demand that in order to make good on the harm that racial discrimination has caused—as a step on the way toward achieving a racial-blind society—it is necessary to rely on racial categories that reinscribe the racial differences responsible in the first place for the harms that were caused.

The problem framed in this way—of whether to sustain social concepts and practices that contributed (and may do so again) to the wrongs they are now being invoked to help right—underscores the way in which socially constructed distinctions enter and shape history to such an extent that the difficulty of "deconstructing" them rivals the difficulty of revising or undoing natural distinctions that have not been constructed at all. The fact that constructed distinctions often seek the cover of nature reflects the undoubted if imprecise power of nature. Racist thinking in its metaphysical varieties has thrived under this cover, and to *un*cover this emerges then as a necessary first step in the undoing of that construction.

« 11 »

Hyphenated-Jews and the Anxiety of Identity

My unlikely starting point here is a trivial item of grammar, or, to slight it further, of punctuation—little noticed even on occasions when grammar or punctuation *do* raise serious conceptual questions. The lowly hyphen is bound by few set rules; it also rests on a convenient escape clause that allows users themselves to decide at times to do away with it, turning hyphenated phrases back into two distinct words (as in "science fiction" or "peer group"); or, in the opposite direction, closing hyphenated phrases into a single word, as in "postmodern" or "subdivision." These shifts are tied closely to history: the more frequent the usage, for instance, the more probable the single-word option (as in the last two examples, often now also in the term "antisemitism"). Unlikely as it may seem, this same link to history in another of its aspects makes the hyphen both informative and provocative on the question of Jewish identity. Or so at least the proposal made here in relation to the syntax of "hyphenated-Jews," as that group-characterization figures in the American-Jewish and other Jewish Diaspora communities, but also as the hyphen in them draws on and shapes Israeli-Jewish identity and, arguably, Jewish identity as such. An alternate title for the discussion here—evoking a longer tradition—might well be "The Hyphen and the Jewish Question."

This account of the hyphen in an uncharacteristically influential role begins with statements by two American presidents speaking from a past when elected officers could still admit openly that political power directly affects public discourse. One statement is by Woodrow Wilson (president of Princeton, after all, before the United States) as he declared that "The hyphen is the most un-American thing in the world," an assertion that, viewed by itself, sounds both cryptic and dogmatic (the more so on both counts since the term "un-American" is itself hyphenated). That mystery recedes, however, when Wilson's statement is juxtaposed to an earlier one by Theodore Roosevelt, as *he* declared that "There is no room in this country [the United States] for hyphenated Americanism."[1]

A number of issues collide in these two assertions, but their common focus is clear. Reacting to the waves of large-scale immigration to the United States, the two presidents were addressing *that* through the medium of punctuation, objecting to the newly arrived immigrants to the United States (a country almost entirely composed of immigrants) who thought to preserve a conjunctive identity between their countries of descent and their new, adoptive home, through hyphenated formulas like "Irish-American," "German-American," "Italian-American," and so on. Roosevelt and Wilson, by contrast, were affirming a project of nation-building in which Americans were to be just that: Americans, without hyphens or any other qualifications, the whole then warmed in the "melting pot" that Israel Zangwill had cast emphatically in his 1908 play by that title. In these presidential views, stirred briskly, the melting pot would produce an undiluted national identity that dissolved or at least dominated other allegiances that new arrivals might have hoped to carry along with them.

It has been objected that for all its vividness as an image, the melting-pot ideal never struck as deeply into American identity as has often been assumed. (Glazer and Moynihan make this claim more bluntly: "The point about the melting pot . . . is that it did not happen.")[2] Whatever its past success, that ideal obviously no longer stands unchallenged, since the principles of diversity and multiculturalism exhibit at least as strong a presence in contemporary policy and practice. Through the latter, moreover, the hyphen has gained a new lease on life, often in applications quite unfamiliar (although perhaps no more likely to have been agreeable) to Roosevelt and Wilson, for example, in relation to Hispanic-Americans or African- (or Afro-) Americans (now, respectively, the first- and second-largest hyphenated groups in the United States).

This change in the direction of social discourse—from melting pot to multi-pot, as it might be—warrants its own discussion, but my interest here is with hyphenated-Jews in particular. And for *them*, I would argue, even the dramatic political and social developments confronting the world Jewish community in the sixty post–World War II years—including the emergence of the State of Israel—have not essentially altered or transformed their hyphenated-Jewish identity: *That* seems to me a modernist feature of Jewish identity not only in the United States and the broader Diaspora but as such. Indeed, the continuity in hyphenated Jewish-identity—in contrast to the changing fortunes of the hyphen elsewhere—suggests that the hyphen in Jewish identity differs from its appearances among its non-Jewish counterparts. (Of which, it should be kept in mind, there are many. The three-volume *Gale Encyclopedia of Multicultural America*, for example, identifies 130 different groups of hyphenated Americans (including both Jewish-Americans [31 pages] and Israeli-Americans [11 pages]).[3] Given the symbolic role of the hyphen in hyphenated identities—as it points both ahead to the word following it and backward to the word preceding it—any question about Israel's effect on diasporic Jewish identity seems unavoidably to evoke its converse as well; that is, the impact of the Diasporic-Jewish community on *Israeli-Jewish* identity, with the latter still another instance of the hyphen hard at work.

Before directly addressing these substantive issues, however, the language of hyphenated identity warrants scrutiny for the order of priority implied about it by the hyphen's use. In the "ontology" of grammar, nouns are more fundamental than adjectives, on the same grounds, presumably, that classical metaphysics claimed that essences precede existence (or attributes or accidents). Furthermore, in the hyphenated-American groups mentioned, the second term in each of them evidently functions as a noun, with the first term a subordinate adjective. Thus, one finds associations or clubs of Polish-Americans, but not of American-Poles; of Greek-Americans, not of American-Greeks, of Swedish-Americans, not of American-Swedes, and the order in these sequences, both linguistically and (I suggest) ontologically, is too constant to be accidental: The second, "American" segment of the hyphenated identity has priority as a noun over the first term, which is, in all its varieties, adjectival. (In some instances, such as "Greek-American," both terms could be nouns on the basis of their respective forms, but since in other examples, such as "Polish-American," the first term *only* can be an adjective, the first terms would be adjectival for the others, even when superficially ambiguous.) The one major exception to this order among American hyphenated groups—typically if not invariably—is that of "American-Jews," with that phrasing characteristically preferred to "Jewish-Americans." So, for example, we find even now—more than 350 years after the first Jewish settlement in the "New World," as that occasion was celebrated a few years ago—the titles of such organizations as the American Jewish Committee, the American Jewish Congress, the American Jewish Historical Society, the American Jewish Joint Distribution Committee, the National Museum of American Jewish Military History, and (in the community's most prominent representative) the Conference of Presidents of Major American Jewish Organizations.

No doubt many contemporary American Jews would prefer to characterize themselves as Jewish-American, and it is clear that the use or preponderance of one or the other of the two designations is open to change.[4] But the continuing tradition suggested by the group titles noted above is significant, the more so, since that same order of priority extends beyond the *American*-Jewish community to other Diasporic countries as well, sometimes with the hyphen physically present, often not, but in any event asserting a conjunctive identity *and* the same pattern articulated in the

"American-Jewish" sequence. Those other expressions invariably prefer to speak of English Jews, Russian Jews, Hungarian Jews, or Argentinean Jews, rather than Jewish Englishmen, Jewish Russians, Jewish Hungarians, or Jewish Argentines.[5]

Again, what this pattern of locutions *means* is open to discussion, an issue that at the same time recalls the reference in this chapter's title to the "anxiety of identity." That "anxiety," it should be emphasized, is not a psychological category, although it includes psychological elements in its composition. Kierkegaard classically distinguished "anxiety" from "fear" on the grounds that, unlike the latter, the former has no specific object, and there hardly could be a surer example of objectless concern than an inquiry in which those initiating it find that it is they themselves who are in question. Understood in this sense, anxiety is a condition, not a feeling, and hyphenated identity dramatizes *its* condition through the divided self it represents between two (or more) vying traditions or allegiances. Kierkegaard goes so far as to claim that the condition of anxiety (and beyond that, despair) is most acute precisely in those who do *not* feel it. A less extreme explanation for the comparative lack of public emphasis on Jewish hyphenated identity in the current groundswell of multiculturalism in the United States is that there has been less need for that emphasis, since, as mentioned, the divided self of hyphenated identity had not been overridden for the American-Jewish community in the first place, notwithstanding the melting pot. (An anecdotal but emblematic example of this is the career of Irving Howe, who, after early changing his name from "Horenstein"—by his own account, as an escape from hyphenated identity—would later attach his new name to such obviously hyphenated books as *A Treasury of Yiddish Stories* and *World of Our Fathers*.)[6]

The sociological analysis of the hyphen in the context of American-Jewish history has been the subject of two conflicting theories. One, called the "Straight-line" or, more polemically, the "Decline" Theory, in which the hyphen marks the first step toward the state of assimilation that would be reached when the "Jewish" half of the hyphenated pair disappears (as, according to the Decline Theory, it surely will). The second, the "Stabilization Theory," finds in the assertion of hyphenated identity the possibility, even the promise of a steady state in which both sides of the hyphen survive (together with the hyphen itself).[7] The conflicts both reflected and provoked by these two theories mark a prime occasion for the "anxiety of identity," as every American Jew, consciously or not, chooses sides individually and thus by implication for the collective. The eventual outcome of these many individual decisions waits on an obviously contingent future, but past history in the United States suggests that notwithstanding the favorable balance in rhetoric for the "Straight-line Theorists," Jewish communal life on the ground has so far supported the Stabilization Theory (perhaps *because* of fears incited by the Decline Theory: a version, as it might be, of the "self-defeating prophecy").

To be sure, various post-Enlightenment Jewish groups and individuals have rejected the concept and the option of hyphenated-Jewish identity: the charge of "divided loyalty" has been a red flag here (in more senses than one), although not the only problem. A "German of the Mosaic faith" is not the equivalent of a "German Jew," and intentionally so, of course.[8] Pressure for what is alleged to be the normalization of Judaism as a religion "like all others" has come from outside as well as within Judaism (it becomes impossible to distinguish in the shaping of collective or even individual identity where the line between external influence and internal assertion can be drawn). One expression of this confluence appears among hyphenated American-Jews who view that designation as analogous not to "Polish-Americans" or "Italian-Americans" but to "American Catholics" or "American Lutherans"; that is, as specifying a religion formally identical to other "faiths." They agree to be American Jews, in other words, just in the sense that American Gentiles fill in *their* religious denominations. And, of course, there are "American-Jews" or "Jewish-Americans" for whom neither locution is relevant in their thinking about it as applied to themselves, and this from a number of different causes. The rejection of "American-Jews," for example, might reflect the Jewish identification as dominating *any* national or political affiliation, leaving only a *single* term of the binary, "Jewish" or "non-Jewish" to build on; from the side of "Jewish-American," the first term might be excluded on grounds of a certain view of patriotism (or *un*divided loyalty), or, more simply, as straightforwardly affirming the effects of assimilation.[9]

To these predictable complications at a formal level in analyzing the hyphenated American-Jewish identity, the existence of Israel as a state adds still others, making concrete and palpable what for centuries had been an abstract possibility or ideal. A principal difficulty in analyzing the impact of Israel on this relation is the continuing, at times radical process of change within both the Israeli- and the American-Jewish communities, beginning with differences among their respective (roughly) three generations during the nearly sixty years of Israel's statehood. An adequate description of the causal interaction among those variables would require a yet-undiscovered historiographic calculus; certainly, what often have been taken as self-evident truths about the impact of Israel on American-Jewish identity often have turned out to be less than obvious and even false. For example, comparison of the responses of the American-Jewish community to the 1948 Declaration (and War) of Independence, on the one hand, and to the run-up and aftermath to the Six-Days War, on the other—in terms of political pressure, public demonstrations, and fundraising—shows notably greater support and interest in relation to the latter than to the former. The more emphatic response to the 1967 war no doubt built on the impact of the earlier one, but interpretation of this difference nonetheless invites questions about the changing nature of American-Jewish identification with Israel. (Such scrutiny would have to consider, for example, the fact that membership in the main American Zionist organization, the ZOA, fell rather than rose in the five years following 1948, and *not*, it seems clear, because of any large-scale Aliyah on the part of its members.)[10] Israel as a state, in contrast to the Yishuv of the Mandate period, obviously has made a difference in the self-definition of the American-Jewish and other Diaspora communities. But the scope and detail of this difference are difficult to measure and far from self-evident; the term "transformation" often applied to the relation seems to me to overstate the difference, although the general problem of judging when the accumulation of individual changes amounts to a transformation applies here as well.

Speculative history is easier to write than empirical history, and this is as true for the history of the American-Jewish community in the post–World War II period as for other groups or periods. A consensus has emerged that the two major events of that history, although they took place elsewhere, were the Holocaust and the establishment of Israel as a state. The various historical and theological hypotheses that assert a link between those two events warrant discussion in their own right, but the appearance of one such connection bears directly on the shaping of contemporary American-Jewish identity; this is the way that the Holocaust came to compete with, and to some extent displace, Zionism in that construction. One can imagine certain likely explanations for this. At least on its surface, Holocaust commemoration is politically nonpartisan and religiously nondenominational, more so, in any event, than Zionism, which has proved emphatically to be *both* partisan and denominational. Zionism, furthermore, entails specific future actions, including, in its normative version, Aliyah.

Holocaust observance and commemoration is no less expressively evocative than Zionism has been; in addition, as it looks rather to the past than to the future, it makes fewer practical demands. As its commemorative gestures add their weight to the "lachrymose view of Jewish history" that Salo Baron both named and criticized, furthermore, they reinforce the tradition of that familiar and evidently seductive reading of Jewish history. And finally, perhaps *because* of what at times has been a struggle between the Jewish communities in Israel and the United States over "Who owns the Holocaust?" (to put the issue as bluntly as it has appeared), the Holocaust has come to occupy a prominent place in American-Jewish communal life virtually independent of reference to Israel. The resources that have gone into building and sustaining the 59 Holocaust museums and study centers in the United States (this is a minimal figure, the actual total is undoubtedly larger), although sometimes incorporating references to the rise of Israel in the aftermath of Holocaust, by and large assert a direct line of cultural and emotional transference between the Holocaust and the American-Jewish community. Israel is viewed in these terms neither as the successor to European Jewry nor as holding special title to its memory. Indeed, the possibility should be considered that the prospect of this independence may itself have been a contributory factor to the emphasis on the Holocaust in the United States. It is a reasonable supposition that the current presence of the Holocaust in the United States—institutionally, as in the museums and monuments; educationally, in the formal courses at all levels devoted to it as an academic subject; and less formally, in the discourse of everyday Jewish life—has served to strengthen the role of the hyphen in American-Jewish consciousness. This occurs partly in the way that communal disaster historically has tended to strengthen communal identity in all cultures or ethnic groups (in the case of American-Jews, it would be the emphasis on the second term that would be strengthened); partly, through that strengthening, the sense of independence or autonomy for the American-Jewish community that the hyphen, sustained along these lines, would bring with it.

On this account, the hyphen turns out to be if not itself a source of strength, at least an indicator of strength on both its sides, rather than the diminution (also on both sides) often attributed to it, as in the criticism of the hyphen by Presidents Roosevelt and Wilson cited earlier). Exactly how much the unifying force of post-Holocaust memory or the establishment of Israel have contributed to this may remain uncertain (and at any rate, in flux), but certainly the inclination to "independence" has loomed increasingly large among initiatives in the American-Jewish community, not so much as a rejection of Jewish collective history or of Israel's importance (although these variables warrant separate consideration) as in a growing interest in that community's internal needs for survival. The most palpable evidence of this—in what now appears as a "third phase" of post–World War II American-Jewish history, after the passing centrality of Zionism and the Holocaust—is the trajectory of American-Jewish fundraising and philanthropy with the proportionate redistribution of funds between Israel and the United States the most notable of its features. The growing perceived needs of Jewish educational, cultural, and lifecycle institutions in the United States, together with a gathering of personal wealth increasingly attentive to the future of the American-Jewish community, has had the result of shifting a substantial part of philanthropic focus from Israel, which not long ago had been its principal beneficiary. A rough estimate finds a shift here on the order of from a half to a third, to which reduction must be added a substantial move within the United States from contributions to communal funds to support of private foundations primarily interested in "local" projects. Certainly the funds devoted to internal "causes" in the United States are now reaching new heights year after year; current expenditures in the United States for Jewish education programs at all levels has been estimated at the substantial amount of 1.5 billion dollars.[11] (The increase and expansion of Jewish Studies programs in American colleges and universities, almost invariably sustained by the contributions of private Jewish donors, is one expression of this.)

These comments may seem a reverse version of the "Negation of the Galuth," but to the contrary: they are intended to describe tendencies, not to evaluate or endorse them, and it is the evidence cited that indicates a growing separation in the construction of American-Jewish identity between the American venue in which it primarily takes place and Israel's contributions or influence (or demands) on it. This point appears in summary—albeit anecdotal—form in Jonathan Sarna's synoptic book, *American Judaism*, which in its 374 pages of American- Jewish history, addresses Israel or Zionism in fewer than thirty pages (and for eight of them, in references to *anti*-Zionism).

I have turned to these indicators of the displacement of Israel and Zionism (or "pro-Israelism") in the hyphenated American-Jewish identity mainly because the imprint of Israel on that identity commonly is viewed as so dominant as to be taken for granted. That this influence cannot be assumed, however, does not dispute the strong presence of Israel for the American-Jewish community in aspects of its construction of identity. A symbolic gesture supporting this claim seems significant. I have yet to be in a synagogue or Jewish community center, the two main current public foci of Jewish identity, where the Israeli flag is not displayed together with the American flag (if any flag is displayed at all). Although this may seem a superficial indicator, the contrast (with only a few exceptions) from the practices of other hyphenated-American groups underscores the point. That this is something more than only a symbolic gesture is emphasized further by the practice in all three major Jewish religious streams of including in the Sabbath service a prayer for Israel in addition to the standard prayer for the American government and its leaders (the prayer for Israel—sometimes supplemented by others related to the Israeli armed forces and to Israeli soldiers held in captivity—varies among the streams).

Material evidence other than ritual practice is also available. Thus, although the Holocaust itself dealt what seems clearly a mortal blow to Yiddish language and culture, the displacement of Yiddish by Hebrew as the second language of Jewish education and communal discourse in the United States is itself an indicator of Israel's importance in the American-Jewish symbiosis. Newly sustained political and philanthropic expressions of support for Israel among otherwise different, even conflicting sectors in religious affiliates of the Jewish community are yet another feature of the emerging American-Jewish identity. The irony that this shift includes previously non- or even anti-Zionist groups in the Reform movement on one side (now the largest American-Jewish denomination), and Chabad, for example, which earlier was strongly anti-Zionist, on the other, should not obscure this common development. As private Jewish Day school enrollment has increased exponentially (more than doubling in the past thirty years, and this at a time of population decline), the growth in those schools—as well as in synagogue, adult education, and college Jewish Studies programs—of what might be characterized broadly as "Israel Studies" has advanced significantly.

Even granting such evidence of the hyphenated status of American-Jewish identity and the anxiety that I have suggested accompanies it, the questions still remain of exactly what the hyphen connects (or separates) in this context and how—going beyond grammar—Israel's impact on that context and on Jewish identity in general fits into the equation. If it does. The conclusion I point to in relation to these questions is that in part through historical circumstance, in part by its own character, contemporary Jewish identity seems *impelled* toward hyphenation—indeed, that in the world of nationalist and democratic modernity in which the worldwide Jewish community finds itself, Jewish identity has become *intrinsically* "hyphenic." This is to say that hyphenation is now the natural condition of Jewish identity, with those who reject this condition obliged (and evidently willing) to give up one or the other side of the hyphen with all the implications that follow from this: assimilation, on one side, or the ideal of theocracy, on the other. (I do not mean to suggest that modernity has been the first or only source of hyphenated Jewish identity, only that it marks a distinctive instance. An especially pointed earlier example appears in the first days of Christianity, when the then-new group of Christian-Jews would have been distinguished from the double-hyphenated "non-Christian-Jews.")

That the hyphenated identity of American-Jews preceded the existence of Israel is evident. To the question of how much the existence of Israel has altered that conjunction, the most common response has been that it added weight to its second side; that is, making American-Jews (arguably, all Diasporic Jews) readier to acknowledge their hyphenated identity *as* Jews, both externally, to others, as well as to themselves. How deep-seated this conjunction is remains a question; the charge of divided loyalty in response to hyphenation (and the increase in both as a consequence of Israel's presence) has resurfaced recently in the United States and elsewhere. But the charge itself had a lengthy history prior to Israel's existence; indeed it pre-dates the modern nation-state and *its* continuing contribution to hyphenation. In any event, the cautionary note it sounds now is hardly startling, although sometimes odd in its expression. For example, when Senator Joseph Lieberman, during his campaign for the Democratic presidential nomination in 2004, addressed a group of Arab-Americans in Detroit, he identified himself as a Jewish-American, reversing the more usual order of his self-reference. Especially at a time when hyphenated identities as such are being celebrated, it might be expected that the existence of Israel would add special emphasis as well as content to the American-Jewish hyphenation.

However, there are reasons why the current realization of that expectation has fallen short and may yet fall shorter still. The most obvious and severe of these reasons is that members of the American-Jewish community do not by and large see their own future in Israel. A reversal of that order of priorities would indeed constitute a transformation, but it has not occurred and, short of a cataclysm, is unlikely to. This matter of fact was itself raised to the level of principle in the early days of Israel's history through the largely forgotten "Blaustein–Ben Gurion Agreement of 1950," which declared (ex cathedra, as it were, but as authoritatively as it ever could be) that "the Jews in the United States do not live in exile." To be sure, not everyone in the United States or Israel, much less in other countries of the Diaspora who go unmentioned, would feel bound by that claim. (The Rabbi of a Young Israel synagogue of which I was at the time a member said in one sermon addressed to his [largely] Orthodox congregation that it was halakhically binding that they should make Aliyah; six years later, the congregation membership is essentially the same, although the Rabbi himself has moved—first, to Denver, and then to Stamford.)

The question thus persists of the degrees and manner of affinity of American Jews for Israel *short* of emigration, and on this point, it seems increasingly clear that the expectations on both sides almost certainly will have to be tempered. Partly although not only because of the ongoing conflict over the status of the Palestininan Arabs, the role of Israel as a potential physical refuge has faded not only for American Jews, most of whom (even the minority who made Aliyah) did not put much weight on that reason in defining their identities, but also for Jews elsewhere who face more explicit and immediate threats. The impasse in Israel itself over the settlements and the prospect of a Palestinina state, furthermore, exacts a distancing price, as those divided opinions affect attitudes about still other features of the Israel-Diaspora relation. The fact of Israel's religious politicization also remains a significant factor in this distancing effect (inside as well as outside Israel). Israel as the spiritual center that Ahad Ha'am envisaged has achieved something like that status for the American (arguably, the worldwide) Orthodox community, but in a very different sense from the secularized Judaism that Ahad Ha'am had in mind; in any event, it holds in religious terms for at most the 10 percent of American Jews identified as Orthodox. Nor does the fact that Israel recently has become the largest single center of Jews numerically assure its centrality in terms of Jewish cultural or social leadership. *That* issue depends on more than numbers and indeed, on something more than place; the land, after all, had an important role for Judaism — arguably no less important then than now — over the millenia prior to the establishment of the state.

It might be argued that Israel appears in this pattern of relations as a victim of its own success. It has become natural rather than miraculous that Israel should exist, and as "normalization" in its various facets increases, less and less extraordinary. Certainly the more fully Israel stands on its own, the less compelling become the unifying motifs of fear or a sense of danger. Alongside the many uncertainties in the process of identity-formation, furthermore, there is the evident need among its requirements for a material base both explicit and substantive. And in these terms, the pressure increases on Israel to demonstrate and not only to assert or assume its relevance to Jews of the Diaspora, the majority of whom accept neither the sacral concept of a "holy" land nor the secular claim of historical continuity as having overriding authority. The Orthodox Jewish community outside Israel requires no such demonstration, but for that community, the symbolic centrality of Eretz Yisroel did not require the *State* of Israel either, and the partial transference that moved the Orthodox community's members from the former view to the latter seems bound to remain just that: partial. Symbolically, the counterpoint between the memory of the Holocaust and the establishment of the State of Israel has had considerable symbolic influence (more than is warranted in strictly historical terms), but the practical consequences of that association seem likely to diminish over time. (When the theologian Emil Fackenheim declared a 614th Commandment affirming Jewish identity *because* of the threat of extermination that had been posed in the Holocaust, he apparently envisioned the hyphen as having a potential permanent — even Halakhic — role.) If, as I have been predicting, the hyphenated identity of contemporary Jews will continue to define them in the foreseeable future, it seems likely that Israel can expect to have a significant part in that identity only to the extent that it recognizes its role as indeed partial, even conditional, with limits to what it can expect to gain acceptance for.

Perhaps still more difficult to bring into this relation is the question of what Israel will be willing to receive or accommodate from the Jewish communities outside it in order to support the relation. I do not refer by this primarily to political or economic factors, although those no doubt will continue to figure significantly in the relationship between Diaspora communities and Israel. Even more pressing for the issue of identity in this back-and-forth, however, is the question of what the two communities can give to and receive from each other culturally and socially, since for the construction of identity, few relationships that hold together can be asymmetrical at their base. There are obvious reasons why this aspect of the relation between Israel and the Jewish communities outside it has received relatively little attention, but that imbalance is bound to be damaging the longer it continues. (This does not mean that "informal" practices have not been in effect; it is estimated, for example, that the percentage of Israeli Jews who have visited the United States is approximately the same as the percentage of American Jews who have visited Israel.)

Earlier in this chapter, I proposed that the tensions of hyphenated identity cited in reference to American Jews apply also to Jewish identity in other Diaspora countries. This is a large claim to make good on, but the principle underlying it should be clear: that as the political unit of post-Enlightenment modernity has been the nation-state, any claim of Jewish identity alongside nationalism, or even instead of it, whether in terms of emotional affinity or the fulfillment of practical need, will in some way fall back on a hyphenated identity of the sort discussed here. For Diasporic Jews living in pre-Israel nation-states, emotional ties exerted pressure largely through the religious tradition; once Israel was established, a significant practical weight—and proportionate anxiety—was added to what already had a hyphenated history. As the circumferences of nations typically (still) mark off decisive boundaries for those who live within them, any other putatively fundamental commitment is bound to join that first one rather than displace or obscure it. Neither the fact of hyphenation nor the problems it raises—or the anxiety it occasions—should come as a surprise. That the nation-state is itself an historical and thus undoubtedly transient institution does not in the slightest diminish its present social reality. Certainly the many recent claims that the nation-state is obsolete, superseded by postnationalism, postcolonialism, or economic globalization, seem more an expression of hope (or fear) than of fact. Of the United Nations' 192 members, some are undoubtedly nominal, but most are not, and very few of them would at the moment consider "uniting" with others by stronger bonds than those loosely present now in the United Nations' structure.

One piece of the composition that I have put together here remains untouched as yet; namely, the question of what the connection is between Diasporic hyphenated identity and Jewish identity in Israel. I cannot address here some of the most complicated aspects of this question, but certain comments about that relation are necessary in order to follow the implications of other claims that I have made. One way of understanding the classical Zionist ideal was as *ending* hyphenated Jewish existence in the Diaspora, with the hyphen appearing there as a weighty symbol of the divided life of Diaspora Jews. But, of course, any such "ending" would come only as the Diaspora itself ended—which has not happened and is unlikely to—*and* as the Israeli version and ideal of the melting pot (the "Mi-zug Gluyoth") also took hold (which *also* has not happened). What I have been proposing is that the source of hyphenated Jewish identity, in addition to the contribution made to it by Diasporic existence, is no less indebted to the structure and dominance of the modern liberal state. This in turn suggests that insofar as the synthesis of nationalism and democracy remains the dominant political template in the world, including both the principal countries of the Diaspora and Israel, it will affect Jewish identity wherever it appears, within Israel as well as outside it.

At least certain rudimentary evidence supports the latter claim. Israeli passports cite the category of "Israeli" as a sufficient indicator of citizenship, but include something more under the heading of "L'om" as attesting to *Jewish* identity. The hyphen implied in this doubling of identity categories (whether one conceives the order of priority as Israeli-Jew or Jewish-Israeli) thus has an official status that is unusual in comparison with other, more commonly recognized hyphenated identities (such as that of American-Jews). Even if the significance of these hyphenic terms continue to be debated, moreover, it seems fair to conclude that whatever this hyphenated category is distinguished from (that is, whatever other hyphenated identities are contrasted with it, e.g., Arab-Israeli or Israeli-Arab), the hyphen nonetheless functions in this context as more than only a grammatical presence. In this sense, the anxiety attending the Jewish identity question within Israel shares formal features and arguably more than that with the anxiety of Jewish identity outside Israel. Thus, again—or still—"The Hyphen and the Jewish Question."

What I have been arguing toward, then, is the conclusion that the hyphen both has been and seems bound to remain a feature of the modern condition of Jewish identity, for Diasporic Jewry first, but also, as things turn out, for Israeli-Jewish identity as well. On the question often raised of how the existence of Israel has altered or transformed issues of Jewish identity in the Diaspora, the implication here suggests that the converse of that formulation has no less significance; that is, the question of the impact of the Diaspora (hyphenated) communities on Israeli-Jewish identity. For the construction of Jewish identity in Israel, with all its distinctiveness, confronts versions of the same issues which that construction faces elsewhere, with the lingering presence of the Holocaust in their common backgrounds still a strong influence on their boundaries and projects. The reciprocal dynamic that emerges here warrants recognition from both sides of those both actual and symbolic places—Israel and the Diaspora—if only because such recognition bears directly on their individual and also, it might be hoped, their common futures.

« 12 »

Reconciliation

Not Revenge, Not Forgiveness, Perhaps Not Even Justice

In a world where globalization is in everybody's mind or waiting to enter it, the country of South Africa may still seem remote in history no less than in geography from centers in the "West." This was even more notable about twenty years ago when a startling sequence of events was set in motion there that, coming at the end of a century marked by atrocities (some in

South Africa itself), culminated in an act requiring an extraordinary effort of political courage and moral imagination. That sequence of events began with a change in the form of the South African government—in effect, a revolution—that was itself as unexpected as it was dramatic. Admittedly, the change took place on a smaller stage than the nearly simultaneous crumbling of the Soviet Union and its empire in Eastern Europe, although much like the latter, the events in South Africa defied the predictions of most expert observers. But much more than the other, the change in South Africa established a moral landmark in an otherwise barren political landscape where large-scale political changes, even for the better, typically seemed due either to large-scale and impersonal historical forces or blatantly personal and self-interested ones. By contrast, the revolution in South Africa, beyond certain evident economic and social pressures, reflected a significant moral dimension on its two sides—in both those revolting and those revolted against. An essential element of this moral dimension was its invocation of a principle of reconciliation or restoration even in the face of atrocity. If the revolution cannot be said to have been due entirely to this principle, it undoubtedly would have followed a very different course without it.

The "scenario" of this sequence of events can be summarized simply. After 1948, a sustained period of white minority rule had hardened the lines of apartheid (the "separation" of races), dividing the 13 percent white populace from the 87 percent Black, colored, and Asians (principally Indian) in a country of 45 million and prescribing this in virtually every aspect of South African social and political life. No pretense was made in this arrangement of a principle of "separate but equal": the differences asserted by the separation were stark, amounting in effect to a form of enslavement for the numerical majority. In 1989, a newly inaugurated president, Frederik Willem de Klerk, an established member of the governing Nationalist Party, set in motion the drafting of a new constitution that called for the dissolution of his government and for a new elective system based on the principle of one person, one vote. The several stages of this initiative's evolution resulted by May 1994 in a new political and legal order that replaced authoritarian rule and official racial discrimination with democracy and universal suffrage. The minority who had ruled as white became a minority in fact; the majority who had *been* ruled because they were not white became a majority, also in fact. The now-past president, De Klerk, agreed to serve in the new government as one of two "deputy" presidents under the newly elected president, Nelson Mandela, who a short time before had been freed from prison by De Klerk after serving 27 years of his life-sentence for "treason." This exchange of roles was as striking a symbol of voluntary political revolution as the twentieth century (and perhaps any other) had seen.

De Klerk's initiative in this process was decisive, although the events leading up to his decision and those accompanying its implementation were complex, difficult, and intermittently violent. In the preceding two decades, South Africa had been a pressure cooker, with both the ruling minority and the disenfranchised majority resorting to violent as well as nonviolent means of asserting themselves within and outside South Africa. Indeed, following what seems a standard pattern in radical political change, the period between 1990 and 1994, from the time that the first steps of implementing the revolution (and thus easing the situation) occurred and the time that it was formally realized, produced more violence (more *deaths*: 14,000) than any similar period in the decades before that. It takes nothing away from the combination of moral imagination and personal courage in De Klerk's initiative to acknowledge that he and his supporters within the Nationalist Party were motivated by their sense of what the future held for South Africa unless some dramatic changes were initiated. Externally, apartheid South Africa had become a pariah state among the world's nations; internally, the frustration of the "legally" repressed majority built steadily. It was understood by *all* the country's inhabitants, whatever their ideological allegiances, that if nothing was done to change the state's political structure, it would be only a matter of time—and not much of that—before civil war broke out. (A substantial step was taken in response to this building pressure—also as proof of it—when the voting franchise was extended in 1983 to "Colored" and "Asian" citizens, although still not to the much larger group of Blacks.)

Although the transition of South Africa from an authoritarian state to a constitutional democracy was marked by violent incidents and bitter disagreements, if one considers the position from which the transition started and what it eventually achieved, the process was relatively peaceful; this was hardly less remarkable than the initial decision to make the effort. But what *followed* the transition seemed at the time and appears still even more radical and distinctive. For it marked a sharp departure from the dominant tradition in Western ethical and legal practice and its "normal" pattern of concluding political, civil, and even individual conflicts. This tradition involves one or another version of the "retributive" model of justice that entails a form of balancing the scales between wrongs committed and the punishment imposed on those responsible—shaping the punishment to fit the crime, but requiring the punishment as a matter of justice. (Certain utilitarian accounts do not conform fully to this pattern, but a "balancing" factor often appears even in them; more about that below.) This model clearly had been the template for the deliberations that followed earlier twentieth-century atrocities and war-making, ranging from the reparations stipulated and the reallocation of territory mandated in the aftermath of World War I to the extensive criminal trials, boundary restructuring, and population exchanges after World War II. In these cases, the individuals or groups responsible for acts judged wrongful were then to be confronted by penalties proportionate to the offense, with the rights of the victim posed against the violation committed by the perpetrator. And if this held to a lesser extent for internal, "civil" conflicts or wars than external ones, the lesser extent was one of degree, not kind. Whether one thinks of this pattern as strict retribution—doing to the wrongdoer exactly as he had done to his victim, as in a literal reading of the Biblical formula of "an eye for an eye, tooth for tooth, life for life"—or if not as literal, righting the imbalance caused by the wrongdoing through a supposed equivalence of compensation, or simply as the due of justice in the abstract, the common thread here was that the wrongdoer should experience something like the loss that his victim had. He should in effect suffer the same loss (objectively no less than experientially), in the economic metaphor that would at times be given literal force, *pay*—and this, as a measure of justice but also for its symbolic social consequences, as a warning to miscreants (including, in the event, the wrongdoer himself). In Kant's "deontological" justice, for the verdicts in which the practical or experiential consequences were irrelevant, it would be unjust, a positive wrong, *not* to balance the scales in this way, since one was obligated to respect the human dignity and rational agency of the wrongdoer. (The penalties imposed after the two world wars evoked the charge of "Victors' Justice," but however one assesses that accusation, it did not challenge the principle of retributive or balancing justice but questioned the decision of who should administer it.)

The radically different model that came to the surface in the South African revolution was adopted notwithstanding recognition of the brutalities that had occurred there and the evidence of responsibility for many of them. Those wrongs had been sanctioned on one side by a willfully undemocratic regime that did not flinch at murder or torture; on the other side, by organizations or individuals among the repressed majority who had also at times turned to violence against the ruling forces but also against its own members. From both points of view, in any event, the precedents of twentieth-century history of justice were clear. And indeed, many South Africans, especially among the newly enfranchised majority, argued for that retributive model in one or another variation, ranging from explicit claims for personal vengeance to more muted pleas for criminal trials and punishments and to requirements of individual compensation. The course finally agreed upon, however, turned sharply against this model. It took shape, rather, in the new constitution's prescription for the formation of a "Truth and Reconciliation Commission," designed as a transitional but legislated agency with two principal charges.[1] The first of these stipulated that the commission was to provide a complete account of all politically motivated "gross human rights violations" committed in South Africa between 1960 and 1994, clearly a large, perhaps impossible order, even given the possibility that many witnesses (relatives, friends) of those harmed by such violations were alive and could be (and in the event were) summoned by the commission. This "truth" part of the commission's charge was not itself extraordinary; it amounted in effect to a national "fact-finding" investigation. But in addition to the project of nation-building that its investigation encompassed, the issues involved here took on added weight in the second, more unusual part of the commission's charge. This was to move toward "reconciliation" by extending amnesty after the finding of truth in cases of human rights violations, on condition that certain other requirements were also met; namely, that the person responsible for the violation(s) should request the amnesty, that the violations scrutinized should have been committed for political reasons, and that the person requesting amnesty should have provided a full account of his actions (the last of these to be supported by all possible evidence).

The keystone of this structure was the provision for amnesty and its relation to the ideal of reconciliation. The latter explicitly was intended to be more than ceremonial or symbolic; it was in fact a central element formulated in the new constitution, emphasized there as a variation on the principle of "*ubuntu*," a Bantu term and concept that recurred in the discussions around the drafting and implementation of the new constitution and the connotations of which amount to a combination of reconciliation and restoration, more concisely, of healing. For example, the summary report submitted in 1994 by the Commission for Truth and Reconciliation described their overriding charge as responding to "a need for understanding but not for vengeance, a need for reparation, but not for retaliation, a need for ubuntu but not for victimization." This ideal did not deny the fact of individual responsibility for moral violations; what it challenged was the assumption that the only appropriate or *just* response to such violations was a repayment in kind rather than an attempt to bring those harmed and those who inflicted it together, to re-establish what had been lost between them or perhaps what had in any particular case never existed, in effect to appeal to a common humanity that included in its circle of concern those who had committed the wrongful acts. The provision thus endorsed a collective goal of justice for the community, one that looked rather to the future than to the past, judging crimes against individuals as if they were to be understand and redressed as crimes against the group; this, in contrast to the basis of the retributive model's traditional focus on individual past wrongs, regarding and judging them as entirely (on both sides) the concern of the individuals involved, as either agents or victims.

To be sure, nothing in the retributive model *precludes* reconciliation as an ideal (more about this issue later); but the offer of amnesty integral to the process in South Africa seems straightforwardly inconsistent with the former model. (Another version of amnesty may be consistent with it, but it ordinarily would take the form of a *pardon*, granted only after a trial and findings of guilt and punishment.) For not only was the commission empowered to extend amnesty, it was obligated to do so once the conditions stated were met. In contrast, then, to a blanket or unconditional amnesty, a full prior account and request by the person seeking amnesty were required, these then to be heard and judged by a three-person panel. Once those conditions were met, the commission *must* erase the prospect of punishment.[2] No prison sentences, no fines or indemnities, no personal reparation—a fortiori no capital punishment—even in the face of evidence that proved "beyond the shadow of a doubt" individual responsibility for atrocity: murder, torture, cruelty in extreme form — any act committed for political reasons. (The requirement that acts eligible for amnesty must have been "politically motivated" was meant to distinguish them from acts committed for personal or other nonpolitical reasons. The odd configuration of this condition extended elsewhere: requests for amnesty for acts in which "innocent [i.e., nonpolitical] bystanders" were killed, for example, were more problematic — and at times disallowed — than acts in which *only* "clear political enemies" were killed.)

The total number of amnesties granted by the commission was relatively small: 849 of the 7,112 petitions submitted (more than 20,000 "witness" testimonies were recorded); and this, remember, in a populace of about 45 million. Why then attach such significance, whether political or moral, to the role of this procedure in the new South African government? To this skeptical question the instrumental reason mentioned before as adding weight to the amnesty provision contributes as well. The view that some such provision was necessary in order to persuade President de Klerk's followers in the parliament to accept the radical changes being proposed was widespread and publicly expressed. Even after the inclusion of this provision, de Klerk faced strong opposition within the Afrikaaner community, many members of which regarded the changes he was urging as a sell-out and him as a traitor, with the amnesty provision a mere sop. Nor was the opposition only to be found on that one side, since a still-larger number of the soon-to-be-enfranchised majority — those who had suffered physical harm themselves or knew it in people close to them, or still others who had not directly suffered but reacted simply to the previous denial of their own political and economic rights within "the law" — argued that the amnesty offer violated the principles of basic justice: the perpetrators guilty of murder or torture would be free to walk the streets and to live their lives unhindered alongside their victims, those who had survived and, in memory, those who had not. This combined opposition was formidable; it led, in fact, to the near-secret and last-minute inclusion of the amnesty provision in the draft constitution, presumably in the hope that public criticism would be muted or at least diminished; the absence of that provision from the transitional legislation that was finally agreed to almost certainly would have been a deal-breaker.

The decision to include the amnesty provision thus mingled practical and moral considerations on both sides of the political divide. On the one hand, without it, the likelihood of a peaceable change of government in South Africa was slight; the thousands of lives already lost would increase manifold. On the other hand, the price of amnesty, even with its goal of "restoration" or nation-building, seemed on the standard model of justice to be itself a form of *in*justice. Justice viewed as embodying a principle of equity or balance in which wrongdoing somehow must be matched by its punishment, the latter shaped "to fit the crime," had had variants in its long history, but its basis, in its insistence on a balancing of the scales, had been constant; in the minds of many South Africans, a failure to act on that basis in the face of the flagrant political atrocities that had occurred there under the apartheid regime would leave a continuing breach if not in nature, certainly in the social texture.

This balancing or retributive conception of justice has not been the only candidate for that title. Utilitarian arguments pitched at various levels (for example, when punishment is justified as a deterrent and thus as protection for society, or where it is viewed as rehabilitative) have had a growing presence in the past two centuries (even with their contradictory outcomes). And well before that, in still different, rationalist terms, Plato had argued that since nobody knowingly does wrong (wrongdoing thus becomes a function of ignorance), just punishment should then be a form of education. At certain points, such analyses of wrongdoing, even on a large scale, would link up with the ideal of reconciliation, but not fully or directly, and not in the specific terms of the South African solution, as it rejects, on the one hand, the retributive or balancing model (a fortiori, any form of revenge), and on the other hand, anything like a blanket amnesty granted impersonally and without conditions. Perhaps most notable in the South African proposal was the absence of any requirement either for requesting forgiveness on the part of the person seeking amnesty or for granting it, on the part either of victims or of the quasi-judicial panel hearing the case.

The most common conception of forgiveness includes the following elements: that someone who has harmed another person recognizes the harm as a wrong for which he is responsible and acknowledges this to the person wronged; he apologizes for having been responsible for the wrong, offering assurance of his intention to avoid repeating the wrong; and he asks the person who had been wronged to forgive him. At that point, the person who suffered the wrong has the choice of forgiving the person responsible or of refusing to. Alternate versions of forgiveness differ on one or more of these conditions (for example, as forgiveness might be granted without any request for it or even without any acknowledgment of wrongdoing). But for the moment I consider only the conception of forgiveness as outlined that in certain respects does resemble the provisions for amnesty set for the Truth and Reconciliation Commission.

A principal condition for the latter's work (as has been mentioned) was the requirement that individuals *request* amnesty, providing with the request a full account of the act(s) for which it was being made. The latter resembles the request for forgiveness (in the scenario given above) where the agent acknowledges the wrong committed, but the resemblance stops almost at this point where it begins. For one thing, the person seeking amnesty as the South African reconciliation legislation defined the process had only to provide the panel that heard the case with a factual account of his actions. This, together with other evidence that might include testimony of victims or witnesses, would be assessed by the panel that was hearing the case for veracity and completeness. The person requesting amnesty was not required to express regret, let alone to ask forgiveness; he had only to acknowledge his role in committing certain acts. And the panel hearing the case had only to determine whether the person making the request had indeed done what he said he did, that he was not concealing other acts, and that these crimes were indeed political crimes—gross human rights violations—in the context of South African politics over the more than thirty-year period to which the possibility of amnesty applied.

The process of amnesty thus differed from that of forgiveness (on the model outlined above) in significant ways. Those empowered to grant amnesty were not the victims themselves or their representatives; they were meant to be disinterested parties appointed to hear the evidence and to judge whether the act(s) described qualified for amnesty. A second difference was that the person seeking amnesty was under no obligation to acknowledge his actions as wrongful; it was sufficient for the purposes of assessment that he admit being responsible for them and that the actions were, by the conventions under which judgment was passed, a human rights violation. In this sense, the impersonality and disinterest required of the panel could be matched by the person *requesting* the amnesty. To be sure, the petitioner *could* express contrition or ask forgiveness, and this sometimes occurred. But it was not a requirement (and there would be no way of testing the sincerity of such expressions if they were given). Nor was there an obligation on the part of the victims or their representatives to grant forgiveness, whether it had been sought or not. In the first months of its fact-finding, the Committee on Human Rights Violations of the Commission (a committee parallel to the Committee on Amnesty) routinely asked victims whose testimony they heard whether they "forgave" the perpetrators responsible; the virtually unanimous negative responses to this question soon led the committee to stop asking the question.[3]

Under these conditions, then, the person seeking amnesty was not obliged to express remorse or to ask forgiveness or to offer personal compensation, all of which are integral to the process of forgiveness (in the version presented). Indeed, in many instances, the most evident motive for the person requesting amnesty appeared the desire to avoid prosecution and any punishment that might follow it if amnesty were *not* applied for and granted—hardly a view of reconciliation sought for its own sake. (Some of those whose requests for amnesty were rejected did face prosecution and subsequent punishment.) In what sense, then, could the "reconciliation" goal of the "Truth and Reconciliation" Commission and its committees, the ideal in it of "*ubuntu*" or restoration be said to have been realized? In what sense, could it *possibly* have been realized?

But consider again the elements of the process. The request for amnesty would be made in a public document and presented at a public hearing. Witnesses could be called and heard on behalf of anyone connected to the events cited, including the victims or their relatives; the setting, in other words, was much like that of a trial. The person requesting amnesty had to be present and to recount publicly the details of his actions. Here it is, then, that "truth" and "reconciliation" begin to come together and to distinguish this process from the standard prosecutorial one. For in the judgment about amnesty, there was no issue of innocence or guilt to be decided; that question was settled when the plea for amnesty and thus acknowledgement of what in the view of the state if not of the perpetrator was a human rights violation were entered. Nor was there an issue concerning the kind or degree of punishment that was warranted; since the granting of amnesty would preempt all punishment, and its denial would shift judgment of the amnesty-seeker to South Africa's regular court system. On more standard systems of law, these two issues—the questions of guilt or innocence and, if guilty, of the punishment to be imposed—focus and intensify the already-antagonistic setting of the prosecutory trial; and whether or not a defendant continues to assert his innocence, much clearly is left unsettled by the process in the relation between the defendant and the society judging him.

This condition would hold even if a confession of guilt were given, accompanied by contrition and the defendant's "throwing himself on the mercy of the court." Nothing in the prosecutory procedure requires such acknowledgement or gives a formal place to it, and it occurs in only a small minority of court cases. (In the United States, victims of the offense or their relatives increasingly have had the opportunity to address the court in trials, but no protocol exists about what they may or may not say.) In short, nothing in the process points to reconciliation as even a subordinate one of its goals. The division that brought the accused and the accuser into court is in effect reinforced by the conclusion of the trial: divided afterward as they were before, with a winner and a loser. Perhaps the consciousness of justice done might itself be viewed as affirming the social contract that holds the society together, as moving beyond the breach introduced by the crime and then overcoming the *agon* of the courtroom process itself, even if none of this is announced as either a goal or an achievement. But this is not anything one would hear about in the courtroom itself or in the definition of the juridical process.

It is this divided, antagonistic opposition that the principle of reconciliation was intended to avoid or to overcome, with its larger purpose to restore or reconstruct, certainly to avoid deepening prior divisions and conflicts. Did it work in principle or in practice in South Africa? *Should* it be taken as a more general ideal? The problems in assessing the policy as a general model, based on the example of South Africa, are clear; such evidence as there is, moreover, is at best equivocal. (For one example: A poll taken soon after the Truth and Reconciliation Commission completed its work found that two-thirds of South Africans believed that the amnesty process had led to a *deterioration* in race relations.) But here as elsewhere in ethical and political decisions, it is not enough to assess the effects of decisions taken without considering what the alternatives had been at the time and their likely consequences. And it is on *that* point, it seems to me, that the importance of reconciliation in South Africa should leave its mark; that is, as an option in the social fabric that differs sharply from the understanding of justice in most contemporary "liberal-democratic" settings, and that yet seems more consistent in certain respects with the latters' aims than their own current practices.

In the Nuremberg Trials—the proceedings of the International Military Tribunal that began in November 1945, soon after the end of World War II—leading members of the Nazi hierarchy were tried for war crimes and crimes against humanity. There was little doubt from the beginning of the trials about whether those accused had contributed to the acts they were charged with, but the trial nonetheless centered on finding and assessing the evidence for those charges, together with the subsequent question of what the punishments were to be for those found guilty. In that setting, the (predictable) stance of the defendants, with one partial exception, was that of denial: rejection of the charges mainly on the grounds that whatever had occurred was done, even if they did it, in the name or at the command of the Nazi government, and so had not been their individual responsibility. In the context of the series of these trials, structured as contests, the one partial exception to this general response (the half-hearted acknowledgement by Albert Speer of *some* responsibility for what went on under his eyes) was perhaps the only surprise. *Could* there have been an alternate trial along the lines followed by the Truth and Reconciliation Commission for these people? *Should* there have been? Such questions do not ask how likely it was that the four countries conducting the trials would have accepted an amnesty proposal along the lines discussed, but speculate on what the outcome of such a procedure would have been (compared to what actually ensued) in the trials of the Nazi officials and functionaries.

There had indeed been disagreement from all sides in South Africa about the process of truth and reconciliation and in the debates afterward of what it did or did not accomplish. But one thing that cannot be said about the process as it was implemented is that it somehow disabled the society that emerged from it. Not, to be sure, that it resolved all or even very many of the deep social problems that affect South Africa to this day, and not even that very many people in South Africa today regard it as having made a significant difference in the contemporary society. It seems, in effect, rather remote. Few in the current society—probably no more than those at the time—would themselves have been willing to say with Nelson Mandela in his new role as president after decades of imprisonment and knowing the identities of those responsible, that even from his new position of power, he did not seek revenge; he would not want anyone else to undergo what he had. But the ideal embodied in that sentiment struck a chord even with others who could not find it in themselves to take the same position, perhaps also with some who sharply disagreed with him.

Admittedly, South Africa had its own distinctive history, and even if the Truth and Reconciliation program had been a clearer success there, that would not mean it would work elsewhere under different conditions. (Versions of the Truth and Reconciliation Commission have been enacted in other countries, some of them only "Truth" commissions; a number of these, principally in South America, were convened prior to the formation of the South African Commission. None, however, had the specific compound structure of the South African model.)[4] Would the procedure have a chance of success, for example, on a smaller scale, in relation to personal, nonpolitical crimes: murder, assault? Or, again at the other extreme, what of the larger-scale political atrocities of the twentieth century, the Holocaust, the Soviet Gulag, the Turkish genocide of the Armenians? The perceived lack of full punishment—or justice—in relation to these instances has remained for many (certainly for many who had been caught up in them) a continuing source of anger; the sense commonly persists that even such trials and punishments as were imposed were not sufficiently rigorous or severe or *just*. And even if the difficulties evident in larger and more severe models of "justice" are recognized (as pointed to above in chapter 8, in relation to the post–World War II "Morgenthau Plan" or in the pre–World War II "Kaufman Plan"), the impulse for enacting justice as based on the balancing or retributive model has continued to express itself. Adding its weight to these formal judicial proposals, we know also that, together with the trials, boundary readjustments, population "exchanges," and reparations that occurred post–World War II, many disorganized, sometimes random, and often arbitrary acts of revenge also occurred in virtually all the countries that the Nazis had occupied with the help of their collaborators. (The "*epuration*" in France is the best-known and most systematic of these, but it was by no means unique; there seems no way even of estimating the number of individual acts of revenge that took place, especially in the closing days of the war or in the chaos of its immediate aftermath.)[5]

But we also know that reconciliation of a *sort*, often unstated or understated as such on both sides and overall never described by anything close to a formal designation, has had an increasingly significant role, internationally but also at the level of individuals, in the post-Holocaust period. This movement has been propelled in part by the combination of voluntary and involuntary reparations or monetary "settlements" sponsored by national governments or business corporations, but something more fundamental also seems at work here—more fundamental than any sense that such settlements do or may right the balance ("make it good," as the German "Wiedergutmachung" has it), and more telling also than the conventional nostrum that the passage of time itself has had, or at least should have, a healing effect.

It may be too much to claim that below the surface of the post-Holocaust, a process of reconciliation has indeed been taking place. But it seems clear that something like that effect has been occurring. A stark measure of this process can be seen in the difference with which the prospect of German reparations was acrimoniously viewed in Israel in 1952 when the first large-scale agreement on that matter between Israel and Germany was being debated ("Over my dead body," Menachem Begin was quoted at the time), and the general attitude, in Israel or anyplace else, toward such gestures at present. To be sure, the economics of the process have influenced this reaction; the substantial difference that German reparations made for Israel in the early years of statehood has since been generally acknowledged even by its then-opponents. But that moral factors as well as practical ones have motivated this shift also seems undeniable: in the European Union, which includes now the dominant opposing powers of Europe in World War II—Germany and Italy, on one side; Great Britain and France, on the other—and to membership in which Israel also aspires; in the breakup of the Soviet Union, which has meant that at least some of its former member states have themselves moved "Westward"; in the ways in which even remaining survivors of the Holocaust and World War II and still more, their following generations, often have redirected the intense and bitter impress of that experience toward the creation of a more inclusive present, not with the intention of forgetting or forgiving, but of finding a way to live in the world in which those events and their agents once ruled.

This does not mean that the the concept of reconciliation, in the context of the immediate post–World War II setting, would have been a viable international (or, for that matter, individual) option. The fact, however, that something that looks very much like reconciliation has begun to occur *notwithstanding* the past that preceded it and the reckonings sought at the time, should, it seems, make some difference in thinking about the process of judgment that did occur then and the process of such judgment more generally, with whatever light can be shed on it by the revolution effected in South Africa. What has been referred to here as a retributive or balancing principle finds its roots in a conception of justice whose locus is in the individual agent and victim—individual injury to be balanced by individual punishment for the perpetrator (whether a person or group or state); the reconciliation model injects the category of social restoration into the process of individual justice, with the effect of producing a potentially different outcome, certainly in the short run but more emphatically in the long run (which the short run inevitably turns into). About that longer run, the retributive model has little to say, since for it the future always, only, resembles the past. To be sure, the comparative prospects and liabilities of these two models would have to be judged in particular historical contexts, and probably, as circumstances differ—sometimes radically—with neither of them having an exclusive claim.

What remains of continuing importance in the example of South Africa, however, is the fact of its posing an alternative to the much more common balancing or retributive principle of justice, thus at the very least asserting the possibility of a choice. And it injects this where the common assumption has been that there *is* no choice, that where justice is concerned, the ideal of reclaiming and reaffirming the past balance, of justice as a form of repayment, is the last as well as the first word. A lesson learned sooner or later, however, whatever values are espoused, is that the hard moral decisions encountered, those that most matter, arise when two values come into conflict, when whatever we do involves the sacrifice of some good for something else that is judged to be a greater good. The easy choices between radical (and obvious) evil and radical (and obvious) good are just that—easy, and also rare. What the example of reconciliation or restoration in South Africa brings into view, it seems, is that for justice in practice, where a society assumes that certain general principles or ideals are settled and fixed, there are indeed choices that can be made. Even allowing for the special circumstances in South Africa, the principle of reconciliation established a presence there, in the end presenting itself if not as a form of justice, as a means toward it. The application of that principle required an act of the moral imagination that saw the good of society placed alongside the good and the rights of the individual—a juxtaposition often asserted but not often followed to its conclusion. Whether or not one accepts that principle as a basis for other deliberations required to bind the fabric of society, the choice it articulates in *thinking* about justice seems itself a valuable contribution.

Afterword

Wound and Scar

One difference between memory and history as it is written is that forgetfulness belongs to one but not to the other. This does not mean that the written record has no gaps, that ideology and repression do not affect its writing or reception, but that the gaps or unexplained swerves that appear in history's accounts may themselves be part of the course of events, as "natural" as any of their other features. Memory, by contrast, is dependent on the act of retrieval, and if the impulse for that is diverted or weakens, what it has in its stores becomes endangered. If the impulse disappears, those vestiges do so as well, and although there may be explanations for that disappearance, no appeals to justice can right it. The imperative "Zachor!" ("Remember!") attests to the fact of forgetting as much as to the possibility of avoiding it.

Perhaps there is indeed a pool of recorded images in our subconscious, individual or collective, to which additions are continually made, as if it were the attic of a house in which we store items we want to hold on to as parts of ourselves but for which we cannot at the moment find a place. We assure ourselves that we will return to them later, and even if that "later" never comes, the significance we attached to them in storing them remains.

Will weakening of this kind mark the future of the Holocaust? It would be extraordinary if shadows of that process did not occur there, as it has for every other historical moment, including the most intense and honored ones. It is important, at any rate, in reflecting now on the Holocaust, to anticipate this as a possibility; that is, to raise for ourselves, even as the impact of that event seems undiminished, the likelihood that this force will weaken. It is the question of mortality itself: What forms can we turn to that are adequate to the historical occurrence but that also bring it into an ongoing present that requires its own sustenance, its own legs.

I am not speaking here about the amber preservation of fossils, although we cannot be afraid to consider that something like that is almost certainly the destiny of most Holocaust monuments, as it has been of so many others. Not that those others have been unheeded or neglected (although that too, at times), but that they eventually have become detached from the history of which they are marks, and then have to sustain themselves, with few of them successful at this. Some, like the pyramids at Luxor, become independently monumental, hardly commemorative at all. More often, as in the memorials marking the Civil War or World War I that dot so many towns and cities in the United States, the monuments become anonymous, identifiable only by the engravings or plaques attached to them that might as well have been placed elsewhere or even gathered collectively together. But one knows, from the list of names inscribed, that those monuments were once fully alive, their dead known and cared for by familiar, devoted visitors for whom the particular names and the particular place mattered greatly.

And why should the present differ in this respect from the past? What is involved here is not a question of concern or effort or good will; there is no more reason to ascribe a deficit of these to the past than to the present. Nor is it our responsibility to bring all of that large past into our own circle of concern. When Donne wrote in his *Meditation* that "Any man's death diminishes me," could he have been referring to *all* the dead of human history? Even "Diminishing," it seems clear, has its limits.

It is difficult—painful and dangerous—to imagine the future in the present, to anticipate experience yet to come in a present that asserts a different, possibly conflicting account. But the presence of the Holocaust also now is striated, with varied and contrasting lines. The shock is still in evidence, like waves moving across an ocean that reach distant shores in their own time, often intensified by the journey itself. Then too, there is the continuing reflection and analysis: Few historical events have been the subject of such persistent and intense scrutiny from so many different angles of vision. And then, beginning and end, there is the constant moral question of how that past is to be drawn into the present, as preserved or as transformed or as both. To some extent, history will have its own way here, independent of human will or decision, impelled by its own requirements that finally assume the role of logic. That still leaves space, however, for human agency at the intersections, and so too, the moral decision repeatedly alluded to in these pages that the Holocaust as presence involves: the question of what to make of that event in the next moment or the moment after that, or then after that—deciding there not for everybody but for ourselves at least *as if* for all others.

Here also, in ourselves, divisions may be discovered. The Holocaust as an enduring wound *should* not be accommodated, assimilated, even if it could be. But the scars that mark—commemorate—wounds have themselves to face the world, and here the moral decisions posed by the continuing presence of the Holocaust, weighing the balance between wound and scar, become most intense.

« Appendix »

Convention on the Prevention and Punishment of the Crime of Genocide

Adopted by Resolution 260 (III) A of the United Nations General Assembly on December 9, 1948.

ARTICLE 1

The Contracting Parties confirm that genocide, whether committed in time of peace or in time of war, is a crime under international law which they undertake to prevent and to punish.

ARTICLE 2

In the present Convention, genocide means any of the following acts committed with intent to destroy, in whole or in part, a national, ethnical, racial or religious group, as such:

a) Killing members of the group;
b) Causing serious bodily or mental harm to members of the group;
c) Deliberately inflicting on the group conditions of life calculated to bring about its physical destruction in whole or in part;
d) Imposing measures intended to prevent births within the group;
e) Forcibly transferring children of the group to another group.

ARTICLE 3

The following acts shall be punishable:

a) Genocide;
b) Conspiracy to commit genocide;
c) Direct and public incitement to commit genocide;
d) Attempt to commit genocide;
e) Complicity in genocide.

ARTICLE 4

Persons committing genocide or any of the other acts enumerated in Article 3 shall be punished, whether they are constitutionally responsible rulers, public officials or private individuals.

ARTICLE 5
The Contracting Parties undertake to enact, in accordance with their respective Constitutions, the necessary legislation to give effect to the provisions of the present Convention and, in particular, to provide effective penalties for persons guilty of genocide or any of the other acts enumerated in Article 3.

ARTICLE 6
Persons charged with genocide or any of the other acts enumerated in Article 3 shall be tried by a competent tribunal of the State in the territory of which the act was committed, or by such international penal tribunal as may have jurisdiction with respect to those Contracting Parties which shall have accepted its jurisdiction.

ARTICLE 7
Genocide and the other acts enumerated in Article 3 shall not be considered as political crimes for the purpose of extradition.

The Contracting Parties pledge themselves in such cases to grant extradition in accordance with their laws and treaties in force.

ARTICLE 8
Any Contracting Party may call upon the competent organs of the United Nations to take such action under the Charter of the United Nations as they consider appropriate for the prevention and suppression of acts of genocide or any of the other acts enumerated in Article 3.

ARTICLE 9
Disputes between the Contracting Parties relating to the interpretation, application or fulfillment of the present Convention, including those relating to the responsibility of a State for genocide or any of the other acts enumerated in Article 3, shall be submitted to the International Court of Justice at the request of any of the parties to the dispute.

ARTICLE 10
The present Convention, of which the Chinese, English, French, Russian and Spanish texts are equally authentic, shall bear the date of 9 December 1948.

ARTICLE 11
The present Convention shall be open until 31 December 1949 for signature on behalf of any Member of the United Nations and of any non-member State to which an invitation to sign has been addressed by the General Assembly.

The present Convention shall be ratified, and the instruments of ratification shall be deposited with the Secretary-General of the United Nations.

After 1 January 1950, the present Convention may be acceded to on behalf of any Member of the United Nations and of any non-member State which has received an invitation as aforesaid.

Instruments of accession shall be deposited with the Secretary-General of the United Nations.

ARTICLE 12

Any Contracting Party may at any time, by notification addressed to the Secretary-General of the United Nations, extend the application of the present Convention to all or any of the territories for the conduct of whose foreign relations that Contracting Party is responsible.

ARTICLE 13

On the day when the first twenty instruments of ratification or accession have been deposited, the Secretary-General shall draw up a process-verbal and transmit a copy of it to each Member of the United Nations and to each of the non-member States contemplated in Article 11.

The present Convention shall come into force on the ninetieth day following the date of deposit of the twentieth instrument of ratification or accession.

Any ratification or accession effected subsequent to the latter date shall become effective on the ninetieth day following the deposit of the instrument of ratification or accession.

ARTICLE 14

The present Convention shall remain in effect for a period of ten years as from the date of its coming into force.

It shall thereafter remain in force for successive periods of five years for such Contracting Parties as have not denounced it at least six months before the expiration of the current period.

Denunciation shall be effected by a written notification addressed to the Secretary-General of the United Nations.

ARTICLE 15

If, as a result of denunciations, the number of Parties to the present Convention should become less than sixteen, the Convention shall cease to be in force as from the date on which the last of these denunciations shall become effective.

ARTICLE 16

A request for the revision of the present Convention may be made at any time by any Contracting Party by means of a notification in writing addressed to the Secretary-General.

The General Assembly shall decide upon the steps, if any, to be taken in respect of such request.

ARTICLE 17

The Secretary-General of the United Nations shall notify all Members of the United Nations and the non-member States contemplated in Article 11 of the following:

a) Signatures, ratifications and accessions received in accordance with Article 11;
b) Notifications received in accordance with Article 12;
c) The date upon which the present Convention comes into force in accordance with Article 13;
d) Denunciations received in accordance with Article 14;
e) The abrogation of the Convention in accordance with Article 15;
f) Notifications received in accordance with Article 16.

ARTICLE 18

The original of the present Convention shall be deposited in the archives of the United Nations.

A certified copy of the Convention shall be transmitted to all Members of the United Nations and to the non-member States contemplated in Article 11.

ARTICLE 19

The present Convention shall be registered by the Secretary-General of the United Nations on the date of its coming into force.

« Notes »

1. PHILOSOPHICAL WITNESSING

(pages 3–16)

1 For an account of the Oneg Shabbos group and the archives (and of Ringelblum himself), see Samuel Kassow, *Who Will Write Our History?* (Bloomington: Indiana University Press, 2007).

2 On issues related to eyewitness testimony as such, see, e.g., Elizabeth F. Loftus, *Eyewitness Testimony* (1979, reprint Cambridge, Mass.: Harvard University Press, 1996); and Laura Engelhardt, "The Problem with Eyewitness Testimony," *Stanford Journal of Legal Studies* 1, no. 1 (1999): 25–29. For issues of eyewitness testimony specifically in relation to the Holocaust, see Machael Bernard-Donals and Richard Glejzer, eds., *Witnessing the Disaster: Essays on Representation and the Holocaust* (Madison: University of Wisconsin Press, 2003); Gary Weissman, *Fantasies of Witnessing* (Ithaca, N.Y.: Cornell University Press, 2004); and Annette Wieviorka, *The Era of the Witness*, trans. Jared Stark (Ithaca, N.Y.: Cornell University Press, 2007).

3 See Primo Levi, *Survival in Auschwitz*, trans. Stuart Woolf (New York: Simon & Schuster, 1993); Thadeusz Borowski, *This Way for the Gas, Ladies and Gentlemen*, trans. Barbara Vedder (New York: Penguin, 1967).

4 On the criteria for nation-building, see, e.g., Anthony D. Smith, *The Ethnic Origins of Nations* (London: Basil Blackwell, 1986), 16–18.

5 As described in James P. Duffy, *Target America: Hitler's Plan to Attack the United States* (Westport, Conn.: Greenwood, 2004). See also Gerhard L. Weinberg, *Visions of Victory: The Hopes of Eight World War II Leaders* (New York: Cambridge University Press, 2005).

6 Buber's most widely circulated statement in relation to Nazism and the Jewish Question appeared in his response to Gandhi's advocacy of non-violent resistance in that context. See *Two Letters to Gandhi from Martin Buber and J. L. Magnes* (Jerusalem: R. Mass, 1939). For other authors mentioned, see, e.g., Karl Popper, *The Open Society and Its Enemies* (London: Routledge, 1945) and *Unended Quest: An Intellectual Autobiography* (London: Fontana, 1976); and Emmanuel Levinas, *Difficult Freedom: Essays in Judaism*, trans. Sean Hand (London: Athlone Press, 1990) and *Quelque reflexion sur la philosophie de l'hitlerism* (Paris: Payot & Rivage, 1997).

7 A. J. Ayer, *Language, Truth and Logic* (London: Victor Gollancz, 1946).

8 David Edmonds and John Eidinow, *Wittgenstein's Poker* (London: Faber & Faber, 2001), 96.

9 See Edmund Husserl, *The Crisis of the European Sciences and Transcendental Phenomenology*, trans. David Carr (Evanston, Ill.: Northwestern University Press, 1954). Notwithstanding its title and the fact that it was first published in Germany in 1936, neither the "crisis" referred to nor anything else in the book gives any indication of the social or political conditions of the time.

10 David Hume warrants mention here as a philosopher who (uniquely, it seems) not only wrote history, but realized in his *History of England* (1754–1762) a work that was for its time and a century afterward a landmark achievement. This was an instance, however, of a philosopher writing history by applying what might be recognized as "philosophical method," not of historical events, singly or collectively, being addressed philosophically or even by way of a philosophy of history.

2. TRUTH AT RISK AND THE HOLOCAUST'S RESPONSE

(pages 17–32)

1 On the elements, form, and afterlife of Renaissance Humanism, see, for example, Paul Oskar Kristeller, *Renaissance Concepts of Man* (New York: Harper & Row, 1977) and *Eight Philosophers of the Italian Renaissance* (Stanford, Calif.: Stanford University Press, 1964); Anthony Grafton, *Defenders of the Text: Traditions of Scholarship in an Age of Science, 1450–1800* (Cambridge, Mass.: Harvard University Press, 1991); and Anthony Grafton and Lisa Jardine, *From Humanism to the Humanities* (London: Duckworth, 1986).

2 So far as I can determine, the phrase "philosophers of suspicion" in the sense used here and often cited elsewhere appears first in Erich Heller, *The Disinherited Mind* (London: Bower & Bower, 1957), but then becomes a common, although at times a shifting designation.

3 Hannah Arendt, *The Origins of Totalitarianism* (New York: Harcourt, Brace, and Jovanovich, 1968), where the charge of the human as "superfluous" under totalitarianism is developed.

4 Specific accounts of this historical "filiation" have varied, although have in common been contentious. See, e.g., Zygmunt Baumann, *Modernity and the Holocaust* (Ithaca, N.Y.: Cornell University Press, 1989); Max Horkheimer and Theodor Adorno, *Dialectic of Enlightenment*, trans. John Cumming (New York: Herder & Herder, 1972); Berel Lang, *Act and Idea in the Nazi Genocide* (Chicago: University of Chicago Press, 1990), chapter 7.

5 See, e.g., Carl Hempel, *Aspects of Scientific Explanation* (New York: Free Press, 1965).

6 As examples, see Carlo Ginzburg, *The Cheese and the Worms: The Cosmos of a Sixteenth Century Miller* (Baltimore: Johns Hopkins University Press, 1980), and *Clues, Myths and the Historical Method* (Baltimore: Johns Hopkins University Press, 1989); also Natalie Zemon Davis, *Women on the Margins* (Cambridge, Mass.: Harvard University Press, 1995).

7 At least on certain levels. The debates continue on what place "the Holocaust" should have among academic disciplines and courses: in history departments in the context of modern "German history"? In German departments? As "Jewish history" in Judaic studies programs? In "human rights" programs in relation to other instances of genocide? More is at stake in this discussion than bookkeeping or college catalogues. It should be recalled, moreover, how long it took for the Holocaust to become a "respectable" academic or scholarly subject. In Raul Hilberg's memoir, *The Politics of Memory* (Chicago: Ivan Dee, 1996), he recounts his advisor's discouraging reaction to Hilberg's dissertation proposal that ultimately gave way to Franz Neumann's grudging consent: "It's your funeral." That dissertation eventually would become the path-breaking work, *The Destruction of the European Jews*, first published in 1961 (Chicago: Quadrangle Books)—but that, too, only after difficulty in finding its marginal publisher.

8 The most serious attempt to establish the claim of Holocaust "uniqueness" on historical grounds appears in Steven T. Katz, *The Holocaust in Historical Context* (New York: Oxford University Press, 1994). In addition to the blurred distinction in Katz's account between "unique" and "unprecedented," most other references to the Holocaust as unique rely as much on rhetorical as historical grounds; see, e.g., George Steiner, *Language and Silence* (New York: Atheneum, 1967); Alan Rosenbaum, ed., *Is the Holocaust Unique?* (Boulder: Westview Press, 1996); John Rawls (on "after Auschwitz"), *The Law of People* (Cambridge, Mass.: Harvard University Press, 1999).

9 As in the "Second Moment" of the "Analytic of the Beautiful," in the *Critique of Judgment*, trans. Werner S. Pluhar (Indianapolis: Hackett, 1987).

10 See Charles Taylor, *Sources of the Self: Making of the Modern Identity* (Cambridge, Mass.: Harvard University Press, 1989).

11 See, for example, Friedrich Nietzsche, *On Truth and Lie in an Extra-Moral Sense*, trans. Walter Kaufman (New York: Viking Penguin, 1976); Michel Foucault, *Power/Knowledge*, ed. and trans. Colin Gordon (New York: Pantheon, 1980). Consider especially Nietzsche's bold formulation in the former of truth as "a mobile army of metaphor, metonym, anthropomorphism—in short, a sum of human relations."

12 Strictly speaking, the constructivist view would be hard put to speak of philosophical *arguments* at all. Richard Rorty makes this point explicitly, replacing

the concept of an argument, with its implication of truth or falsity with "looking bad" or "looking good"—that is, by judging the "looks" of positions. Rorty, however, left quite untouched the question of what the criteria are for assessing "looks." See his *Contingency, Irony, and Solidarity* (Cambridge: Cambridge University Press, 1989).

13 The immediate occasion for this controversy was the article intended as a "send-up" by Alan D. Sokal, "Transgressing the Boundaries: Towards a Transformative Hermeneutics of Quantum Gravity," *Social Text* 46/47 (1996): 217–52. See also his *Beyond the Hoax: Science, Philosophy and Culture* (Oxford: Oxford University Press, 2008).

14 For an early summary and critique of Holocaust denial, see Deborah Lipstadt, *Denying the Holocaust* (New York: Free Press, 1993); and for a more sustained account, Richard Evans, *Lying about Hitler: History, Holocaust, and the David Irving Trial* (New York: Basic Books, 2001). Two "standard" works advocating the view are Arthur R. Butz, *The Hoax of the Twentieth Century* (Torrance, Calif.: Noontide Press, 1977); and Robert Faurisson, *Memoir en defense: Contre ceux qui m'accusent de falsifier l'histoire* [with an Introduction by Noam Chomsky] (Paris: La Vieille Taupe, 1980).

15 See the "Besprechungsprotokoll" of the Wannsee Conference, in the House of the Wannsee Conference Memorial (Wannsee); see also Christopher Browning, *The Origins of the Final Solution* (Lincoln: University of Nebraska Press, 2004); David Caesarani, *Eichmann: His Life and Crimes* (New York: Vintage, 2005); and John Mendelsohn, ed., *Documents of the Holocaust*, vol. 11 (New York: Garland, 1982).

16 See Rorty's response to Umberto Eco in the multi-authored volume, *Interpretation and Overinterpretation* (Cambridge: Cambridge University Press, 1992), and then, too, Eco's response in the same volume to Rorty's response.

17 Hayden White, *Metahistory: The Historical Image in Nineteenth-Century Europe* (Baltimore: Johns Hopkins University Press, 1973).

18 Jean Baudrillard published a book before the first Iraq war under the title *The Gulf War Will Not Take Place*, a title to which he conceded little even after the war broke out, when he altered the title to *The Gulf War Did Not Take Place*, trans. Paul Patton (Bloomington: Indiana University Press, 1995, original French edition 1991). History may be as arbitrary as Baudrillard would have it, but for better or worse, it did not answer to him. For an exchange of views explicitly on this issue in relation to the Holocaust, see "The Holocaust and Problems of Historical Representation," in *History and Theory* 33 (1994): 127–97, and the response by Berel Lang, "Is It Possible to Misrepresent the Holocaust?" *History and Theory* 34 (1995): 84–89.

19 The classic formulation of this distinction between descriptive and moral reasoning is the "Naturalistic Fallacy," defined and named by G. E. Moore in his *Principia Ethica* (Cambridge: Cambridge University Press, 1903), although very much the same claim was made by Hume over a hundred years earlier.

20 In *Le Monde* (February 21, 1979), thirty-four French historians published a statement about Holocaust "revisionism," which bases their moral "outrage" over the view—still as though the historical claim and the moral issue were separate, arguing basically that: "It is impossible to have a debate on the existence of the gas chambers. . . ." The latter form of response, often taken in relation to Holocaust-denial (as when, at the first "Lessons and Legacies" Conference, held in a public university forum, Saul Friedländer refused to address a question raised from the floor by Arthur Butz) seems to me at least debatable on a number of grounds, among them the one emphasized here: a failure to give due weight to the connection between the modalities of the historical and the ethical.

3. EVIL AND UNDERSTANDING

(pages 33–56)

1 *The Book of Theodicy*, translated and with a commentary by L. E. Goodman (New Haven, Conn.: Yale University Press, 1988).

2 See G. E. Moore, *Principia Ethica* (Cambridge: Cambridge University Press, 1903); see also for a later summary, William Frankena, *Ethics* (Englewood Cliffs, N.J.: Prentice-Hall, 1963). Plato's *Theaetetus* remains a locus classicus for both the presentation and critique of this view.

3 That societies invariably find gradations among acts of wrongdoing and their related punishments has largely been unnoticed in the search for "cultural universals," of which it is clearly one.

4 On this comparison, see Helmut Dubiel and Gabriel Motzkin, eds., *The Lesser Evil* (London: Frank Cass, 2003).

5 Susan Neiman sees Rousseau as "historicizing" evil, but she seems here to be speaking about the history of the individual agent (in a social context), not the structural history of evil through its acts. See *Evil in Modern Thought* (Princeton, N.J.: Princeton University Press, 2002), 36–46.

6 For a variety of examples, see Arthur A. Cohen, *The Tremendum: A Theological Intepretation of the Holocaust* (New York: Crossroads, 1981), 21; Emil Fackenheim, "Leo Baeck and Other Jewish Thinkers in Dark Times," *Judaism* 51 (2002): 288; Irving Greenberg, *Living in the Image of God* (Northvale, N.J.: Jason Aronson, 1998), 234. In his 2002 Nobel Prize speech, Imre Kertesz

speaks of the "break" caused by the Holocaust, with Auschwitz "the end point of a great adventure." *PMLA* 118 (2003): 607.

7 As, for example, in such books (and titles) as Sara Horowitz, *Voicing the Void* (Albany: SUNY Press, 1997); Andy Leak and George Paizis, eds., *The Holocaust and the Text: Speaking the Unspeakable* (London: Macmillan, 1999); George Steiner, *Language and Silence* (New York: Atheneum, 1967). See also below, chapter 5.

8 Consider, as one of many examples, the statement by Werner Hamacher: "We do not just write 'after Auschwitz.' There is no historical or experiential 'after' to an absolute trauma. The continuum being disrupted, any attempt to restore it would be a vain act of denegation . . . This 'history' cannot enter into history. It deranges all dates and destroys the ways to understand them." Werner Hamacher, Neil Hertz, and Thomas Keenan, eds., *On Paul deMan's Wartime Journalism* (Lincoln: University of Nebraska Press, 1989), 458–59. See also John Rawls, on "after Auschwitz," in *The Law of Peoples* (Cambridge, Mass.: Harvard University Press, 1999), 20.

9 Alan Mintz, *Hurban: Responses to Jewish Catastrophe in Hebrew Literature* (New York: Columbia University Press, 1984), 98. See also Jacob Katz, *Tradition and Crisis,* trans. Dov Bernard Cooperman (New York: New York University Press, 1993): ". . . The essential attitude toward tradition did not change" (184).

10 In the range of possible "moral" consequences, see, for example, Yisroel Yuval's controversial suggestion, as part of that aftermath, of a possible causal connection between suicidal martyrdom (including the killing of their children by Jewish parents) and the medieval emergence of the blood libel ("Ha'Nakam v'Haklalah" [Hebrew], *Zion* 58 (1993): 33–90.

11 See Primo Levi, *The Drowned and the Saved*, trans. Raymond Rosenthal (New York: Summit, 1988). On the claim of Holocaust-uniqueness, see especially Steven T. Katz, *The Holocaust in Historical Perspective* (New York: Oxford University Press, 1994, vol. 1. Katz's arguments for the *historical* uniqueness of the Holocaust leaves unaddressed the question of what, if any, moral or philosophical implications would follow if that *were* the case.

12 Eliezer Berkovitz, *Faith after the Holocaust* (New York: Ktav, 1973), 90, 98.

13 I would relate this to a question that seems to me indicated for "uniqueness" claims for the Holocaust quite apart from the issue of their historical basis: the question of what difference it makes if the Holocaust *is* unique, or more bluntly, "So what?" See Berel Lang, *The Future of the Holocaust* (Ithaca, N.Y.: Cornell University Press, 1999), 77–91.

14 G. W. Leibniz, *Theodicy: Essays on the Goodness of God, the Freedom of Man,*

and the Origin of Evil, trans. E. M. Huggard (New Haven, Conn.: Yale University Press, 1952).

15 Maimonides, *Guide of the Perplexed*, vol. 3, section 17, trans. Shlomo Pines (Chicago: University of Chicago Press, 1963), 469. Maimonides distinguishes his own position from this communal and traditional one, although *how much* difference his own formulation entails is arguable. Ibid., section 51, 625.

16 Shabbath 55a. Cited by Maimonides, *Guide*, loc. cit., 470.

17 The Art Scroll prayer book adds its own gloss to the statement: "This is a cardinal principle of Jewish faith. History is not haphazard. Israel's exile and centuries-long distress is a result of its sins." *The Art Scroll Siddur*, trans. Nosson Scherman (Brooklyn: Mesorah, 1984), 678.

18 Eliezer Berkovitz, *Faith after the Holocaust*, 94. See also, e.g., Amos Funkenstein, "Theological Responses to the Holocaust," in *Perceptions of Jewish History* (Berkeley: University of California Press, 1993), 311.

19 Taitlebaum and Wasserman as cited in Yosef Roth, "The Jewish Fate and the Holocaust," in *I Will Be Sanctified: Religious Responses to the Holocaust*, ed. Yehezkel Fogel (Northvale, N.J.: Jason Aronson, 1952), 58–59.

20 Reported in *New York Times*, August 7, 2001.

21 For other examples (and analysis) of the "punishment-reward" view in Orthodox and Haredi sources, see especially the writings of Gershon Greenberg, "Orthodox Jewish Thought in the Wake of the Holocaust," in *In God's Name: Genocide and Religion in the Twentieth Century*, ed. Omer Bartov and Phyliss Mack (New York: Berghahn, 2001), and "Jewish Religious Thought in the Wake of the Catastrophe," in *Thinking in the Shadow of Hell*, ed. Jacques B. Doukhan (Berrien Springs, Mich.: Andrews University Press, 2002).

22 Ignaz Maybaum openly affirms this (admittedly, as a rhetorical question): "Would it shock you if I were to imitate . . . [Isaiah's] prophetic style and formulate the phrase 'Hitler, my [God's] servant'?" *Ignaz Maybaum: A Reader*, ed. Nicholas De Lange (New York: Berghahn Books, 2001), 165.

23 Berkovitz, *Faith after the Holocaust*, 105.

24 Norman Lamm, "The Face of God: Thoughts, on the Holocaust," in *Theological and Halakhic Reflections on the Holocaust*, ed. B. H. Rosenberg and F. Heuman (Hoboken, N.J.: Ktav, 1999), 191–92.

25 Berkovitz, *Faith after the Holocaust*, 105, 107.

26 Maimonides preempts this explanatory effort in favor of the literalist view of punishment and reward: "It is clear that *we* [emphasis added] are the cause of this '*hiding of the face*', and we are the agents of this separation . . . If, however, his God is within him, no evil at all will befall him." Maimonides, *Guide of the Perplexed*, 626.

27 Sanhedrin, 101a.

28 Cited in Arthur Green, *The Tormented Master* (Tuscaloosa: University of Alabama Press, 1977), 175.

29 "Kol Dodi Dofek," trans. L. Kaplan, in *Theological and Halakhic Reflections*, 56. The value posited would presumably hold also for people who did not survive their suffering; in any event, the statement is presumably not a prediction about human behavior, since no evidence (here or elsewhere) suggests that suffering typically *has* the effects described.

30 David Weiss Halivni offers an intriguing variation on this thesis in his application of the concept of "Tsimtsum" ["contraction"] to the question of God's presence; see "Prayer in the Shoah," *Judaism* 50 (2001): 268–91. Halivni emphasizes differences between "Tsimtsum" and "Hester Panim," but a common element in their logical structures holds that at some historical moments, divine nonintervention, no matter how severe the context, is preferable to intervention. Eliezer Schweid argues that since free choice does not *require* "Hester Panim," this line of explanation as a whole seems either redundant or beside the point. See *Wrestling until Daybreak: Searching for Meaning in Thinking about the Holocaust* (Lanham, Md.: University Press of America, 1994), 390. See also David Weiss Halivni, *Breaking the Tablets*, ed. Peter Ochs (Lanham, Md.: Rowman & Littlefield, 2007).

31 Hugh Rice, *God and Goodness* (New York: Oxford University Press, 2000), 92.

32 Emmanuel Levinas, *Entre Nous: Thinking-of-the-Other*, trans. Michael B. Smith and Barbara Harshav (New York: Columbia University Press, 1998), 241.

33 Arthur A. Cohen and Paul Mendes-Flohr, eds., *Contemporary Jewish Religious Thought* (New York: Scribners, 1987), 945.

34 Berkowitz, *Faith after the Holocaust*, 128.

35 Richard Rubenstein, *After Auschwitz* (Indianapolis: Bobbs-Merrill, 1966); see also *The Cunning of History: The Holocaust and the American Future* (New York: Harper, 1978). For a fuller account of Rubenstein and especially of Emil Fackenheim, see Michael Morgan, *Beyond Auschwitz: Post-Holocaust Jewish Thought in America* (New York: Oxford University Press, 2001).

36 E.g., Thomas J. J. Altizer and William Hamilton, *Radical Theology and the Death of God* (Indianapolis: Bobbs-Merrill, 1966); Harvey Cox, *The Secular City* (New York: Macmillan, 1965); William Hamilton, *The New Essence of Christianity* (New York: Associated Books, 1965).

37 Richard Rubenstein, *The Age of Triage: Fear and Hope in an Overcrowded World* (Boston: Beacon Press, 1983).

38 Hans Jonas, "The Concept of God after Auschwitz: A Jewish Voice," in *Mor-*

tality and Morality: A Search for God after Auschwitz (Evanston, Ill.: Northwestern University Press, 1996), 140.

39 See, e.g., Emil Fackenheim, *Quest for Past and Future* (Bloomington: Indiana University Press, 1968), chapter 1.

40 See, e.g., Michael Wyschogrod, "Faith and the Holocaust," *Judaism* 20 (1971): 250.

41 Emil Fackenheim, "Leo Baeck and Other Jewish Thinkers in Dark Times," *Judaism* 51 (2002): 288. For earlier and fuller accounts of the Commandment, see *God's Presence in History: Jewish Affirmations and Philosophical Reflections* (New York: New York University Press, 1970), 70ff; and *The Jewish Return into History* (New York: Schocken, 1978), 27–29.

42 Irving Greenberg, who speaks of the Holocaust as a breach in the Covenant—to be repaired only by a new, "Voluntary Covenant"—articulates a "principle" (not, as he conceives of it, a law) with some of the force of Fackenheim's commandment: "No statement, theological or otherwise, should be made that would not be credible in the presence of burning children." (Quoted in Eva Fleischner, ed., *Auschwitz: Beginning of a New Era* (New York: Ktav, 1977), 22. See also Greenberg's "Voluntary Covenant," in *Perspectives* (New York: National Jewish Resource Center, 1982).

43 Arthur A. Cohen, *The Tremendum: A Theological Interpretation of the Holocaust* (New York: Crossroads, 1981), 8.

44 See on Arendt's relation to Jewish sources, Richard Bernstein, *Hannah Arendt and the Jewish Question* (Cambridge: MIT Press, 1994), 6–13.

45 Letter dated July 24, 1963, in *The Jew as Pariah*, ed. Ron H. Feldman (New York: Grove, 1978), 251. Arendt elaborates on this view in the opening pages of *The Life of the Mind* (New York: Harcourt, Brace, and Jovanovich, 1978). Richard Bernstein emphasizes the vagary in Arendt's distinction between "judgment" and "thinking"; an arguably more basic issue is justification for the power that Arendt ascribes to thinking—*apart* from the question of its relation to judging (*Hannah Arendt*).

46 Hannah Arendt, *The Origins of Totalitarianism* (New York: Harcourt, Brace, and Jovanovich, 1951).

4. KARL JASPERS' *DIE SCHULDFRAGE*

(pages 57–74)

1 Karl Jaspers, *Die Schuldfrage* (Heidelberg: Lambert Schneider, 1946). Quotations here are taken from Karl Jaspers, *The Question of German Guilt*, trans. E. B. Ashton (New York: Fordham University Press, 2000).

2 This relationship affected not only Jaspers' career but threatened his life (in addition to his wife's), to the extent that they obtained poison pills that they agreed to use in the event of their deportation. Indeed, although they survived the years of Nazi rule until then with no physical harm, the liberation of Heidelberg by the American forces (April 1, 1945) anticipated by only two weeks the date that had been set for their deportation. (Viktor von Klemperer and his non-Jewish wife had a comparable experience, avoiding *their* scheduled deportation only because of the chaos resulting from the mass bombing of Dresden in mid-February 1945.)

3 The first postwar course that Jaspers offered—beginning in November 1945 in the faculty of Theology—was on "Proofs of God's Existence." At that time, Jaspers not only was preparing the lectures that later became *Die Schuldfrage*, but was participating in a more pressing, quasi-judicial review: responding to the request of a special faculty committee at the University of Freiburg who had requested Jaspers' opinion on what should be done about Martin Heidegger's status at the University, given Heidegger's conduct during the Nazi years. Jaspers' response (letter of December 22, 1945) was to propose continuation of Heidegger's pension, but to "suspend him from teaching for several years pending review of his subsequent published work." Jaspers' letter to the special committee included a statement that he requested should not be shown to Heidegger: "Heidegger's mode of thinking, which seems to me fundamentally unfree, dictatorial, and uncommunicative, would have a very damaging effect on students at the present time."

4 On the external evidence, see Suzanne Kirkbright, *Karl Jaspers: A Biography* (New Haven, Conn.: Yale University Press, 2004), 39–42.

5 Jaspers goes so far in presenting this theme as to claim that of all those who suffered in the war, German distress "is comparatively the greatest"; he never provides the "comparative" evidence to support this claim, but he does contextualize it with the qualification "that we Germans . . . also bear the greatest responsibility for the course of events until 1945" (108).

6 Jaspers seriously considered the possibility of leaving Germany during the war on at least two occasions, once for a potential position at Oxford, once for a position at Basel. (The latter opportunity came up twice, and all that apparently deterred him from accepting the second of those was the Nazi denial of an exit visa for his wife.) Did Jaspers find a *moral* difference (or difference in guilt) between leaving Germany or remaining there under the Nazi regime? It does not seem so; the only considerations he discusses in relation to his opportunities for positions outside Germany concern the terms of the offers, not moral reasons for or against emigration (neither of which would in

his view count as active opposition). He does condemn himself for his conduct while remaining in Germany, for what he refers to as "my silence under Nazism." Letter to Hannah Arendt, May 16, 1947, in *Hannah Arendt–Karl Jaspers: Correspondence, 1926–1969*, ed. L. Kohler and H. Saner, trans. Robert and Rita Kimber (New York: Harcourt Brace and Jovanovich, 1992), 88. In a letter to Arendt soon after that (July 20, 1947; 94), however, he says that "I would act again just as I did in the past"—a puzzling commentary on the earlier judgment.

7 Jaspers is so conscious of his audience *as* Germans that he writes to Hannah Arendt, in connection with the possibility she had raised of publishing a translation of *Die Schuldfrage* in the United States, "I can't imagine it [as worth translating] . . . It is too much directed at my German readers." June 9, 1946, in *Hannah Arendt–Karl Jaspers*, 43.

8 The concept of the "bystander"—or in Jaspers' term, the "other"—is ambiguous. It has been used in its broadest sense to include everyone who was not both a "formal" and actual adversary; in this view, citizens of countries occupied by Germany (and noncombatant Germans themselves), as well as the citizens of countries and the countries that officially declared "neutrality," would count as "bystanders." The semantic issue here is a substantive one: the question of the moral responsibility of onlookers in situations where human lives are at stake.

9 Although speaking of guilt and purification, Jaspers does not in *Die Schuldfrage* refer to evil itself as the objective property it is in the main philosophical traditions on which he draws. Jaspers himself is sometimes held to have been the source of Hannah Arendt's reference in the subtitle of her book on Eichmann to "the banality of evil," but in a letter to Arendt (December 13, 1963), he mentions Arendt's husband, Heinrich Blucher, as the source for that phrase; about the concept as such, he writes that "this [Eichmann's? Nazi?] evil, not evil per se, is banal." (Arendt, in her acrimonious exchange about the Eichmann book with Gershom Scholem, subsequently concluded—contrary to Jaspers—that indeed, *all* evil is banal.)

10 So he writes generally of Germany's role "in the extermination of populations" (47) and of Nazi "race mania" (63); in two different places (13 and 65–66), he refers to Kristallnacht and the "Jewish" progroms, but again, these references are slight in comparison to his general emphasis on Nazi crimes. (The phrase "the Holocaust" is absent—it became current only decades after Jaspers wrote—and is absent also from the 1962 "Afterword" that he appended to a new edition of *Die Schuldfrage* in which he does refer to the "gassing" of the Jews.) As mentioned before, it would be important to know

exactly how much Jaspers himself had learned about the extent of Nazi crimes before the end of the war as well as at the time of his writing *Die Schuldfrage* in 1945.

5. HOLOCAUST-REPRESENTATION IN THE GENRE OF SILENCE

(pages 77–91)

1 Babel, even during his productive and "nonsilent" periods, preferred not to speak about his writing; asked once about the work he was planning, he replied, "I'm thinking seriously about getting a goat."

2 Leo Strauss, *Persecution and the Art of Writing* (Glencoe, Ill.: Free Press, 1972). A figure of speech that acts in a way similar to the aporia is the "preteritio," which at once disavows a position and makes the opposite, more basic commitment clear: thus, "I do not mean at all to question my opponent's patriotism, but . . ." Similarly, in relation to the Holocaust: "I cannot describe the degradation and inhumane treatment inflicted on concentration camp inmates. This included, etc. . . ."

3 For a more extensive account of this structural feature, see Sara Horowitz, *Voicing the Void* (Albany: SUNY Press, 1997).

4 See Berel Lang, *Holocaust-Representation: Art within the Limits of History and Ethics* (Baltimore: Johns Hopkins University Press, 2000), chapter 2.

5 "Oskar Rosenfeld and the Realism of Holocaust-History: On Sex, Shit, and Status," *History and Theory*, 43 (2004).

6 Terrence Des Pres' account of the "excremental universe" remains one of the few sustained efforts to address this aspect of the camps. See his *The Survivor: An Anatomy of Life in the Death Camps* (New York: Oxford University Press, 1976). Contrary to a common assumption, it has been shown that most birds have, and use, the sense of smell.

7 Vassily Grossman, *Life and Fate: A Novel*, trans. Robert Chandler (London: Collins Harvill, 1985).

8 See, e.g., the Introduction to *Nazi Germany and the Jews: 1939–1945* (New York: Harper Collins, 2007).

9 For a conspectus of Holocaust films, see Annette Insdorf, *Indelible Shadows: Film and the Holocaust* (New York: Cambridge University Press, 2003); Lawrence Baron, *Projecting the Holocaust into the Present: The Changing Focus of Contemporary Holocaust Cinema* (Lanham, Md.: Rowman & Littlefield, 2005).

6. REPRESENTATION AND *MIS*REPRESENTATION

(pages 92–111)

1 On this point, see Hegel, *Introductory Lectures on Aesthetics* (London, 2004), 12–13; also Arthur Danto, *The Abuse of Beauty* (Chicago: Open Court, 2003), 136–37.

2 In an essay on this issue, "Hamlet's Grandmother" in *The Anatomy of Philosophical Style* (Oxford: Basil Blackwell, 1990), I have argued that although a speaker in the drama explicitly acknowledges only Hamlet's grandfather ("Your father had a father, and that father had his . . ."), Hamlet would surely have had a grandmother as well (two of them). Think only of the consequences if he did not.

3 See the striking analysis of this example of misrepresentation—which he himself argues is *not* that—in Julian Barnes's novel, *Flaubert's Parrot* (New York: Vintage International, 1990).

4 See Elie Wiesel, "Looking Back," in *Lessons and Legacies*, vol. 3: *Memory, Memorialization, and Denial*, ed. Peter Hayes (Evanston, Ill.: Northwestern University Press, 1999), 15. Wiesel also posed the objection in the context (on separate and ad hominem grounds) that Kazin was not himself a survivor.

5 William Cutter has suggested the need within the framework of misrepresentation formulated here for an additional (fourth) level of "artistic" or "aesthetic" misrepresentation, and it seems clear that the compass of judgment on works of art (including those with the Holocaust as a subject) should—would—include aesthetic criteria. However the three types of misrepresentation cited impinge, as they do, on aesthetic evaluation, they do not fully cover its grounds. On the other hand, the history of aesthetics repeatedly has shown the difficulty, if not the impossibility, of distinguishing the issue of aesthetic evaluation from the boundary question bearing on the line between art and non-art (e.g., at what point does "bad" art become "non-art"? (This question has a special point in relation to Holocaust art because of a common tendency to avoid its aesthetic evaluation altogether, just because of its subject, as though that were itself a guarantee of its quality or an immunization against criticism.) It seems to me impossible, however, to address here the array of questions related to this issue. Thus, a fourth level of misrepresentation is acknowledged, but in absentia.

6 The categorization of a "Holocaust-writer" can work the other way as well, in establishing writers whose "non-Holocaust" writings otherwise might receive less notice or whose Holocaust-writings benefit in their circulation from the

independent importance of the subject rather than from aesthetic criteria. Another Czernowitz author, Rosa Auslander, is arguably an example of this.

7. APPLIED ETHICS, POST-HOLOCAUST

(pages 112–124)

1 For a more systematic analysis of this issue, see Berel Lang, *The Future of the Holocaust* (Ithaca, N.Y.: Cornell University Press, 1999), chapter 8.

2 See, e.g., Peter Novick, *The Holocaust in American Life* (Boston: Houghton Mifflin, 1999); Norman G. Finkelstein, *The Holocaust Industry: Reflections on the Exploitation of Jewish Suffering* (London: Verso, 2000).

3 This account initially was written in response to a question posed about the difficulties that a scholar might anticipate in writing about the Holocaust for a contemporary Polish audience.

4 On the post-Holocaust pogroms in Poland, see Jan T. Gross, *Fear: Anti-Semitism in Poland after Auschwitz* (New York: Random House, 2006).

8. THE JEWISH DECLARATION OF WAR AGAINST THE NAZIS

(pages 125–136)

1 Also published by Kaufman were *A Will and Way to Peace* (Newark, N.J.: American Federation of Peace, 1939) and *No More German Wars! Being an Outline of Suggestions for Their Permanent Cessation* (Newark, N.J.: Argyle Press, 1942).

2 In his 1939 book, Kaufman proposed the sterilization of *Americans*—so that their children, as soldiers, would not become "murderers." References to *Germany Must Perish* appeared quickly in the German press (e.g., *Völkischer Beobachter*, July 24, 1941, and *Frankfurter Zeitung*, July 24, 1941. On these references, see Wolfgang Benz, "Judenvernichtung aus Notwehr?" in *Viertel-Jahrsheft für Zeitgeschichte* 29 (1981): 615–30. The Nazi edition of *Germany Must Perish* was published under the title *Das Kriegziel der Weltplutokratie*, ed. Wolfgang Diewerge (Berlin: Zentral Verlag der NSDAP, 1941).

3 Cited in Christopher Browning, *The Path to Genocide* (New York: Cambridge University Press, 1992), 71.

4 See on this the 1985 German translation: *Deutschland müsst Vernichtet Werden* (Bremen: Faksimile-Verlag). See also, e.g., M. R. Johnson, "The First Shot Fired in WWII," *The Barnes Review* 7.1 (2001): 40–46; David Irving, *Goebbels: Mastermind of the Third Reich* (London: Focal Point Publications, 1996), 269ff.

5 Joseph Goebbels, *Die Tagebucher von Joseph Goebbels*, ed. Elke Frolich (Munich: Saur, 1987–2007).

9. FROM THE HOLOCAUST TO GROUP RIGHTS

(pages 139–155)

1 Nietzsche, with his usual combination of ingenuity and perversity, imagines prohibition and punishment as preceding rather than following violation. Once there is prohibition, it may at times have the effect Nietzsche ascribes to it, but the question of why the prohibition was first formulated requires more evidence than that.

2 It is even more difficult to prove what people did not intend than what they did intend, but when Hitler wrote in *Mein Kampf*, blaming Germany's World War I defeat on the Jews, that the course of the war might have been different if "twelve or fifteen thousand Hebrew corrupters of the people had been poisoned by gas before or during the war," he surely was citing what seemed to him at the time a large number. For detailed analysis of the developmental account of the "Final Solution," see, e.g., Christopher Browning, *The Origins of the Final Solution: The Evolution of Nazi Jewish Policies* (Lincoln: University of Nebraska Press, 2004).

3 Raphael Lemkin, *Axis Rule in Occupied Europe* (Washington, D.C.: Carnegie Endowment for International Peace, 1944).

4 Raul Hilberg in private correspondence called my attention to what he takes to be the earliest judicial use of the charge of genocide, in a trial in Poland, still in 1944.

5 For the text of the U.N. Convention on the Prevention and Punishment of the Crime of Genocide, see the Appendix.

6 On the history of rights, see, e.g., John Finnis, *Natural Law and Natural Right* (Oxford: Claredon Press, 1980); Fred D. Miller, *Nature, Justice, and Rights in Aristotle's Politics* (Oxford: Claredon Press, 1995); and Francis Oakley, *Natural Law, Laws of Nature, Natural Rights* (New York: Continuum, 2005).

7 For discussions of issues related to group rights, see, e.g., Judith Baker, ed., *Group Rights* (Toronto: University of Toronto Press, 1994); Will Kymlicka, ed., *The Rights of Minority Cultures* (New York: Oxford University Press, 1995) and *A Liberal Theory of Minority Rights* (Oxford: Claredon Press, 1995); Ian Shapiro and Will Kymlicka, eds., *Ethnicity and Group Rights* (New York: New York University Press, 1997).

8 The justification for Affirmative Action programs based on the value of diversity is a latecomer on the scene, intended to finesse the charges of racial

discrimination that had been raised against such programs. Perhaps an independent argument can be made for diversity as a value—but diversity itself seems as likely to be a function of groups as of individuals.

10. METAPHYSICAL RACISM

(pages 156–170)

1 Cited in Stephen J. Gould, *The Mismeasure of Man* (New York: W. W. Norton, 1981), 45.

2 Kwame Anthony Appiah, *In My Father's House* (Cambridge, Mass.: Harvard University Press, 1992), 13–14.

3 Which has not been much of a hindrance to dogmatism: "A combination of processes thus gave rise to the modern races, which must at the very least [!] include Mongoloids, Caucasians, Negroids, and Australoids, the native peoples of Asia, Europe, Africa, and Australia." Pat Shipman, "Facing Racial Differences—Together," *Chronicle of Higher Education,* August 3, 1994, 9. B2. For a concise summary of biological arguments disputing the genetic significance of race, see Daniel G. Blackburn, "Why Race Is Not a Biological Concept," in *Race and Racism in Theory and Practice*, ed. Berel Lang (Lanham, Md.: Rowman & Littlefield, 2000), 3–26.

4 Letter to J. D. Hooker, September 25, 1853, in Francis Darwin, ed., *The Life and Letters of Charles Darwin* (New York: Appleton, 1898), vol. I, 400–401.

5 J. Noakes and G. Pridham, eds., *Nazism 1919–1945*, vol. 1 (New York: Schocken, 1984), 495; see also Berel Lang, *Act and Idea in the Nazi Genocide* (Syracuse: Syracuse University Press, 2003), chapter 1.

6 On the "one-drop" rule, see Naomi Zack, *Race and Mixed Race* (Philadelphia: Temple University Press, 1994), 128–30.

7 Stanley Elkins, *Slavery* (New York: Universal Library, 1963), 61.

8 Benzion Netanyahu gives an extreme view of this "proto-racism" in his *Origins of the Inquisition in Fifteenth Century Spain* (New York: New York Review Books, 2001).

9 See Moshe Zimmerman, *Wilhelm Marr, The Patriarch of Antisemitism* (New York: Oxford University Press, 1986).

10 For a summary of recent analyses of "Nazi Science," see Volker R. Rennert, "What's Nazi about Nazi Science?" *Perspectives in Science* 12 (2004): 454–75.

11 Richard Wolin, *The Heidegger Controversy* (Cambridge, Mass.: MIT Press, 1992), 62, 64.

12 See entry for June 18, 1945, in Nigel Nicolson, ed., *The Harold Nicolson Diaries* (London: Weidenfeld & Nicolson, 2004).

13 Cited in W. E. B. Du Bois, *The Autobiography of W. E. Burghardt Du Bois* (New York: International Publishers, 1968), 230.

14 From a letter by George Pierson, quoted in Dan A. Oren, *Joining the Club* (New Haven, Conn.: Yale University Press, 1985), 121.

15 Paul Gilroy in *The Black Atlantic* (Cambridge, Mass.: Harvard University Press, 1993) calls attention to a claim of this sort in Edmund Burke's *Inquiry into the Origins of Our Ideas of the Sublime and the Beautiful.* The psychologist, L. Hirschfeld, has entered a claim for race as a "natural" conceptual category, in Hirschfeld, *Race in the Making: Cognition, Culture, and the Child's Construction of Human Kinds* (Cambridge, Mass.: MIT Press, 1996).

16 One could move still farther back to Aristotle's metaphysics, in his claim that matter exists *only* in species (*Physics*, II:8).

17 See Lawrence Wright, "One Drop of Blood," *The New Yorker*, July 25, 1994, 46–55.

11. HYPHENATED-JEWS AND THE ANXIETY OF IDENTITY

(pages 171–186)

1 A statement soon afterward reiterated by Justice Brandeis in a speech before the New Century Club, "What Loyalty Demands," on the *250th* anniversary of Jewish settlement in the New World: "There is no place [here] for what President Roosevelt has called hyphenated Americans."

2 Nathan Glazer and Daniel Patrick Moynihan, *Beyond the Melting Pot* (Cambridge, Mass.: MIT Press, 1963), v.

3 Jeffrey Lehman, ed., *Gale Encyclopedia of Multicultural America* (Detroit: Gale Group, 2000).

4 The (premature, in my view) claim has been made that a radical change in these proportions already has occurred: S. Daniel Elazar writes, "Today there are very few American Jews left. Instead there are Jewish Americans, no longer hyphenated." "The Future of American Jewry," Jerusalem, Center for Public Affairs, 1995.

5 The locutions cited here have varied as a function of "point of view"; so, for example, the phrase typically applied from outside a country may have differed from the locution used within it, and has at times differed within a country, as between the term applied by Jews to themselves or in references by non-Jews to Jews. (In some cases, the *possibility* of hyphenated identity, where Jews are concerned, has been itself a large, and indeed continuing, issue, as within Hungary.)

6 Gerald Sorin suggests something in the way of a "hyphenated" retention in

the fact that Howe, changing his last name, held on to what was at the time a characteristically "Jewish" *first* name. Gerald Sorin, *Irving Howe: A Life of Passionate Dissent* (New York: New York University Press, 2002), 27. The history and ideology (and wit) of name changes in relation to issues of hyphenated identity warrant volumes of their own (including first as well as family names: Consider the special case of the Marx brothers: Groucho from Julius, Chico from Leonard, Gummo from Milton, Zeppo from Herbert, Harpo from Adolph.)

7 See Steven Cohen, *American Modernity and Jewish Identity* (New York: Tavistock, 1983), 49–51.

8 It is worth noting that the locution of "Deutsche Juden" that had been a common referent in pre-Nazi Germany was replaced, under Nazi pressure, in all official citations by "Juden in Deutschland," a usage that predominates in Germany now, although "Deutsche Juden" is now making something of a comeback. (The issue is complicated, of course, by the significant numbers of new Jewish "immigrants" to Germany.) According to a Google search, "Deutsche Juden" exceeds "Judische Deutsche" by a ratio of 8 to 1. (I am indebted to Joerg Riegel for this information.)

9 Two indicative if anecdotal instances of how misleading the externally imposed disappearance of such reference can be appear in a sampling of newspaper obituary notices. One was in the *New York Times*, where the obituary of Samuel Dash, who was U.S. Senate Chief Counsel in the Watergate investigation, described him as "the son of émigrés from the Soviet Union." A week later, a commemorative item in the *International Herald Tribune* noted that on that date in 1952, "a Ukrainian-born microbiologist, Selman Waksman, was awarded the Nobel Prize in medicine for the co-discovery of Streptomycin." Both these identifying statements were strictly speaking true, but the absence of reference to the hyphenated-Jewish identities in the two accounts left them incomplete and arguably misleading.

10 Report of the 46th Annual Meeting of the American Jewish Committee in 1953 (New York: American Jewish Committee, 1953), 81.

11 Jonathan Sarna, *American Judaism* (New Haven, Conn.: Yale University Press, 2004), 328.

12. RECONCILIATION

(pages 187–202)

1 For a full account of the formation and structure of the Truth and Reconciliation Commission, see especially Richard A. Wilson, *The Politics of Truth*

and Reconciliation in South Africa (Cambridge: Cambridge University Press, 2001). For further elaboration of issues involved in and raised by the Proceedings of the Commission itself, see also Deborah Posel and Graeme Simpson, eds., *Commisioning the Past: Understanding South Africa's Truth and Reconciliation Commission* (Johannesburg: Witwatersand University Press, 2002).

2 The Truth and Reconciliation Commission did authorize a single "blanket amnesty," granted to 37 members of the African National Congress leadership; this exceptional step caused (and reflected) great controversy both within and outside the commission.

3 The importance and relevance of forgiveness remained an ideal for many of the figures involved in the conceptualization and implementation of the Truth and Reconciliation Commission, including Nelson Mandela and Desmond Tutu (see especially Desmond Tutu, *No Reconciliation Without Forgiveness* (New York: Doubleday, 1999).

4 On the structure of other truth commissions and their comparison to the South African commission, see Teresa Godwin Phelps, *Shattered Voices: Language, Violence, and the Work of Truth Commissions* (Philadelphia: University of Pennsylvania Press, 2004); and Chandra Lekha Sriram, *Confronting Past Human Rights Violations* (New York: Frank Cass, 2004).

5 On the "epuration," see Robert O. Paxton, *Vichy France: Old Guard and New Order* (New York: Columbia University Press, 2001); and Henri Rousso, *The Vichy Syndrome: History and Memory in France since 1944* (Cambridge, Mass.: Harvard University Press, 2006). On the troubled issue of revenge in the Jewish reaction to the Nazi genocide, see Berel Lang, "Revenge and Holocaust-Memory: The Presence of the Past," *Jewish Social Studies* 3 (1996): 5–31.

« Index »